TRANSFORMING PROBATION

Social theories and the criminal justice system

Philip Whitehead

First published in Great Britain in 2017 by

Policy Press
University of Bristol
1-9 Old Park Hill
Bristol
BS2 8BB
UK
t: +44 (0)117 954 5940
pp-info@bristol.ac.uk
www.policypress.co.uk

North America office:
Policy Press
c/o The University of Chicago Press
1427 East 60th Street
Chicago, IL 60637, USA
t: +1 773 702 7700
f: +1 773-702-9756
sales@press.uchicago.edu
www.press.uchicago.edu

British Library Cataloguing in Publication Data
A catalogue record for this book is available from the British Library

Library of Congress Cataloging-in-Publication Data
A catalog record for this book has been requested

ISBN 978-1-4473-2766-0 paperback
ISBN 978-1-4473-2765-3 hardcover
ISBN 978-1-4473-2770-7 ePub
ISBN 978-1-4473-2769-1 Mobi
ISBN 978-1-4473-2768-4 ePdf

Cover design by Liam Roberts
Front cover image: istock
Printed and bound in Great Britain by CMP, Poole
Policy Press uses environmentally responsible print partners

Contents

List of tables

Acknowledgements

I have incurred many debts of unconditional generosity over nearly four decades, through my association with the criminal justice system and, since 2007, Teesside University. I am indebted to Roger Statham, whom I have known and worked with since the 1980s, as well as many former probation colleagues. I have learned much from David Faulkner, Rob Canton and Mike Nellis. I thank Georgios Antonopoulos, Georgios Papanicolaou and Paul Crawshaw. Evi Boukli and Anthony Lloyd allowed me to share their office, the location for valued conversations. It is right and proper to mention Eric Baumgartner, and other colleagues in the School of Social Sciences, Business and Law, especially the Teesside Centre for Realist Criminology. I owe a considerable intellectual debt to Steve Hall and Simon Winlow, who enabled me to expand and refine the theoretical resources in this revised and expanded edition.

It remains appropriate to mention Judge Peter Fox and all those solicitors, court clerks, magistrates, barristers and crown court judges without whom it would not have been possible to undertake the research retained in this edition. In fact, there remains a paucity of research on these criminal justice professionals.

I must express my gratitude to Ishmael Hussain, MSc student, for checking the in-text citations against the references. This was an invaluable source of assistance during the early part of 2016 that contributed to the completion of the book. It would be remiss of me not to mention Policy Press and their interest in this updated text.

As always, my deepest debt of gratitude is to Carolyn, Alex, Tim and Jenny. My life with them has always been the platform for my probation and academic work.

Finally, I dedicate this book to all those probation colleagues that I have worked with since 1977 – those who taught me the history and culture of the organisation, and who operated as the social workers of the courts. Many former colleagues have endured much, too much, over recent years.

Stokesley, North Yorkshire, March 2016

About the author

Philip Whitehead is Professor in criminal and social justice at Teesside University. After studying theology at Manchester University and later qualifying as a social worker/probation officer at Lancaster University, Philip worked for the Probation Service in the North East of England before being appointed lecturer at Teesside University. He has written widely on the history and modernisation of the probation service, co-edited a collection of papers on managerial issues, and co-authored a book on the education of Trainee Probation Officers. His recent books are *Organising neoliberalism: Markets, privatisation and justice* (Anthem Press 2012), and *Reconceptualising the moral economy of criminal justice: a new perspective* (Palgrave 2015).

Introduction

The first epiphany of this book was published in 2010: *Exploring Modern Probation: Social Theory and Organisational Complexity*. It spanned the years from the election of New Labour in 1997 to 2009. The current edition has substantively rewritten, revised and updated the original text. It is chronologically extended to include 1997–2015, which witnessed the eruption of the rehabilitation revolution. It is also theoretically enriched. Authors are not the best judge of their own work, just as parents are not the best judge of their own children. Nevertheless, I advance the bold, perhaps reckless, claim that this is a better book primarily because of its extended chronology, theoretical additions and refinements.

I have been associated with the probation service since 1977 (approaching 40 years), when I first worked as a volunteer at the Lancaster probation office. One of my tasks was to explore employment opportunities for borstal boys released on licence. Since 1979, the criminal justice system in general, and probation in particular, have been confronted with a series of critical events or hinge moments: in 1979, the conservative government; in 1992/93, prison works; in 1997, New Labour; in 2001, the National Probation Service (NPS); in 2003, the National Offender Management Service (NOMS); and in 2010, the move towards transforming rehabilitation. This book covers the period of the New Labour and Coalition governments, 18 years that culminated in the privatisation of a proportion of probation work by 21 Community Rehabilitation Companies. This politically imposed process was driven relentlessly forward through time, but backward ethically, by the ideological and material interests of neoliberal capitalism and its New Public Management. One serious casualty is the probation service.

I proceed as follows. Chapter One moves around within an extended chronology that embodies the New Labour governments from 1997 to 2010, followed by the Coalition government from 2010 to 2015. The first substantive period disturbingly *modernised*, the second convulsively *transformed*, probation services and the criminal justice system. Chapter Two assembles the theoretical resources to excavate and critique developments since 1997: Durkheim, Weber, Marx and Foucault, in addition to the conceptual framework of Lacan and Žižek that is conducive to organisational analysis and critique. Chapter Three turns to the religious and personalist tradition to promote reflections on the conceptual device of moral economy (see Whitehead, 2015b).

This puts into sharp relief the contestation between the ideological and material interests of neoliberal political economy, and the ethico-cultural duties and demands of people facing organisations. Next, Chapter Four puts the extended and refined grid of social theory and moral sensibilities to work to elucidate and critique the thematics of modernisation and transformation. Importantly, Chapter Five retains the substantive research insights contained in the first edition. There remains a paucity of empirical research on solicitors, clerks, magistrates, barristers and judges. This continues to represent a slice of criminal justice history in the north-east of England at what was a critical historical and organisational juncture. I have constructed a new final chapter, Chapter Six, on what can legitimately be described as modernising monstrosities and transformational traumas, in order to expose the penetrative reach of political impositions and associated organisational reconfigurations over 18 years. These monstrosities and traumas have had serious implications for probation staff and their practices: 21 Community Rehabilitation Companies, community supervision, the prison system and the moral foundations of criminal and social justice.

Essentially, this critical excavation of probation, criminal justice and penal policy is a detailed case study of politico-economic, ideological and material organisational reconstruction under the harsh and harmful realities of neoliberal capitalist arrangements.

ONE

Probation and criminal justice, 1997–2015: from New Labour to the Coalition government

Introduction

This chapter schematically plots transformations in probation, criminal justice and penal policy from the election of New Labour in 1997 to the period of the Coalition government that ended in May 2015. As a preliminary contextual marker, it should be acknowledged that from 1945 until the 1970s, the UK experienced a 'golden age' of inclusivist welfare and criminal justice services that supported rehabilitation rather than punishment and prison (see Garland, 1985, 2001). By the late 1970s, there were signs of dislocation within the post-war Keynesian order, manifested in attempts to reduce welfare provision and the emergence of tougher attitudes towards crime and justice (Hall et al, 1978; Brake and Hale, 1992; Cavadino and Dignan, 2006). From the onset of the Conservative era in 1979, the rhetoric of law and order was tempered by the Criminal Justice Act 1982, which introduced criteria to restrict the use of custody for juveniles (Whitehead and MacMillan, 1985; Charman and Savage, 1999). During 1987–92, Douglas Hurd's pragmatism moderated the Conservative motif of law and order as criminal justice became more managerialist, contiguous with a strategy of punishment in the community ostensibly to control the prison population (Downes and Morgan, 1997). Between 1992 and 1997, the Howard–Major axis advanced punitive law and order in straitened economic circumstances, with the New Labour phenomenon appearing in the distance. With little warning, the gloves came off to expose a more visceral message that prison works!

New Labour's election victory in 1997 released a melange of contradictory penal and social forces. There was no wholesale abandonment of the link between socio-economic conditions and crime because of the salience awarded to tackling social exclusion. Equally, there was no dilution of punitive toughness when responding to offenders. New Public Management (Whitehead, 2007, p 34), inherited from previous Conservative administrations, cohabited with evidence-based 'What Works' and the renaissance of rehabilitation (Raynor 2002; Clarke et al, 2000). Prisons may not 'work' as effectively as community sentences, but there was no concerted policy to curb imprisonment in a climate of US-style zero tolerance, with young people singled out for special attention. There remained an ongoing commitment to neoliberal political economy as the only credible platform, and a penchant for a generous dose of punishment; however, restorative justice was a sentencing option. Consequently, New Labour did not revert to some halcyon period dominated by inclusivist welfare and anti-punishment sensibilities. Rather, it presented itself as a modern political force, pursuing a 'Third Way' (Jones and Newburn, 2004), with a mandate to modernise the country and its public institutions. The political foundations of criminal justice were expressed as 'We must be tough; we must be modern; we must get value for money; we must be re-elected' (Cavadino and Dignan, 2006, p 75). Then, after 13 years of New Labour, the Coalition of Conservatives and Liberals, from 2010 to 2015, embarked upon a rehabilitation revolution that constituted the deeper penetration of modernisation, privatisation, marketisation and disruptive competition into the criminal justice domain. We need to track our way back to 1997 before plotting our way towards the present.

New Labour's modernising turn, 1997–2001

The politico-electoral phenomenon of New Labour, in contradistinction to pre-1990s' social-democratic old Labour,[1] associated itself with the thematics of modernisation and cultural change. Enshrined within New Labour's manifesto before the general election of May 1997 after 18 years of conservative administrations – *New Labour: Because Britain Deserves Better*[2] – modernisation was the summons for a new bond of trust between the political establishment and British people, exemplified in 10 specific commitments. These were enumerated as education, tax, the economy, getting the unemployed into work, and rebuilding the National Health Service. At number six was a reference to being tough on crime and its causes by halving the time it takes persistent juvenile offenders to come to court.[3] The remaining four were families and communities in a modernised welfare state, the environment, the imperative to clean up politics, and leadership in the modern world.

New Labour's evangelical theology of making all things new was in the process of being shaped before election to governmental office. This set the nation on a new course in a spirit of rebuilding and renewing, on the solid foundation of belief in progress and justice, the value of equal worth (a theme resonating with old Labour), and with no one cast aside in what would be a fairer and safer society (for a critique, see Wilkinson and Pickett, 2009). Additionally, the politics of crime was constructed according to a narrative of personal responsibility, which necessitated a more punitive riposte. This approach set it apart from the tenets of former Labour administrations; it also continued to forge a new consensus with Conservative penal philosophy since the punitive turn of 1992–93. New Labour had transformed its criminal justice philosophy since the early 1990s so that the claim could be made in 1997 that it had become the natural party of law and order. In other words, it would no longer be outflanked by the political Right. This was a critical selling point to secure electoral legitimacy. If the National Health Service was safe in New Labour's hands, the country could feel secure that the punishment of offenders would be equally safe. Modernising influences would: fast-track the punishment of recalcitrant young people; reform the Crown Prosecution Service to convict more criminals; put more police in uniform on the beat; and crackdown on petty crimes, including the malaise of disorder. To maintain evidential balance, it should be acknowledged that a tougher and more punitive approach to offenders would not eschew the relationship between behavioural repertoires, differential opportunities, social deprivation and exclusion.[4]

Although there is no overt reference to probation in Campbell's (2007) journalistic apologia of the Blair era, it is difficult to entertain the view that probation was never mentioned prior to 1997 within political debates appertaining to the modernising agenda. We step from speculation onto solid ground by 1998 because the proposal for a modernised probation service was contained in the consultative document *Prisons–Probation: Joining Forces to Protect the Public* (Home Office, 1998). After decades of ideological, philosophical and self-evident organisational distinctions between the primary task of prisons and probation, a period of consultation was established in 1997 to explore closer integration in order to improve efficiency and enhance performance. Was it possible for these two organisations, which had for decades largely pursued their own distinctive penal-welfare trajectories, to work more closely together to: reduce reoffending; better prepare prisoners for release; share resources, information, knowledge and skills; and reconfigure organisational structures to provide value for money on the platform of New Public Management?

In the second chapter of the 1998 consultation document, there is a reference to modernising the organisational framework of probation.

Significantly, it is stated that legislation continues to direct employees to advise, assist and befriend (originally stated in the Probation of Offenders Act 1907), which, without supporting evidence, is boldly claimed to be out of touch with the expectations of the courts and transformations in probation work. The service had become more oriented towards public protection and a modernised service must confront, challenge and change offenders, rather than advise, assist and befriend. Accordingly, a harsher and more punitive discourse is tantamount to modernisation.[5] The document states that there is a lack of probation accountability to central government due to fragmented governance arrangements, which would have been disputed in the 56 local area services by chief probation officers. Consequently, it needs to be better organised and forge closer links with central government, the prison system, police, mental health services, local authorities and the Crown Prosecution Service. Interestingly, the theme of modernisation and cultural transformation involves, it is argued, much clearer national direction and stronger national leadership, and the Home Secretary must be able to have political responsibility – centrally imposed command, power and control – over local area probation services. Windlesham (2001, p 245) concurs when stating that in the area of criminal policy, as in other areas of public administration, 'the demands of modernisation called for models of central control, rather than delegated authority and local accountability'.

Finally, at paragraph 2.11, the suggestion is made for a new organisational name to accompany the new nomenclature in order to convey modernised messages. It was suggested that the organisation should be rebadged from the Probation Service to the Public Protection Service or perhaps the Community Justice Enforcement Agency. The Criminal Justice and Court Services Act 2000 signalled the culmination of a process beginning in the document under discussion, which saw the establishment of the National Probation Service (NPS) in 2001. Eventually, 'probation' was preserved after much lobbying and deliberation between the organisation and government. From 1997 to 1998, probation was inextricably enmeshed in the politics of modernisation at the behest of New Labour modernisers (Nellis, 1999; Windlesham, 2001). This was confirmed in 1999, when it was asserted that government had a mission to modernise, renewing the country for the new millennium: we are 'modernising our schools, our hospitals, our economy and our criminal justice system' (Cabinet Office, 1999). Before proceeding, it is of interest to acknowledge Raynor and Vanstone's (2007, p 71) analysis. Even though the *Prisons–Probation* review gave due consideration to the merging of two organisations into a single service in order to *reduce the cultural divide*, at this juncture, it was a step too far (a step too far in 1998 but not by 2003, as we will see later).

A new urgency, 2001–05

By 2001, after a four-year term in office, New Labour's manifesto – *Ambitions for Britain* – included a number of pledges for the next five years on economics, schools and health. There was also a pledge for 6000 extra police recruits to tackle drugs and crime and to build upon the claim that crime is down by 10% compared to 1997 (in fact, *conventional* crime had been falling overall since the mid-1990s; see Reiner, 2007a; Office for National Statistics, 2015). Again, attention is drawn to more radical public service reform, which included renewing public services to provide front-line staff with the freedom to respond to the needs of the public, particularly nurses, doctors, teachers and police officers – probation officers were not included on this list. The language of being tough on crime was repeated, as were the related themes of punishment and individual responsibility for one's actions, regardless of differential social circumstances. Outbursts of criminality are constructed in millenarian-apocalyptic terms as a battle that has to be fought and won by the government on behalf of the people. This is a war against crime, or more specifically a war in support of a specific definition of crime, against a specific section of the community, to benefit the law abiding (see Durkheim later). The war on crime, including the war on terror and war on poverty, became a cogent motif of political governance in the US, which legitimated the expansion of governmental power, punishment and authoritarian control. By doing so, it drained away the real causes of social conflicts rooted in the 'asymmetrical effects of power' (Simon, 2007, p 14). This tone was duplicated in the UK when the Casey Report vacuously stated that crime is tackled most effectively when the law-abiding majority 'stand together against the minority who commit it' (Cabinet Office, 2008, p 4).

Reforming and modernising impulses towards the criminal justice system were the subject of a White Paper to: speed up the prosecution of offenders; take victims much more seriously; continue the fight against crime; and develop Crime Reduction Partnerships. The fight would also be directed against anti-social behaviour and what was emotively referred to in 19th-century terms as 'yob culture'. There was a greater sense of urgency to reform and modernise after the election victory in 2001 (Windlesham, 2003). Accordingly, *Criminal*

Justice: The Way Ahead (Home Office, 2001a), published in February 2001, acknowledged in structuralist, social exclusion terminology that the increase in crime over the previous 25 years was partly a result of unemployment and a lack of opportunities for the unskilled, the blight of drugs, and the availability of consumer goods. Even though the mechanisms for the creation of a responsible and law-abiding society do not inhere solely within criminal justice systems – socio-economic forces and wider structural factors must be factored into an analysis of human behaviour – nevertheless, a modernised criminal justice system must function instrumentally to prevent crime and reduce reoffending, efficiently deal with cases, respond appropriately to victims, and be more accountable for its decisions. Fundamentally, what is desirable is a criminal justice system that delivers *justice for all* (Home Office, 2001a, p 5).

Parts 1 and 2 of the White Paper from February 2001 summarised the reforms that had been introduced since 1997,[6] in addition to continuing the theme of modernisation. It is explained that the criminal justice system will continue to be modernised in response to transformations in society and associated patterns of crime. This will be achieved by apprehending and convicting more persistent offenders expeditiously (100,000 hard-core offenders could be responsible for half of all crime); tough and effective punishments will become more intense for persistence. The more you offend, the tougher it will be – a theme contained in the Criminal Justice Act 2003, which reflects a different penal philosophy to the Criminal Justice Act 1991. Modernisation is also associated with giving the police, Crown Prosecution Service, courts and other agencies what they require to do the job defined by central government, and to build public confidence. Moreover, modernisation encapsulates: the Auld (2001) review of, and reforms to, the criminal law (began in 1999); the Halliday review of sentencing practices (began in 2000, but see Home Office, 2001b); reducing delays in the system; bringing more people to justice; establishing a better deal for witnesses and victims; and facilitating more effective partnerships to enhance the delivery of services. It also involved the creation of the NPS in 2001. Attention is drawn to the political importance attached to enforcement practices that resonate throughout many of the documents under consideration during this period (Home Office, 2001a, para 2.78). However, if these changes were not challenging enough for the criminal justice system to absorb, along came another set of reforms that established the National Offender Management Service (NOMS) as the veritable exemplar of modernisation.

In 2002, Patrick Carter was asked to undertake a review of correctional services. Subsequently, if 2003 saw the arrival of the latest Criminal Justice Act that had significant implications probation (following the Halliday review but not implemented until 2005), it also revealed Carter's deliberations, as laid out in *Managing Offenders, Reducing Crime: A New Approach* (Carter, 2003). This report analysed the state of prisons, overcrowding and the lack of help available for short-term prisoners following release. Carter proposed the linear concept of end-to-end management of offender services and the creation of a single agency to deliver it through NOMS (Hough et al, 2006; Gelsthorpe and Morgan, 2007). It would consist of a chief executive and national offender manager, as well as 10 regional offender managers responsible for commissioning services – custodial provision and in the community – for the management of offenders in that region. The goals of effectiveness, better performance and target achievement would be sharpened up by a mechanism of contestability in a marketised mixed economy of provision. In other words, it is possible that the work being undertaken by probation could be awarded to other organisations within the public, private and voluntary sectors. This was not a novel policy as during the early 1990s, a decade before NOMS, the monopoly position of probation was challenged by the rise of a pluralism of offender service providers (Fullwood, 1994).

It should be confirmed that help and support for offenders remain part of the NOMS structure as services exist to respond to problems related to accommodation, education, training and employment, finances, and addictions. Nevertheless, the new organisation was criticised for sustaining a politics of punitive controlism, depersonalisation and deprofessionalisation. On the theme of punitive controlism, it was explained that the retributive penal agenda, fuelled by punitive populism, radically threatened to shift the purpose of probation 'from one of caring control to one of punitive control' (Burnett et al, 2007, p 228). Furthermore, a number of concerns were raised in response to developments associated with privatisation and contestability by the National Association of Probation Officers and the Probation Boards Association (Gelsthorpe and Morgan, 2007). This became acute between 2010 and 2015, as we will see towards the end of this chapter.

By 2004, the strategic aim of *Confident Communities* (Home Office, 2004a) was articulated as social change to achieve enhanced security (whatever this means). Also, the objectives of the Home Office for a safe, just, tolerant society included helping people to feel more secure in their homes and communities. The interests of the law-abiding citizen must come first and they will be protected from the threat of terrorism, illegal immigration and criminal disorder on the streets. The theme of modernisation reverberated throughout this document when addressing ongoing reforms within the criminal justice system, the programme of structural and organisational changes that commenced in 1997, and elevating the status of victims. There are supporting references to Halliday and the Criminal Justice Act 2003, the delivery of effective punishments, the creation of NOMS, enforcement, and crime prevention. It is important to acknowledge, though, that offenders will not be unsupported to achieve behavioural change. However, if offenders do not respond positively to the offer of support, negative consequences will follow in the form of tougher enforcement practices. The prevailing tonal discussion on criminality is directed at low-level street crime rather than, for example, the harms inflicted by the powerful, even though a number of publications under discussion in this chapter include discrete sections on organised crime.

According to *Cutting Crime, Delivering Justice* (Home Office, 2004b), published concurrently with *Confident Communities*, the vision for the criminal justice system for the next five years (2004–09) is: increased public confidence in the system; that victims and witnesses should receive a high standard of service; bringing more offenders to justice; rigorous enforcement, which warrants another mention; joined-up services; and reducing delays – all of which constitute the normative contours of modernisation. Again, modernising reforms that have occurred since 1997 are reprised and there is a specific reference to probation within the context of more resources being allocated to the police, Crown Prosecution Service and prisons. In fact, when turning to probation, it is lamented that the training of new probation officers ceased under the Conservatives between 1995 and 1998. No newly qualified staff entered the profession for several years in the 56 local area services (Whitehead and Statham, 2006). Moreover, breach/enforcement action had been problemmatic until the system was tightened up in the 2000–02 National Standards.[7] It should be acknowledged that the documents published during 2004 signalled an end to the 1960s' liberal consensus on law and order. Creating safer communities will be pursued through a punitive war on crime, rather than ameliorative social policies to reduce the deleterious effects of inequality (Wilkinson and Pickett, 2009), which would entail systematically dismantling the neoliberal order. In other words, New Labour retreated from the solidaristic thinking on crime of old Labour (Sim, 2009).

Beyond 2005: drifting towards the end of New Labour

New Labour's 2005 manifesto, *Britain Forward Not Back*, repeated the refrain of tough on crime and its causes and proudly asserted that sentences had become tougher, illustrated by 16,000 more prison places compared to 1997. It also confirmed that NOMS ensured that every offender would be case-managed from the beginning to the end of their sentence. Furthermore, the Respect agenda was increasingly important at this juncture, but in his book *Penal Populism*, John Pratt (2007) persuasively argued that respect has contingent social conditions. These were enumerated as commitment, trust, tolerance, loyalty, stability and security, which were being systematically eroded by a neoliberal economics that fosters fearful competition, in the interests of the few over the many (Pratt, 2007, p 121). The manifesto referred to: Anti-Social Behaviour Orders (ASBOs), which resulted in the criminalisation of low-level disorderliness; a proper focus on victims and the law-abiding majority; and the commitment to cut crime and send dangerous offenders to prison. There was also a reference to making community sentences more effective, which is a persistent theme over the last two decades.

On 19 September 2005, Home Secretary Charles Clarke made a speech to the Prison Reform Trust, entitled *Where Next for Penal Policy*. While sentencing within the reformed criminal justice system is conducted according to various sentencing philosophies,[8] Clarke affirmed that the government would be tough on crime and criminals, particularly dangerous and persistent offenders. The Home Secretary proceeded to refer to a contract between the offender and the state that would involve a commitment not to reoffend. Importantly, the provision of help and support to offenders should be provided not only by statutory services, but also by the voluntary/faith sector in the form of community chaplaincies (see Whitehead, 2011). In other words, the provision of help to offenders and families on release from prison could be enhanced by building links between churches and communities[9] as an integral component of the NOMS strategy (see Chapter Five). However, when turning to discuss prisons, it is idiotically stated that the central strategy must be to take all possible steps 'to encourage prisons to become colleges for constructive citizenship rather than recruiting sergeant for crime'. This is naive because the prison system has not managed to achieve this objective in 200 years.[10]

The Home Secretary's speech addressed NOMS within the context of organisational change and the modernisation agenda by bringing prisons and probation closer together. The central priority was to reduce reoffending by 5% by 2008 and then 10% by 2010. The role of the new offender manager is considered – note the change of job designation from probation officer to offender manager – as is the plan to develop a mixed economy of provision, thus breaking up the monopoly position of the probation service in the delivery of offender services. It is asserted that NOMS is committed to rehabilitation, but while a number of prison and probation areas had made a positive response to the prevailing challenges and improved, there are other areas that had not achieved as much as government considered necessary. This is why Charles Clarke was personally committed to the creation of a vibrant mixed economy within NOMS. The policy being reinforced is that encouraging contestability between the public, private and voluntary sectors will enhance and improve the delivery of offender services. Consequently, the vision for the future consisted of regional offender managers purchasing services from different providers (this may no longer be a probation organisation), who will be expected to achieve targets and provide value for money, the rationale being to drive up standards of performance within a market-driven criminal justice system. Once again, rigorous enforcement is advanced as a symbolic cause célèbre during the modernising programme of New Labour.

During 2005, updated in 2006, the Home Office was involved in producing the NOMS Offender Management Model (National Offender Management Service, 2006). Included within this document was guidance to probation areas on the tiering (stacking) of cases in order to relate resources to the assessed category of risk – low, medium, high and very high risk. There are four substantive tiers, all of which will deliver some form of punishment to offenders, even though the document articulates the importance of social work relationships as well: Tier 1 – punish; Tier 2 – punish and help; Tier 3 – punish and help and change; Tier 4 – punish and help and change and control. Tier 1 cases comprise low- to medium-risk categories; by contrast, tier 4 contains high- to very high-risk categories, including public protection cases. Tiers 3 and 4 will attract most of the resources and be the preserve of trained and professionally qualified staff. The reconfiguration of resources and services by risk status anticipates the rehabilitation revolution of 2010–15. A spate of documents appeared during 2006.

Notwithstanding the complexities involved in obtaining an accurate picture of crime statistics, the *Five Year Strategy for Protecting the Public and Reducing Re-Offending* (Home Office, 2006a) restated the claim that while crime was decreasing, the strategic aim remained to cut reoffending, protect the public, keep the right people in prison and manage the risks posed by offenders (Reiner 2006). The offender manager is responsible for the punishment and rehabilitation of offenders, including the promotion of closer links with the prison system via the newly emerging NOMS structure. This document underlines the political message that while the language of punishment, reparation and rehabilitation overlap, punishment is a legitimate activity in prison and the community and that both organisations should prevent reoffending. The context remains one of being tough on crime, illustrated by the assertion that we are 'catching and convicting more criminals' (Home Office, 2006a, para 1.4). It is imperative that the public is kept safe from serious, violent, dangerous and persistent offenders. Risks must be identified and managed via the Offender Assessment System (OASys; but see Mair et al, 2006), which is considered one of the most advanced systems of its kind in the world (Home Office, 2006a, para 2.2). Once again, key political messages are delivered on enforcement (Home Office, 2006a, para 3.12) when it is specified that when offenders breach their community orders, over 90% are enforced (the process of returning them to the sentencing court normally after two failed appointments) within 10 working days. Nevertheless, managing offenders to prevent reoffending and improve compliance can be enhanced by confronting and resolving factors related to obtaining work, housing and drugs (Home Office, 2006a, para 4.3). In other words, there remains an uneasy alliance between the discourses of punitive toughness and ongoing support for some of the underlying causes of unlawful behaviour, which OASys is expected to identify.

Much had been achieved since 1997 when the modernisers came to power. Nevertheless, the modernisation of the criminal justice system was not completed. This was the dominant message of *Rebalancing the Criminal Justice System* (Home Office, 2006b). It was claimed that crime had fallen by 35% since 1997 and the risk of becoming a victim of crime was the lowest since the British Crime Survey began in 1981. Public confidence in the criminal justice system was on the rise, and worry about anti-social behaviour had fallen since the commencement of the Respect programme alluded to earlier. Modernisation, which assumed the quality of a permanent revolution, was constructed positively by recourse to the provision of more resources for criminal justice agencies, investment, improved performance, partnerships, NOMS, stricter enforcement, new laws, ASBOs and bringing more people to justice. While much had been achieved, the system must be *rebalanced* in favour of victims rather than offenders. On compliance and enforcement (Home Office, 2006b, para 2.32) it was reinforced that in addition to ensuring that appropriate sentences are imposed, the public continues to expect the criminal justice system to enforce them effectively, with robust measures to secure compliance. Accordingly, the Criminal Justice Act 2003 and accompanying National Standards introduced more onerous requirements. Paragraph 3.29 of the *Rebalancing* document addressed probation specifically by stating that resources should target serious not minor offenders, underpinned by the new tiering system. Also, the intention remained to break up probation's monopoly by creating a mixed economy of provision through the NOMS structure, which requires new legislation to enable other potential providers to get involved. Finally, the document turned to the aspiration of *Delivering Simple, Speedy, Summary Justice* (Home Office, 2006c), and its implications for the probation service will now be considered.

This document, another integral component of the modernising agenda, attempted to push ahead with a more effective and efficient criminal justice system, particularly within the magistrates' courts, which deal with 95% of criminal cases. It is further clarified that the latest vision for the criminal justice system must include the following categories:

- *Simple*: dealing with specific cases transparently by way of warning, caution or some other effective remedy to prevent reoffending without recourse to the court process.
- *Speedy*: those cases that need the court process will be dealt with fairly but as quickly as possible.
- *Summary*: a much more proportionate approach involving due process – for example, dealing with appropriate cases the day after charge or during the same week – which would constitute a change in the way cases are dealt with in magistrates' courts.

This had profound implications for the work of probation, primarily because the pressure to deal with more and more cases expeditiously touched the organisation at the point where reports (written documents) were being prepared for the courts, particularly magistrates' courts. In other words, one of the aims of the 'Triple S' agenda was to reduce the average number of hearings before a case is finally sentenced from five or six to an expectation of one for guilty pleas, which would eradicate costly adjournments; if the court requires more information on the offender, then this will be in the form of a Fast Delivery Report rather than a full and detailed Pre-Sentence Report. Therefore, modernisation can be construed positively as effective and efficient case management (the application of New Public Management principles; see Whitehead and Statham, 2006). By contrast, speed may have moral implications that appertain to the delivery of criminal and social justice (Cook, 2006).

By 2006, it had been over two years since the Carter Report resulted in the emergence of NOMS and proposals to utilise the diverse talents of public, private and voluntary agencies. As John Reid stated in *Public Value Partnerships*, the public sector is valued and will have a continuing role to play: 'However, all current providers should be open to challenge and able to demonstrate that the services they offer are the best available' (Home Office, 2006d, p 3). The rationale was the development of NOMS and its mixed economy of offender services. If the probation service was seen to be failing under the reconstituted arrangements, it could be taken over by another organisation to deliver effective and efficient services. It was stated that government plans for extending contestability are not to cut costs or even to have competition for its own sake. Rather, its primary policy objective was to improve standards of service by encouraging innovative practices that would result in less crime and getting the best mix of services and service providers.

The Cabinet Office Prime Minister's Strategy Unit (2006) published an interesting document, initially confirming that there has been a regime of tougher sentencing since 1997; the average length of custodial sentences at the crown court increased from 20 to 30 months between 1994 and 2004. Moreover, there was an increase in community sentences that were more demanding, but they displaced fines rather than were alternatives to custodial sentences. A more punitive culture had been created within the criminal justice system. Equally important is the assessment that recent decreases in crime were due to positive economic factors. Alternatively, we read how the Home Office was predicting that crime would begin to rise because the economy was slowing down (Cabinet Office Prime Minister's Strategy Unit, 2006, p 13). This point raises important questions that touch directly upon the efficacy of the criminal justice system, contrasted with an inclusive and protective social policy response during adverse socio-economic conditions (Garland, 1985; 2001, p 90; Young, 2007; Wacquant, 2008, 2009). This is reinforced by Zedner (2006, p 153) when she persuasively argues that the 'social, economic, and cultural sources of crime control thus extend deep into social policy and cannot be supplied by the criminal justice system alone'. During September 2008, a leaked Home Office letter – *Responding to Economic Challenges* – warned that the global economic downturn is expected to result in more crime, fewer police and more illegal immigration, coupled with Far Right extremism. After studying previous recessions and the effects on crime and policing, Home Office computer modelling indicated that an economic downturn 'would place significant upward pressure on acquisitive crime and therefore overall crime figures' (reported in the *Telegraph*, 1 September 2008; see also Reiner, 2007b, and his analysis of how the rise in crime since the 1970s and accompanying law-and-order responses must take account of neoliberal policies).

'Ten years of criminal justice under Labour' (Solomon et al, 2007) is a significant publication because it constitutes an independent audit of events since 1997. Since 1997, the intentions of New Labour were clear: tough on crime and its causes, and introducing modernising reforms across the public sector, which included the criminal justice system, manifested by more investment and a harsher nomenclature, and resulting in cultural transformations and ideological dislocations (Whitehead, 2007). The priorities of the New Labour phenomenon were to narrow the justice gap (bringing more offenders to justice), reduce reoffending and respond to anti-social behaviour. Central concerns were policing, youth justice and drugs. Indubitably, more resources were allocated to the criminal justice system[11] but the critical question remains – has it all worked? The audit results are somewhat mixed, notwithstanding the reforms that were pushed through at a relentless pace. Significantly, this echoes the aforementioned Cabinet Office Prime Minister's Strategy Unit (2006) document, and questions remain about the efficacy of the criminal justice system to achieve its objectives. In other words, is it the right or most effective instrument to respond to illegal forms of behaviour, particularly when some of these are associated with socio-economic structural factors?

Next, the importance of the *Carter Review of Prisons*, published in December 2007, was not the proposal for Titan establishments to expand the capacity of the prison estate (Titans were abandoned in April 2009). Rather, we should be interested in the analysis of those *drivers* behind the 60% (more than 30,000) rise in the prison population in England and Wales between June 1995 and November 2007, by which time it stood at 81,547. First, Carter addressed changes in public attitudes and the political climate from the law-and-order themes of the 1980s: the break-up of consensus, economic decline, rising crime and the retreat from rehabilitation; the Jamie Bulger and Stephen Lawrence murders in 1993 and accompanying media responses; and developments within community punishment and the Prison Works debate in the 1990s. Consequently, there was a greater public preoccupation with crime, fuelled by media reporting, accompanied by a heightened emotional tone in the way crime issues were presented (Freiberg and Gelb, 2008). Second, legislation and the sentencing framework, including the drift towards more punitive sentencing, were alluded to, particularly the 66 pieces of legislation since 1995. It is of interest to refer to the comments of Lord Justice Auld when he said that the public's confidence in the criminal justice system is damaged if, as happened all too often over recent years, legislative reforms are insufficiently considered and 'hurried through in seeming response to political pressures or for quick political advantage' (Auld, 2001, p 19). Third, custody rates and sentence lengths, with greater sentencer demand for probation and prison, were alluded to. In fact, the number of community penalties at all courts increased from 129,922 in 1995 to 190,837 in 2006. Fourth, alluded to earlier, there was a much greater focus on harsher enforcement practices and more emphasis on risk, harm and public protection. When turning to the newly created Suspended Sentence Order, introduced by the Criminal Justice Act 2003, Carter recounted that a significant number of suspended prison sentences were being given for summary offences and that 'a significant number of these would previously have received non-custodial sentences' (Carter, 2007, p 51).

The Ministry of Justice was created in May 2007, which assumed responsibility for probation and prisons following restructuring within the Home Office. By the end of 2007, Patrick Carter published his review on prisons. One of the proposals contained in the review was to reappraise the headquarters function of NOMS, which would have implications for both prisons and probation. The restructuring of offender services associated with the creation of NOMS during 2003–04 was itself now restructured. This was initiated during January 2008 to improve the efficiency and effectiveness of managing offenders and the refocusing of resources to enhance front-line delivery. By March 2008, this amounted to bringing probation and prisons even closer together within a streamlined headquarters function, and the rationalisation of regional structures. With this latest bout of restructuring, Phil Wheatley, Director General of Her Majesty's Prison Service, became Director General of NOMS. Consequently, there were material changes to the upper managerial and strategic reaches of the organisation. One significant outcome of this restructuring was that probation no longer existed separately from, or even on equal terms with, the prison system. Instead, it was subsumed beneath, rather than residing alongside, the Director General. The organisational map of the restructured NOMS, produced in July 2008, revealed that the Director of Probation, Roger Hill, no longer occupied a position coequal to Phil Wheatley. Rather, he was relocated *below* the Director General and alongside seven directors, who were responsible for operations, high security, finance and performance, human resources, the capacity programme, commissioning, and offender health. By the autumn of 2008, it became clear that the Director of Probation would not be replaced when Roger Hill became the Director of Offender Management in the South East region. Therefore, streamlining had greater implications for probation than prisons, even though the Minister of State, David Hanson, denied that this was a merger or even the prison takeover of probation at the National Association of Probation Officers Conference on 17 October 2008. Both agencies would remain as individual delivery services with their own governance and employment structures. It became increasingly difficult to reconcile these disarming ministerial intentions with the NOMS organisational structure, or what occurred after 2010.

Changes at the national level were established on 1 April 2008 and further changes to regional structures were introduced by April 2009. This meant that each of the 10 regions appointed a Director of Offender Management (from 'ROM' to 'DOM') to coordinate and commission all probation and prison services from the public, private and third/voluntary sectors, consistent with the legislative provisions contained in the Offender Management Act 2007. In fact, these arrangements were put in place in London and Wales during 2008 and the Prison Service London Area Office and the office of the Regional Offender Manager were formally merged into the office of Director of Offender Management. It may be suggested that these changes were largely cosmetic, primarily concerned with reducing costs and would hardly be noticed lower down the organisational structure by prison officers and probation offender managers. On the other hand, senior managerial and organisational reconfigurations within NOMS could culminate in the declining influence of the probation ethos throughout the whole of the criminal justice system. If this transpires, the following reflections on *restructuring the restructuring* are offered for consideration.

First, the point can be advanced that changes that affected probation after 1997 were not the result of organic evolutionary processes *initiated from within*, but swift and decisive revolutionary changes *imposed from without* by government for political more than penological reasons. These are not the changes that would have been chosen by the organisation for itself, then slowly introduced over a period of time after a careful analysis of their likely implications. Rather, probation was subjected to a series of convulsions that rapidly transformed the character of the organisation, which continued under the latest phase of restructuring. There was opposition to these enforced changes, particularly by the National Association of Probation Officers. Could the leadership of the service have done anything, something, to prevent the imposition of these transformational convulsions?

Second, it may be suggested that initiatives to encourage organisations to work more closely together to *reduce cultural divides* (the language of partnership arrangements) can be perceived as a laudable objective with more positive than negative features. Contrastingly, when organisations are 'forced' to move closer together at the behest of political and strategic imperatives, the result could be that the distinctive contribution of each institution is diluted. Such developments can damage those mediating checks and balances within the criminal justice system that rely on the disparate influences and contributions of its component parts. Competing and sometimes discordant voices from within different organisational domains can be a sign of dialectical health rather than malaise (from prisons *and* probation, magistrates *and* judges, police, court clerks *and* defence solicitors). Testing out cogent arguments; the challenge of different perspectives; listening to and learning from each other's organisational perspective, values and responsibilities; steering a course through contrasting positions, including critiques of central government policies – all are necessary mechanisms to maintain the strength of different organisations and democratic institutions. This perspective received support from a barrister in the north-east of England who participated in the research project recounted in Chapter Five:

> "The probation service has changed beyond recognition over the course of the last 10 years. The shift of the probation service has left the criminal justice system unbalanced. There is too much emphasis on punishment and a void where there should be an agency dedicated to values of befriending and assisting."

Probation should have a clearly articulated and different organisational rationale to other criminal justice organisations, and this difference should arguably be strengthened rather than diluted through streamlining, modernising and coalescing.

Third, it is possible to argue that rationalisation and streamlining organisational functions to conserve limited financial resources is another laudable objective. It is reasonable to suggest that organisations should guard against becoming bloated on the back of taxpayers' money, so the principles of economy and efficiency can be compelling. However, criminal justice should not solely be guided by fiscal principles embedded within the New Public Management, the contours of which reflect and reproduce the managerial logic of neoliberal capitalism. Working with people who offend, justifying punishment and recourse to community or custodial sentences raise moral issues that advance the debate beyond financial, bureaucratic and managerial priorities. Probation, until relatively recently, constituted a challenge to punishment and imprisonment and, by doing so, made a distinctive historico-cultural contribution throughout the 20th century to criminal and social justice. However, this distinctive sphere of influence has been eroded by modernising and restructuring, which has damaged probation's historic mission. Those features that set probation apart have been denigrated by the politics of disavowal, and an accompanying discourse of punitive excess has displaced sociological understanding and explication. Therefore, what occurred under New Labour after 1997 was not in the organisational interest of either probation or prisons, or the dialectics of criminal and social justice. A separate and distinctive probation voice within NOMS to promote the probation ideal[12] can ensure that prisons are used appropriately for the most serious offenders, reduce costs and also reduce pressure on increasingly hard-pressed staff within overcrowded custodial facilities without compromising the goals of efficiency and effectiveness. Self-evidently, this did not occur if we look back on events from the vantage point of the present. Accordingly, we need to update this account by approaching the period of the Coalition government.

On the cusp of the Coalition government

In 2008, two years before the general election, the Conservative Party (2008) published *Prisons with a Purpose*. This document refers to energy supplies, pollution, economic stability, national security, immigration, transport and development, before turning to crime and prisons. Students of criminal justice are inured to consulting the crisis literature on crime, prison overcrowding and longer prison sentences since 1993, reoffending rates,[13] community sentences that lack credibility, and the volume of crime committed by offenders with previous convictions. Accordingly, the 'right way to reduce the prison population is to break the cycle of re-offending and reduce crime' (Conservative Party, 2008, p 4). It is imperative to restore confidence in the criminal justice system, which will be achieved by launching a rehabilitative revolution in which community and prison sentences reflect four basic principles: punishment, rehabilitation, employment and reparation for victims. Community sentences must be tough and demanding to enhance their credibility and to improve compliance, which repeats familiar themes. *Prisons with a Purpose* also threatens benefit withdrawal for non-compliance with community sentences, a policy previously introduced, then abandoned, by New Labour (see Chapter Five). Furthermore, the ongoing crisis in criminal justice is explained by insufficient prison capacity and the imposition of centrally imposed targets that paralysed prison governors and probation officers. In fact, the 'Probation Service in particular has been burdened with too many targets' (Conservative Party, 2008, p 25). This analysis admits to organisational weaknesses but also proffers liberating possibilities after the stultifying, target-driven and bureaucratically obsessed governmental regimes since 1997. However, it is intriguingly reinforced that 'We want to see new providers brought in to *aid* the probation service' (Conservative Party, 2008, p 80, emphasis added).

There is a vestige of hope for probation services after nationalisation in 2001, which established the NPS, then NOMS after 2003, because of the tantalising prospect of energising professional autonomy and discretion. Nevertheless, a closer reading of the text precipitates a number of niggling concerns: subjecting prison regimes to payment by results (PbR) (the first of many references in the literature between 2008 and 2014; see Whitehead, 2015a), expanding the role of the voluntary and private sectors, and incentivising performance. Some features were innovative in tone, for example, PbR; others were continuous with previous developments, such as value for money and the deeper penetration of privatisation and market expansion. However, there are two significant omissions.

First, analysis and responses are not intellectually embedded within an explanatory historical, politico-economic and ethico-cultural context. The document fails to consider political decisions affecting criminal justice during the previous 30 years, the impact of governmental policies, material conditions leading to the economic crisis in 2007–08, neoliberal ideology and the moral implications of prioritising fiscal efficiencies. This lacuna distorts the analysis compared, for example, to a much earlier Home Office review (Home Office, 1977). Second, there is an air of silence on the content of, and arguments for, the moral coordinates of criminal justice and penal policy. Canton (2007, p 236, cited in Faulkner and Burnett, 2012, p 132) argues that work with offenders is a *morally significant activity* that cannot be reduced to technical gimmicks for achieving efficiency and effectiveness. The dialectic of criminal justice combines fiscal considerations *and* personalist ethics, but *Prisons with a Purpose* is silent on the latter. In 2008, the latest battle lines were sketched to differentiate New Labour from Conservative criminal justice policies during the period leading up to the general election in May 2010. In December 2010, a Green Paper was published by the Coalition government.

The Coalition government and criminal justice, 2010–15

Breaking the Cycle (Ministry of Justice, 2010) is a significant document because it proposes fundamental changes to the criminal justice system to ensure 'improved public safety through more effective punishments that reduce the prospect of criminals reoffending time and time again' (Ministry of Justice, 2010, p 5). The thematic focus is local solutions for local problems and to utilise expertise wherever it can be found, which juxtaposes the Big Society with the rehabilitation revolution. *Breaking the Cycle* repeats the refrain that the prison population had doubled since 1993 (but fails to come clean that this followed the decision of a previous Conservative administration). Retribution displaced rehabilitation; reconviction rates were too high and costly, at £7–10 billion annually; and there were 16,000 active offenders at any one time, each with 75 previous convictions. There was also the admission that the weight of criminal legislation since 1997 had been excessive rather than measured. The principles of reform underpinning the rehabilitation revolution are public protection, punishment *and* rehabilitation, transparency and accountability, and the decentralisation of services. It is creditably acknowledged that crime is committed by offenders with a surfeit of problems, and the proposed reforms offer a once in a generation opportunity to make a difference.

There are five substantive sections in the Green Paper.[14] Importantly, PbR is foregrounded as a radical reform that signals the transference of financial risks from taxpayers to the new providers. Consequently, there will be a competition strategy to determine the provision of services according to commercial and market principles (on the transition from a *market economy* to *market society*, see Sandel, 2012). In other words, the Ministry of Justice will no longer pay for good intentions. Again, silence enshrouds the moral foundations of criminal justice, nor does *Breaking the Cycle* consider the theoretical possibility that services to offenders may have value even though they achieve 'nothing'. Rather than weave a nomenclature establishing the intellectual and moral coordinates of the moral responsibility of the government and the corresponding ethical duties of criminal justice organisations, the Green Paper foregrounds future business opportunities, commercial interests and fiscal rewards for achieving reductions in reoffending. At no point is sufficient consideration given to the archaeological deposits, historical traditions or ethico-cultural contribution of probation work to the system of criminal and social justice. A narrow-minded and market-oriented perspective invades the criminal justice domain, which penetratively extends the direction of New Labour adumbrated earlier.

Modernising Commissioning (Cabinet Office, 2010) comments on the rehabilitation revolution and associated plans for commissioning services through the expansion of mutuals, cooperatives, charities and social enterprises in running public services. At this early stage, the Coalition government was actively turning towards profit-making businesses with commercial objectives to assume an enhanced role in public service reform. The accumulating documentary evidence provided a strong steer on how public services should be delivered in future: the relentless demand to improve efficiency and effectiveness; investment opportunities; private is superior to public provision; the expansion of markets; and reducing risks to taxpayers through PbR. Accordingly, 'As announced in the Spending Review, the Government intends to identify particular opportunities to expand the use of payment by results across particular service areas' (Cabinet Office, 2010, p 9). Nevertheless, *Modernising Commissioning* does not ask moral questions appertaining to the state disposing of its ethico-cultural responsibilities to diverse providers, or the implications for probation. The scythe of privatisation, marketisation and diversification is penetratively struck at the moral and cultural fabric of criminal justice, without rigorous intellectual consideration. This was a serious omission and neglect of duty.

The following year *Open Public Services* (HM Government, 2011, p 5) asserted that the reform of public services is a 'key progressive cause'. It conflated reform with the task of civilising society, but omitted the problematic of reconciling the future commercial platform with the ethical provision of services. In other words, is it possible to create good public services to enhance the social domain if the forces and influences of symbolic efficiency are coercively relegated into the *Real* (see chapter Two), if the ideological and material forces of neoliberal capitalism stifle the reproduction of ethico-cultural phenomena? This document continues the thematic trend of reform through the fiscal mechanism of PbR, which was applied to numerous organisational spheres, including the Work Programme, public health, drug and alcohol recovery services, children's centres, and vulnerable people, as well as the rehabilitation revolution in prisons and probation (HM Government, 2011, para 5.14). Five additional principles of reform are cited: increased choice, decentralisation, the diversity of providers, fair access to services, and accountability to taxpayers. With no supporting evidence, it is ideologically asserted that 'Our reforms are the best way to deliver better services; indeed, they are the only way we can deliver improved, modern public services in a time of fiscal consolidation and growing demand' (HM Government, 2011, para 1.27).

Next, the *Competition Strategy* (Ministry of Justice, 2011) reinforced the aforementioned documentary themes, confirming that competition in offender services can be traced to 1992, with the first private prison at HMP Wolds (currently 14 private and 130 public prisons including 16 youth offenders institutions). However, the market in non-custodial sentences was much less developed. Therefore, the Ministry of Justice aspired to build on the platform of competition, inchoate privatisation, the private finance initiative (PFI) prison building programme, better value for money (VfM) in the delivery of prison escort and custody services, bail accommodation, and the expansion of electronic monitoring. A competition strategy was required to identify the most suitable providers to deliver offender services, which include custodial provision, community services, health, substance misuse and learning skills. When shifting the focus from custody to the community, 'The starting point here is different, as the use of competition in delivering core probation services is less developed, as is the market for providing these services' (Ministry of Justice, 2011, p 15). The drivers of public service and criminal justice reform are elucidated as financial rationalisation, VfM, outcomes, target achievement, risk and reward, business models and commercial practices, the diversity of providers, privatisation, and markets and competition between the sectors. Again, for comparative purposes, this operating framework is incompatible with the aforementioned *Review* (Home Office, 1977). It is also discernibly different to the 1980s and 1990s, primarily because the nature and scale of reform is more penetrative. The past was a different place, intellectually and morally, compared to the period under consideration here.

Two significant documents were published in March 2012: *Punishment and Reform: Effective Community Sentences* (Ministry of Justice, 2012a); and *Punishment and Reform: Effective Probation Services* (Ministry of Justice, 2012b). Previously, in 2008, *Prisons with a Purpose* stated that reconviction rates were too high, indicative of a lamentable failure. Now, four years later, this problem would be remedied by allowing probation to retain responsibility for approximately 40,000 high-risk offenders and the production of court reports for magistrates and judges. The remaining low- to medium-risk offenders, approximately 220,000, would be the subject of market competition between the public, private and voluntary sectors. Consequently, 'The aim of all this is to free up a traditional, old-fashioned system and introduce new ways of operating and delivering that will help drive a reduction in reoffending' (Ministry of Justice, 2012a, p 3). The accompanying publication, *Effective Probation Services*, extends the principle of competition in the Offender Management Act 2007. On reflection, it would have been beneficial to reflect with greater intellectual perspicacity on why: the 'modern' is presumed to be superior to established historical traditions; new superior to old; competition better than cooperation; and private enterprise superior and more efficient than public duty and service. Additionally, there is the problematic of efficiency targets swamping moral questions, and restructuring and rebalancing unbalancing the dialectics of criminal justice by eroding former historical, cultural and ethico-cultural conventions. Finally, also during 2012, the White Paper *Swift and Sure Justice* (Ministry of Justice, 2012c) supported the intellectual justification for reforming the criminal justice system in England and Wales by repeating the arguments for modernisation of an outdated infrastructure that delivers justice too slowly and costly.

The year 2013 is significant for *Transforming Rehabilitation*, which began in January (Ministry of Justice, 2013a), with a period of consultation until 22 February. This New Year document provides further detail on the structural mechanisms required to deliver reform, and 19 questions are posed for consultation. These questions refer to: PbR; the pricing structure and incentives for providers; bureaucracy; incentivising performance; managing poor performance; the supply chain of offender services; integrating the public, private and voluntary sectors; relevant legislation; non-compliance; probation and other delivery systems; maximising local expertise; maintaining professional standards; and the role of the inspectorate. None of these questions initiate reasoned discussion and public debate on the intellectual and moral foundations of criminal justice, a prerequisite of people-facing organisations. Subsequently, the Ministry of Justice (2013b) published its response to the consultation in *Transforming Rehabilitation: A Strategy for Reform*. First, under the rubric of *Reducing Reoffending*, rehabilitation and mentoring services would be statutorily provided to all offenders, including those sentenced to less than 12 months. Consequently, 'Competing services will allow us to use innovative payment mechanisms which drive a focus on reducing reoffending. Providers' level of payment will therefore be dependent on the reductions in reoffending they achieve' (Ministry of Justice, 2013b, p 14). PbR is elucidated as a mechanism to facilitate fiscal incentives: providers must assist *all* offenders not just those who will 'succeed', which would rig payment in favour of investors' vested interests; providers will be financially rewarded for success when offenders and former prisoners achieve complete desistance for 12 months; and payment mechanisms will take account of the total number of offences committed by offenders. Therefore, 'The combined payment mechanism, including "fee for service" and "payment by results" elements will mean that providers need to work successfully with all offenders, in order to get paid in full' (Ministry of Justice, 2013b, p 15). Next, the section on *Protecting the Public* proposes a new public sector probation service after 60–70% of its work had been opened up to competition. Then, *Making the System Work* indicates that some probation staff will transfer into the private and voluntary sectors. This signals the end of probation trusts through the creation of a new NPS managed by the Ministry of Justice and NOMS. By the autumn of 2014, it was envisaged that there would be 21 Contract Package Areas of diverse providers called Community Rehabilitation Companies (CRCs) to deliver criminal justice services alongside a truncated probation system. Between May 2013 and the autumn of 2014, potential providers, including large private companies (Interserve, G4S and Sodexo Justice Services), were encouraged to bid for Ministry of Justice contracts.

In September 2013, the Ministry of Justice (2013c) issued the *Target Operating Manual*, which consolidated the structure to deliver more effective rehabilitative outcomes. It included through-the-gate services for offenders sentenced to less than 12 months' imprisonment that necessitated new licence arrangements. Furthermore, the reformed structure endorsed marketised competition between the sectors, the flexibility to innovate, a new NPS and 21 CRCs. It is specified that payment to the CRCs 'will be based on a weighted annual volume of offender starts, with a proportion of the payment at risk, dependent on their performance in reducing reoffending' (Ministry of Justice, 2013c, p 5). The NPS would be responsible for writing court reports on offenders and sentencing advice to the courts, risk assessment, allocating cases, the management of high-risk cases, the enforcement of community orders and licences, Parole Board duties, and Multi-Agency Public Protection Arrangements (MAPPA). Accordingly, existing probation trusts would be dissolved on 31 March 2014 and staff allocated to either the NPS or CRCs. Nevertheless, a number of concerns were articulated during the transitional phase before the new arrangements were finally determined: the necessity for and pace of reforms; their rationale; making the transitional arrangements work; tender processes; how the market will work and the relationship between NPS and CRC if there is a change in the risk status of offenders, as assuredly there will be; PbR and penalties for failure;

the risks and costs of reform; and staff retention and the potential loss of skills.

After much activity between *Breaking the Cycle* of December 2010 and the cumulative events of 2013, 30 bidders passed the first stage of the competition process to win the 21 CRC contracts to lead the new era in a fight against offending (announced on 13 December 2013 in Ministry of Justice, 2013d). The bids were submitted by a melange of organisations and partnerships who wanted to lead the rehabilitation revolution, such as private firms, charities, businesses and multinationals. It was anticipated that the successful bidders would be announced during the autumn of 2014. For the Ministry of Justice, the rehabilitation revolution exemplified innovative ways of doing business differently and the best way of using taxpayers' money: the contracts are worth £450 million annually, and in addition to bids from lead providers, 800 organisations expressed an interest in the delivery supply chain.

The proposals for reform were scrutinised by the House of Commons Justice Committee (2014). Some committee members expressed approbation at the direction of travel since 2008, but others expressed concern that reducing the role of the public sector probation service is unconvincing, too risky, untested and unpiloted, and unlikely to deliver better results. Furthermore, there were divergent views from witnesses appearing before the committee. It was acknowledged that there were gaps in current practice, such as support being unavailable to offenders leaving prison after serving less than 12 months (erstwhile prison voluntary aftercare cases (PVACs)). Consequently, the evidence presented to the committee during 2013, including from Ministry of Justice officials, consolidated the position that *Transforming Rehabilitation* has four elements:

- extend statutory rehabilitation to those sentenced to less than 12 months – an extra 50,000 offenders;
- open up rehabilitation services to a diverse market of providers and new payment mechanisms;
- create a new NPS primarily involved in public protection; and
- reorganise the prison estate.

Most of the proposals could be undertaken through the Offender Management Act 2007, but new legislation was required to extend supervision to short-term prisoners, beginning with the Offender Rehabilitation Bill. The conclusions and recommendations from the committee report are enumerated as follows:

- Extending statutory supervision for offenders sentenced to 12 months imprisonment or less is a positive reform;
- There remain serious questions about the evidence-base for reform, ironic given the emphasis on What Works since 1992;
- Witnesses expressed apprehension at the pace, scale, architecture, detail, and likely consequences of reform;
- Risks to the system and costs;
- Retention of skills and the development of staff in the 21 CRCs;
- Payment by Results: is the principle of reward for success and punishment for failure morally acceptable? It is worth stating the following in full:

The Ministry has high expectations of what can be achieved in the way of efficiency savings and extension of services through contracting out the management of low and medium risk offenders within existing resources. It seems entirely feasible to us that as the competition progresses and details are refined, the attractiveness of these contracts might wane, resulting in incomplete or inadequate provision in certain areas or types of service. (House of Commons Justice Committee, 2014, para 25 of 'Conclusions and recommendations')

On Wednesday, 29 October 2014, Chris Grayling, Justice Secretary, announced the decision on the successful bidders for the 21 CRCs: Sodexo Justice Services in partnership with NACRO (six areas), Achieving Real Change for Communities (ARCC) (one), Purple Futures (five), The Reducing Reoffending Partnership (two), Working Links (three), Geo Mercia Willowdene (one), MTCNovo (two) and Seetec (one). Fuller details are as follows (but also refer to note 15):[15]

- Northumbria: Sodexo Justice Services in partnership with NACRO.
- Cumbria and Lancashire: Sodexo Justice Services in partnership with NACRO.
- Durham and Tees Valley: ARCC.
- Humberside, Lincolnshire and North Yorkshire: Purple Futures.
- West Yorkshire: Purple Futures.
- Cheshire and Greater Manchester: Purple Futures.
- Merseyside: Purple Futures.

- South Yorkshire: Sodexo Justice Services in partnership with NACRO.
- Staffordshire and West Midlands: The Reducing Reoffending Partnership.
- Derbyshire, Leicestershire, Nottinghamshire and Rutland: The Reducing Reoffending Partnership.
- Wales: Working Links.
- Warwickshire and West Mercia: Geo Mercia Willowdene.
- Bristol, Gloucestershire, Somerset and Wiltshire: Working Links.
- Dorset, Devon and Cornwall: Working Links.
- Hampshire and Isle and Wight: Purple Futures.
- Thames Valley: MTCNovo.
- Bedfordshire, Northamptonshire, Cambridgeshire and Hertforshire: Sodexo Justice Services in partnership with NACRO.
- Norfolk and Suffolk: Sodexo Justice Services in partnership with NACRO.
- Essex: Sodexo Justice Services in partnership with NACRO.
- London: MTCNovo.
- Kent, Surrey and Sussex: Seetec.

Additional comment on payment by results

The documents cited earlier incorporate frequent references to PbR. Due to its semiotic significance in the new dispensation, an additional explanatory comment is required. The first substantive application of PbR to the criminal justice system is the six-year pilot that began in 2010 at HMP Peterborough (Ministry of Justice, 2013f). This project provides rehabilitation and mentoring services to 3000 offenders serving sentences of less than 12 months, which commences in prison and continues beyond release. Peterborough is a Category B establishment operated by Sodexo Justice Services, one of 11 private prisons in England and Wales (also 111 public prisons), that won the contract to run six out of 21 CRCs. The point for emphasis is that the Ministry of Justice contracted with Social Finance (see its dedicated website), which was established in 2007 to build a social investment market in the UK. Its rationale is to raise capital to fund social projects according to measures of success and failure determined by market principles. Funds can be raised from a variety of sources, including local authorities, private/commercial investors, philanthropists and associated charitable foundations, as well as national lottery funds. The next step was for Social Finance to fund the St. Giles Trust to deliver the intervention to reduce reoffending beyond release, in addition to which, the Ormiston Trust provides support to prisoners' families. If the intervention delivers a reduction in reoffending by 7.5% or more, then the Social Impact Bond, the outcome-based contract mechanism, results in investors receiving a return of up to 13% on the original investment. The premium will be funded by the Ministry of Justice from anticipated savings accrued in the overall reduction in reoffending (Cabinet Office, 2010). However, if the 7.5% outcome target is not achieved, then investors must bear the risks and costs, rather than the taxpayer/treasury. Under PbR, the Ministry of Justice only pays for demonstrable and measurable successful outcomes in reducing reoffending. The interim results at Peterborough were encouraging, in fact, more encouraging than the Doncaster pilot (Ministry of Justice, 2013e). However, what about offenders sentenced to community supervision? Although, as explained earlier, the probation service will retain responsibility for offenders on community orders and prison licences who present a serious risk of harm to the public, most community-based services will be delivered by the 21 CRCs for low- and medium-risk offenders. These services, locked into the parameters of the internal market by political fiat, will deliver accommodation, mentoring, employment, training and education, and alcohol and drug addiction support, as well as supervising community orders and appropriate low-risk prison licences. They will also be subjected to PbR. For further information, see: Chambers (2013) on the case for expanding PbR; Knight-Markiegi and Quinn (2013) for a comparison of the implementation of PbR across public services; and Whitehead (2015a). Finally, in addition to open source material, one should also refer to associated websites, tweets and blogs, for example, Russell Webster (see: http://www.russellwebster.com) on what is quickly becoming a discrete industry of the new organisational orthodoxy. If the documents from 2008 make repeated references to the new funding mechanism, by contrast, they omit to locate developments in criminal justice within a broader historical and political context, which is a serious deficiency rectified in this book.

Conclusion

This chapter excavated the chronological parameters of modernisation that brought into view politically imposed ideological, material and cultural transformations in probation, criminal justice and penal policy from the accession of New Labour in May 1997 to the end of the Coalition government in May 2015. It is possible to suggest that the first bout of modernisation can be traced to the Criminal Justice Act 1948, or perhaps the 1980s has a better claim on the term. Nevertheless, the starting point for this book is deliberately established at 1997, earlier periods are covered in previous work (Whitehead and Statham, 2006; Whitehead, 2007). Towards the end of the New Labour dispensation in 2008, Jack Straw, Justice Secretary, gave a speech at the Royal Society of Arts in London on the theme of punishment and reform (on 27 October 2008). The speech was constructed as a justificatory reprise of New Labour's achievements in the field of criminal justice, which included an unseemly boast on the policy of punitive toughness pursued towards offenders, which constituted the criterion of political success. There was also a litany of predictable themes, for example, 14,000 more police and 30% more prison places, but even this was not enough because 12,500 additional places would be required by 2014 to increase capacity to 96,000, even though adult offending was down by 23% and youth offending by 19%. However, there is an analytical drought when it comes to explaining the circumstances in which many of these features were deemed necessary, and there is little in this speech that was novel; in fact, it was much more of the same (Goodman, 2003).

In another speech in the following month (17/18 November 2008), this time to the influential Magistrates' Association, Straw made it clear that the Comprehensive Spending Review of 2007 meant that by March 2011, there should be £1 billion worth of savings across the Ministry of Justice. The aim remained to deliver a fair system of justice, but can this be achieved if there are 10,000 job cuts in probation, prison and court services? Nevertheless, the expansion of punishment talk, organisational restructuring associated with NOMS, New Public Management, centralisation and the accompanying deprofessionalisation within local probation areas, and the erosion of social work encapsulated within advise, assist and befriend remain as some of the talismanic fixtures of the new penal heaven and earth created between 1997 and 2010. Modernisation was given a splash of colour in the fluorescent vests adorning offenders on community payback. As the Jews were ghettoised in Renaissance Europe (Venice provides a pertinent illustration) and much later forced to wear the distinguishing yellow star as the mark of a racially excluded and denigrated *other*, so offenders undertaking unpaid work in the community were symbolically represented as a deviant and exclusionary *other*. The New Jerusalem of modernisation and cultural change, *extraordinarily cemented in place by what was formerly the political Left rather than Right*, had taken a nastier turn.

However, there was much more to come because the then Justice Secretary, in a speech to Trainee Probation Officers at the University of Portsmouth on 4 February 2009, stated that community sentences still have an image problem by appearing too 'soft' (Straw, 2009). Does this mean that probation employees will be transmuted into 'soft cops' to enhance their credibility with the public (Goodman, 2003, p 219), or perhaps muscular attack dogs of the repressive state apparatus snapping at the heels of offenders in the community? Finally, this chapter concluded with a preliminary account of criminal justice policy and practice under the Coalition government between 2010 and 2015. This section drew attention to a rehabilitation revolution, the mechanisms of which are competition, privatisation and marketisation. This has profound implications for probation, manifested clearly in the construction of 21 CRCs.

The motif of modernisation and transformation, threading its way through this chapter, exemplifies a more emotionally charged, politically induced, expressive criminal justice policy (Durkheim); there is more management and bureaucracy (Weber); and probation has been reconfigured by the ideological and material forces of neoliberal capitalism (Marx), and webs of disciplinary control (Foucault). We have witnessed the decline of symbolic efficiency by the obscene *Real* (Lacan and Žižek), precipitating the collapse of moral conventions (personalism and moral economy). Before developing these themes, Table 1.1 summarises key events.

Table 1.1: Summary of significant developments, 1997–2015

1997	Labour manifesto: *New Labour Because Britain Deserves Better*
1998	*Prisons–Probation: Joining Forces to Protect the Public*
1999	Cabinet Office: *Modernising Government*
	Lord Justice Auld's review of the courts
2000	Halliday review of sentencing (culminated in the Criminal Justice Act 2003)
	National Standards (revised 2002) introduced stricter enforcement
2001	Home Office: *Criminal Justice: The Way Ahead*
	NPS commenced on 1 April
	Labour manifesto: *Ambitions for Britain*
2002	Patrick Carter reviewed correctional services
2003	Criminal Justice Act (partially implemented 4 April 2005)
	Carter report: *Managing Offenders, Reducing Crime: A New Approach*, which established NOMS
2004	Home Office: *Confident Communities in a Secure Britain*, Strategic Plan 2004–08
	Home Office: *Cutting Crime, Delivering Justice*, Strategic Plan 2004–08
2005	Labour manifesto: *Britain Forward Not Back*
	National Standards revised
	NOMS National Offender Management Model
2006	*Five Year Strategy for Protecting the Public and Reducing Re-Offending*
	Rebalancing the Criminal Justice System in Favour of the Law-Abiding Majority
	Delivering Simple, Speedy, Summary Justice
	Improving Prison and Probation Services: Public Value Partnerships
	Prime Minister's Strategy Unit Policy Review: *Crime, Justice and Cohesion*
2007	*Ten Years of criminal justice under Labour: An Independent Audit*
	Ministry of Justice created
	National Standards updated
	Offender Management Bill received Royal Assent on 26 July
	Carter review of prisons published in December
2008	NOMS restructuring
	Casey Report: *Engaging Communities in Fighting Crime*
	David Hanson's speech to National Association of Probation Officers Conference on 17 October
	Jack Straw's speech during October on punishment and victims
	Ministry of Justice: *Punishment and Reform*
	Conservative Party: *Prisons with a Purpose* (important document)
2009	NOMS *Strategic Business Plan 2009–2011*
	Jack Straw's speech to trainee probation officers at Portsmouth University
2010	Coalition government elected in May
	Ministry of Justice: *Breaking the Cycle* (December)
	Modernising Commissioning
2011	*Open Public Services*
	Competition Strategy
2012	*Punishment and Reform: Effective Community Sentences*
	Punishment and Reform: Effective Probation Services
	Legal Aid, Sentencing and Punishment of Offenders Act
	Between 1993 and 2012, the prison population in England and Wales increased by 41,800 to 86,000
2013	*Transforming Rehabilitation: A Strategy for Reform*
	Target Operating Manual
	Crime and Courts Act
2014	House of Commons Justice Committee Transforming Rehabilitation
	29 October decision on the 21 CRCs
	Offender Rehabilitation Act
2015	General election – Conservative government elected (to 2020)
	Prison population 85,884 (November) but predicted to rise to approximately 90,000 by June 2020 (see Ministry of Justice [2013e] *Story of the Prison Population 1993–2012*; Ministry of Justice (2014) *Prison Population Projections 2014–2020*

Notes

[1] A clear distinction should be established between 'old' and New Labour. It is worth recalling that the Labour Party was out of office for 18 years between 1979 and 1997, a period in which there were four consecutive general election defeats at the hands of Conservative governments. Consequently, it is argued that a critical factor in the reconstruction of Labour, particularly after 1992, was a significant change in the direction of penal policy. What had been an antipathy towards the police and a predisposition for explaining offending behaviour by reference to socio-economic disadvantage were now seen 'by the modernisers as being increasingly out of step with the public demand for greater protection from the consequences of criminal acts' (Windlesham, 2003, p 61). It is also helpful to be acquainted with the material contained in the book by Robert Reiner (2007a) on this theme. Additionally, there was a retreat from old Labour *solidaristic* thinking (Sim, 2009, p 81) in the endorsement of Conservative ideology that blamed the individual to construct a criminological *other*.

[2] For more information on party political manifestos since 1945, see: www.psr.keele. ac.uk/area/uk/man.htm. Another useful resource is the excellent chapter in the *Oxford Handbook of Criminology* by Downes and Morgan (1997).

[3] There is a collection of useful texts on the subject of youth justice, for example, Muncie (2009) and Burke (2008) *Young People, Crime and Justice*. Moreover, the assessment by Solomon and Garside (2008) 'Ten years of Labour's youth justice reforms: an independent audit' is particularly instructive. My book primarily explores and explains modernisation and cultural change in probation. Nevertheless, it should be acknowledged that one of the first acts of modernisation by New Labour was undertaken in the field of youth justice. Prior to 1997, the youth justice system was deemed to be uneconomic, inefficient and ineffective. After 1997, the system was reformed, which can be illustrated as follows: a number of consultation documents were produced; and the Crime and Disorder Act 1998 established the new Youth Justice System, Youth Justice Board and Youth Offending Teams in local authorities. It was also stated at section 37 of the Crime and Disorder Act 1998 that 'It shall be the principal aim of the youth justice system to prevent reoffending by children and young persons'. Reform was a key priority from 1997 to 2001, but modernisation is associated with a punitive turn (Pratt et al, 2005): more resources accompanied by performance indicators, National Standards, value for money and economy, efficiency and effectiveness (the New Public Management agenda). There has been a focus upon system management, procedures and processes, including target setting, some of which have not been met. All these matters are critically reviewed in this document. For an exploration of modernisation in the prison system, see Sim (2009) and particularly Chapter Five.

[4] Jock Young (2007, ch 6) touches upon New Labour politics and the creation of the Social Exclusion Unit. He argues that New Labour acknowledged the structural causes of crime, but that this did not result in changes being made to the politico-economic structures of society. Rather the focus was placed upon 'managing the problem' rather than initiating necessary transformations. The 'analysis of crime, therefore, emphasises agency over structure, and management and the administration of life's difficulties over the structural inequalities which generates these difficulties' (Young, 2007, p 112). This analysis resonates with arguments advanced in Wilkinson and Pickett (2009).

[5] Norman Fairclough (2000) *New Labour, New Language?* is worth consulting. It contains an interesting thesis that, among other things, looks at the way in which changing the culture of an organisation is inextricably bound up with transforming its language. It is also worth noting how Fairclough provides examples of modernising features associated with New Labour, some of which resonate with what has occurred within probation: introducing an annual report on the progress of government; devolution; the centralisation of power and the role of special advisors; bypassing the cabinet; coordinating the presentation of policies across government departments; discipline and control within the party in addition to public sector organisations; and focus groups, spin and media manipulation.

[6] Some of the key features contained in the White Paper *Criminal Justice: The Way Ahead* (Home Office, 2001a) should be alluded to. First, the White Paper acknowledged that the increase in crime over the previous 25 years is associated with unemployment, a lack of opportunities for the unskilled, drug taking, the availability of consumer goods and changes within social attitudes. Even though the formal structures of the criminal justice system cannot, on their own, create a law-abiding and cohesive society, the system must nevertheless prevent crime and reoffending, effectively deal with criminal cases, be responsive to victims and the law-abiding, and be accountable for its decisions. Accordingly, it should deliver 'justice for all' by catching, trying, convicting, punishing and rehabilitating offenders. Some of the reforms since 1997 were reprised, primarily to the youth justice system and Crown Prosecution Service, including establishing 376 Crime and Disorder Reduction Partnerships in England and Wales. There is also a reference to Neighbourhood Watch Schemes – 160,000 separate local schemes involving 6 million households – victim support, additional resources, and expressions of concern for minority ethnic groups being over-represented in the criminal justice system. Significantly, modernisation is juxtaposed with being *tough*.

[7] National Standards were initially introduced into probation in 1988 with a view to creating a more consistent and accountable service. Since then, they have been periodically reviewed and new versions were produced, for example, in 1992, 1995, 2000–02, 2005 and 2007.

[8] The Criminal Justice Act 2003 was the first piece of legislation to set out the aims of sentencing, of which there are five:
- punishment;
- reduction of crime, including deterrence;
- reform and rehabilitation;
- public protection; and
- reparation.

The discussion contained in Taylor, Wasik and Leng (2004, p 173), on what are deemed to be incompatible philosophies of sentencing, is worth consulting.

[9] Additional material on encouraging faith communities to participate more fully in the delivery of services to offenders will be considered in Chapters Three and Four. Suffice it to say that this constitutes an important development within NOMS because of the way in which the third sector is attracting a degree of prominence.

[10] Foucault's thesis that the prison does not prevent recidivism, in fact, that the reverse is the case, can be found in *Discipline and Punish* (Foucault, 1977). Some data indicate that the reoffending rate following short custodial sentences was 59.7%, compared with 37.9% for community sentences (Straw, 2009, p 3). For more information on Foucault, see the discussion towards the end of Chapter Two, which covers this

subject in rather more detail. Additionally, see the critique of the carceral boom, primarily in the US, in *Punishing the Poor* (Wacquant, 2009).

[11] 'Ten years of criminal justice under Labour: an independent audit', by Solomon, Eades, Garside and Rutherford (2007), is an important document. It explores a number of issues, including spending on the criminal justice system since 1997 and Labour's record on crime reduction. The document proceeds to look at three New Labour priorities – the justice gap (bringing more people to justice), reoffending and anti-social behaviour – before turning to the police, youth justice and drugs. In relation to political intentions and targets, this independent audit comes to the conclusion that the results are *mixed* after 10 years. The criminal justice system has been overhauled since 1997, major changes have been imposed and more resources were provided, particularly since 2000, when probation did quite well (an increase of 70% in real terms since 1997; see Straw, 2009, p 3). By contrast, the Ministry of Justice pursued savings of £1 billion between 2008 and 2011, which affected probation, prisons and the courts. One observation of the independent audit is that 'Questions remain about whether government is placing too much emphasis on finding criminal justice solutions to complex social and economic problems' (Solomon et al, 2007, p 13). This document is a useful summary of events prior to the rehabilitation revolution of 2010–15.

[12] In a previous publication, the main features of what can be described as the probation ideal were summarised as follows: take victims seriously; offenders have the potential to change; work with other agencies to keep offenders out of the criminal justice system and custody because of the labelling effects of both; a clear set of values rooted in tolerance, decency, care, compassion and *sociological* understanding; the importance of social work relationships; an awareness of the adverse effects of social circumstances on human behaviour; and the promotion of criminal and social justice (Whitehead, 2007, 2015b).

[13] See Home Office (2007), where two-year reconviction rates data controlled for offender characteristics: prison 64.7%, community rehabilitation order 56.9%; drug treatment and testing order 82.3%; community punishment order 37.9%; and community punishment and rehabilitation order 52.2%. See also McNeil and Weaver (2010) and Ministry of Justice (2013) *Transforming Rehabilitation: A Summary of Evidence on Reducing Reoffending*, which summarises evidence on reducing reoffending.

[14] It is stated that 'The Green Paper provides a once in a generation opportunity for new providers from all sectors to work alongside staff in the criminal justice system to make a real difference' (Ministry of Justice, 2010, p 9). The five substantive sections are: (1) Punishment and Payback; (2) Rehabilitate Offenders to Reduce Crime; (3) Payment by Results; (4) Reform Sentencing; and (5) Youth Justice. At page 24 we read that 'Evidence indicates that the *relationship* between an offender and the person managing them is an important factor in successful rehabilitation'.

[15] Sodexo Justice Services (see: http://uk.sodexo.com/uken/services/on-site/justice-services/) is in partnership with NACRO in six areas. Formerly Kalyx, Sodexo has been running justice services since 1993 in 120 sites across the world, including five prisons in the UK (Peterborough, Northumberland, Forest Bank, Bronzfield and Addiewell). Its values are safety, dignity and opportunity, in addition to which 'Everyone has the right to be treated humanely, decently, respectfully and fairly'. ARCC (see: http://www.stockton.gov.uk/communitysafety/arcc/) is comprised of eight partners and is a not-for-profit organisation delivering quality services in the north-east of England. At a conference at Police Headquarters, Ladgate

Lane, on 25 January 2014 for the Voluntary, Community and Enterprise (VCE) sector, Achieving Real Change for Communities (ARCC) was confirmed as one of 13 local bidders. ARCC is in partnership with Fabrick Housing, the Wise Group, Safe in Tees Valley, Tees Esk and Wear Valleys Foundation Trust, the Vardy Foundation, Changing Lives in the North East Company Incorporated (CIC), Stockton Borough Council, and Darlington Borough Council. Purple Futures is an Interserve-led partnership (see: http://purplefutures.sites.interserve.com/), where staff will be managed by Interserve on behalf of Purple Futures to provide rehabilitative services in conjunction with voluntary groups. Interserve, the majority partner, is 'one of the world's foremost support services and construction companies operating in the UK and internationally'. In 2011, it created a justice team to respond to the emerging *Transforming Rehabilitation* agenda to deliver a 'Theory of Change' model. It is listed on FTSE 250 Index, with gross revenue of £3.4 billion and a workforce of over 80,000 worldwide. The Reducing Reoffending Partnership (see: http://rrpartnership.com/) is described as a 'groundbreaking new partnership' between Ingeus (work programme), Crime Reduction Initiatives (CRI) (health and social care charity) and St Giles Trust (work with offenders), combining experience from the voluntary and private sectors to deliver the government's rehabilitation revolution agenda. Working Links (see: http://www.workinglinks.co.uk/) provides services to people to create better futures. Geo Mercia Willowdene (see: http://geomerciawillowdene.co.uk/) is a partnership between the Geo Group Ltd, Mercia Community Action Ltd and Willowdene Rehabilitation Ltd. The Geo group provides custody, detainee transport and offender management across the world (US, UK, South Africa and Australia). MTCNovo (see: http://www.londoncrc.org.uk/news/) seeks to embody the best of probation in a joint innovative venture that embodies the third, public and private sectors to provide rehabilitation services. Seetec (see: http://www.seetec.co.uk/) has, since 1984, grown to be one of the UK's largest and most experienced providers of government-funded welfare to work and skills training programmes. It is expected that the new arrangements will be established by February 2015.

TWO

Assembling the resources to theorise probation and criminal justice

Approaches to excavating probation

It is possible to construct different approaches to exploring and explaining the probation service throughout its long association with the criminal justice system. The first, unilluminatingly descriptive, sequentially presents a number of significant events beginning in late-Victorian society with the missionary forerunners of probation officers. This approach is illustrated in the texts by Joan King (1964), Fred Jarvis (1972) and Dorothy Bochel (1976). The second identifies a series of discontinuous ideologies that can be slotted into definable time frames: 1876–1930s, a theology of saving souls; 1930s–1970s, 'scientific' curing by casework to rehabilitate offenders; 1980s, alternatives to custody; 1990s, punishment in the community; and after 2001, bureaucratic managerialism and more expressive forms of punishment (McWilliams, 1983, 1985, 1986, 1987). More recent (2010–15) is the deeper ideological and material penetration of neoliberal restructuring by marketisation and privatisation. This is more tantalising because it is more analytical than descriptive, drawing attention to the significance of changing ideas and accompanying discourses within probation practice, associated with different politico-economic formations. In other words, changing ideologies are related to transformations within state formation in support of different socio-economic systems, which, in turn, shape penal responses (Garland, 1985, 2001; Cavadino and Dignan, 2006).

A third approach, refined in this book, is grounded in and informed by disparate bodies of social theory, some of which have profitably been applied to the sociology of punishment to achieve illuminating effects (Garland, 1990; Hudson, 2003). As there are different approaches to understanding the phenomenon of punishment that draw theoretical inspiration from classical and contemporary social theory, it may also be suggested that the modernised and transformed probation domain since 1997 can profit from an exploration as theoretically diverse.

The probation service is not a monolithic structure, a self-contained autonomous entity, immune from forces pressing in upon it from the *outside*, such as: changing public attitudes towards crime; the politics of will to power and latest fashions in management and bureaucracy; the problematic of maintaining order in circumstances of advanced marginality (Wacquant, 2009); and crime stories generated by the media that fuel fear of crime. Rather, it is a complex organisation, involved in a multiplicity of tasks, which bodies of social theory can excavate and explain. To illuminate the contemporary and modernised complexities introduced in Chapter One, and to turn from description to rigorous analysis, a theoretically nuanced approach is required, which, in turn, establishes a solid basis for insightful understanding and sustained critique. For my purposes, a predominantly descriptive approach is singularly ill-equipped for the exploratory and explanatory task required by this book. Bodies of social theory should be flushed to the surface to undertake the intellectual task. This chapter begins with classical sociological theory in the company of Durkheim, Weber and Marx, before proceeding to Foucault, Lacan and Žižek. Accordingly, I have extended and refined the theoretical grid contained in the first edition of 2010.

Brief note on social theory

Social theory constitutes an essential tool in scholarly activity to explore and analyse some feature of social phenomena, including institutional practices. These diverse practices, operating within the criminal justice system, cannot support a single approach or interpretation, any more than the phenomenon of crime can be theorised by one criminological theory. It has been suggested that theories involve constructing 'abstract interpretations which can be used to explain a wide variety of empirical situations … they represent attempts to explain particular sets of social conditions or types of occurrence' (Giddens, 1989, pp 17, 711). Additionally, theories are the 'conceptual means of interpreting and explicating information. They come into competition only when they offer alternative and incompatible explanations of the same data' (Garland, 1990, p 13; see also Duffee and Maguire, 2007). If it is possible to theorise the work of the police and the prison system from different perspectives (Zedner, 2004), then a similar approach can be adopted towards probation. The task, in this and the next chapter, is to establish an extended and refined theoretical grid to facilitate the rigorous exploration of events recounted in Chapter One from 1997 to 2015. Some of these events are: emotionally charged; bureaucratically constraining; ideologically and materially influenced by neoliberal restructuring; manifestations of strategic politics contained within a disciplinary play of forces; and an evidential display of the decline of symbolic efficiency and moral sensibilities.

Emile Durkheim, 1858–1917

Introduction and some biographical references

Auguste Comte (1798–1857) (see Thompson, 1976) constructed the term 'social physics' to describe the newly emerging science of society. Later, he supplanted social physics with sociology because he thought the earlier construction had been purloined by Adolphe Quetelet (1796–1874).[1] According to Comte, the newly emerging *science of society* should follow the pattern of the natural sciences, not only in its 'empirical methods and epistemological underpinnings, but also in the functions it would serve for mankind' (Coser, 1977, p 3). Sociology offered the prospect of extrapolating from the past a predictable future by the appliance of positive science, which would benefit society (Simon, 1963). Accordingly, Durkheim could not claim to be the founder of the intellectual discipline preoccupied with the science of society. Although Comte is the acknowledged founder, Durkheim cultivated the discipline as one of his descendants. Attention can be steered towards Durkheim's sociological approach influencing the Chicago School of criminology and the thesis that the level of crime is linked to social disorganisation (Smith, 1988; Newburn, 2007, p 170). Furthermore, Durkheim's anomie assumed the hue of strain theory in Robert Merton (Sztompka, 1986) and crime is defined as a social phenomenon that offends the collective conscience, which requires a sociological rather than psychological explanation. It should also be emphasised that Durkheim had much to say about crime and punishment, as we will see later. For what probably remains the definitive biography of Durkheim, covering details of his life, academic interests and outputs, the reader can be guided towards Steven Lukes (1973). If new to the subject, an accessible starting point is Kenneth Thompson (1982). Both texts provide detailed information on Durkheim's contribution to the following thematics: family, morality, law, crime and punishment, education, and religion. He was also the founder of the Journal *L'Année Sociologique*, published between 1898 and 1925. This journal is the source of *The Two Laws of Penal Evolution*, which will be examined in due course.

Some key sources – primary
- *The Division of Labour in Society* (Durkheim, 1984 [1893]).
- *The Rules of Sociological Method* (Durkheim, 1938 [1895]).
- *Suicide: A Study in Sociology* (Durkheim, 1952 [1897]).
- *The Elementary Forms of the Religious Life* (Durkheim, 1915 [1912]).
- See also texts on Montesquieu, moral education and published lecture courses, including *The Two Laws of Penal Evolution*.

Lukes (1973, p 561) provides a comprehensive bibliography of all of Durkheim's publications. Thompson (1982, p 167) provides a similar service, including a bibliography of Durkheim's major original works in French and their English translations.

Secondary sources
- Simon (1963).
- Giddens (1971, 1972, 1989).
- Taylor et al (1973).
- Coser (1977).
- Callinicos (2007).
- Garland (1990).
- Morrison (1995).
- Hudson (2003).
- Emirbayer (2003).

Durkheimian themes

The scholarly contributions of Lukes (1973), Thompson (1982) and Morrison (1995), provide excellent introductions to the sociological themes running throughout the Durkheimian corpus. Morrison's exposition and critique, pertinent for our introductory purposes, begins with an account of some of the major intellectual influences on Durkheim's work. This is a good place to begin. First, as indicated earlier, Comte lurks in the background, casting a long positivistic shadow (Simon, 1963) that applies the methodology established within the orbit of the natural sciences to the social domain. It purports to be the scientific study of society, comprising human beings and their social arrangements, rather than the world of inanimate objects and things. This methodology pursues the independent/objective 'facts' based upon empirical observation, the search for law-like regularities and patterns to establish causal, predictive and invariant laws of how things work and will continue to work. Mazlish (1968, p 210) underlines this point by stating that it follows from the 'scientific' nature of Comte's work, just as it does not follow from that of Hegel's, that Comte's sociology is an attempt to predict future social phenomena. Consequently, if, by the 19th century, human beings were establishing laws to account for natural phenomena, the emerging discipline of sociology was expected to render the same intellectual benefits to social phenomena. This substantiates the claim to the unity of the scientific method, or the orthodox consensus between the natural and social-human sciences (Giddens, 1982).[2] In *The Rules of Sociological Method*, Durkheim (1938 [1895], p 159) expressed an assimilative summation:

> Since the law of causality has been verified in the other domains of nature and has progressively extended its authority from the physical and chemical world to the biological world, and from the latter to the psychological world, one may justifiably grant that it is likewise true of the social world.

Second, Durkheim was operating against the intellectual background of the 18th-century European Enlightenment, or Age of Reason, mainly characterised by the replacement of: supernatural by natural explanations; religion by science; divine decree by natural law; and priests by the critical thinking of philosophers. Additionally, we can draw attention to the exaltation of human reason and experience to solve human problems, and the belief in the perfectibility of human beings through scientific progress, which mirrors the Comtean triadic stages of progression from theological, through metaphysical, to scientific positivism. We may also refer to those humanitarian concerns for human rights that culminated in the French Revolution of 1789. A related manifestation was the liberal crusade and accompanying pursuit of justice associated with Beccaria and the application of reason and humanity to penal policy in *Dei delitti e delle pene* (for additional information on all these Enlightenment features, see Sampson, 1956; Mack, 1962; Porter, 2000; Outram, 2013; see also Peter Gay's [1967, 1969] excellent two volumes).

Another Enlightenment motif was that human beings were assumed to be free, responsible, equal, autonomous, rational and self-directed. This is illustrated by the doctrine of utilitarianism, a rational calculator anthropology that influenced the classical criminological perspective, whereby the offender is psychologically constructed as someone who pursues pleasure and avoids pain, thus weighing up the costs and benefits of various repertoires of behaviour prior to selecting a specific course of action (Garland, 1985). The utilitarianism of Beccaria and Bentham gave prominence to an individualistic perspective when accounting for criminal behaviour.[3] By contrast, the sociological theorising of Durkheim advocated that human beings cannot be reduced to a set of atomistic or biological-psychological explanations. By doing so, his work constituted a discernible break with 'analytical individualism' (Taylor et al, 1973) because he questioned the degree to which individuals are the free, rational calculators of utilitarian theory and Kantian rationality. According to Durkheim, the latter is curtailed because of the constraining force of social facts that impose themselves upon the individual. In *The Division of Labour* (Durkheim, 1984 [1893]), the defining characteristics of a social fact were externality, constraint and generality.

Next, Durkheim did not concur with Hobbes, Rousseau and Spencer that social order was based upon the free decisions and motivations of self-seeking atomistic individuals. He rejected the utilitarian view that the pursuit of one's own economic self-interest formed the basic unity of society. In other words, a social contract between autonomous individuals is not the basis of social solidarity and cohesion. The social world is self-evidently comprised of individuals, but individuals are influenced and constrained by, as well as reflect and reproduce, prevailing politico-economic and social forces. Consistent with a tradition traced through St Simon, Comte and Renouvier in France (Simon, 1963), Schaffle and Wundt in Germany, and even English and American influences if the discussion is extended to religious phenomena (Thompson, 1982), for Durkheim, there is a discrete realm of social facts that can be studied empirically, just as the objects of nature can be studied empirically. These social facts constitute a discrete realm of social phenomena that exist independently of individuals. It is possible, therefore, to consider the social realm as an artefact, rather than a phenomenological perspective constructed by individual consciousness (the social as object rather than product). Lukes (1973) advances the view that Durkheim's epistemology follows Descartes.[4] This means that phenomena are purported to exist independently of the observer, which the mind can grasp clearly and with certainty. Descartes's rationalism expatiated upon the relationship between the content of the human mind and the external world being reliable (Grayling, 2005). In other words, the contents of the human mind mirror that which exist outside of itself accurately, producing a mirror-like image of what objectively 'is' the case.

One issue for mention at this point is how individuals are purported to be constrained by Durkheimian social forces and facts. In other words, to what extent are individuals free and responsible human beings? This is the sociological conundrum between structure and agency, expressed philosophically as determinism versus free will, and how the individual is circumscribed in Durkheim's sociology. Suffice to say, and by way of illustration, Durkheim turned to suicide rates to explain them by referring to social phenomena such as religion and economic conditions, rather than individual predilection. Consequently, suicide rates were higher during periods of economic recession, caused by a lack of moral-social regulation.[5] It was the lack of organisation, the decline of moral regulation and solidarity, in the 19th century – associated with the Industrial Revolution, the release of egoistic individualism, rapid urbanisation and class divisions under transformed social arrangements created by capitalism – which constituted a central theme in Durkheim's sociology. These are some of the factors that established the background for the rise of socio-theoretical perspectives associated with Durkheim, Weber and Marx. There are other Durkheimian themes that should be alluded to prior to turning to crime and punishment: the division of labour; mechanical and organic solidarity; anomie; collective conscience; individual versus social facts; the constraining influence of morality; religion and the sacred; and repressive and restitutive sanctions. Some of these will surface in what follows.

Crime and the sociology of punishment

For Durkheim, the discussion on crime is rooted in the collective feelings and sentiments prevailing within society. Crime is not a fixed artefact, or phenomenon, which possesses an inherent, objective, definable and unchanging essence (which finds an echo with the labelling perspective of the 1960s).[6] Rather, it is a phenomenon which changes over time, more social product than fixed object, so that crime and law provide valuable insights into the changing nature of society, the prevailing forms of social solidarity. In other words, law constitutes a visible symbol or index, an empirical indicator, of the nature of society, moral phenomena and type of social solidarity, the collective conscience and social change.

According to Durkheim, the perfect social order, that is, a form of order based upon a spontaneous rather than a forced division of labour, which characterised 19th-century industrial capitalism, is conducive to producing social solidarity. This can be explicated as a set of arrangements in which occupational status accords with individual abilities or, to put it another way, roles are distributed according to biologically endowed talents. However, the lack of such socio-economic perfection during the 19th century created conditions conducive to deviance. The following exposition contained in the work of Taylor, Walton and Young (1973) of Durkheim's typology of deviance is as follows:

- *Biological deviant* – it is suggested that even if there was a spontaneous and perfect division of labour, if deviance occurred, it can be explained by genetic and psychological malfunctioning. However, it is difficult to conceive of a perfect and therefore completely deviance-free society.
- *Functional rebel* – a form of behaviour that constitutes a response to the forced division of labour. This response challenges the lack of fit between biological faculties/talents and occupational status.
- *Skewed deviant* – if the preceding category is a consequence of a normal person responding to a pathological division of labour, by contrast, the skewed deviant is un-socialised within a sick society. According to Durkheim, there are two sources for this condition: anomie, which is a lack of a normative moral-regulative framework; and egoism, associated with excessive individualism.

It is worth repeating how the Durkheimian thesis explicated that during the 19th century, rapid socio-economic developments ran ahead of moral regulation, formerly provided by the cohesive nature of religion, creating anomic conditions. Anomie involves a 'lack of social regulation, and a situation in which the unrestricted appetites of the individual conscience are no longer held in check' (Taylor et al, 1973, p 87). In what follows, I expand upon Durkheim's understanding of crime and punishment to establish one of the theoretical perspectives that can be applied to the excavation of probation and the criminal justice domains later. The three main texts for consideration are: *The Division of Labour in Society* (Durkheim, 1984 [1893]); *Two Laws of Penal Education*; and *Moral Education* (Durkheim, 2002) (which was a course delivered at Bordeaux between 1889 and 1912; see Lukes, 1973, p 110).

The Division of Labour in Society

In Book One and Chapter Two of *The Division of Labour in Society*, Durkheim turns his attention to mechanical solidarity, or solidarity by familiarities. This prepares the ground for a discussion about crime. Durkheim says that the word 'crime' applies to those acts that elicit a punitive response by society, so that 'Universally they strike the moral consciousness of nations…. All are crimes, that is, acts repressed by punishment' (Durkheim, 1984 [1893], p 31). He proceeds to argue that crime 'disturbs those feelings that in any one type of society are to be found in every healthy consciousness' (Durkheim, 1984 [1893], p 34). Therefore, in a passage familiar to those acquainted with Durkheim's work, and often quoted, crime is tantamount to a form of behaviour that offends the collective consciousness. We should not say that an act 'offends the common consciousness because it is criminal, but that it is criminal because it offends that consciousness. We do not condemn it because it is a crime; but it is a crime because we condemn it' (Durkheim, 1984 [1893], p 40).

Durkheim advances the discussion by stating that under conditions of mechanical solidarity, a number of distinguishable features can be identified: a homogeneous population (united by sameness rather than difference); most of the population being engaged in the same form of employment (eg hunting); minimum specialisation in the division of labour; strong religious sentiments; the uniformity of beliefs; and strong values conducive to social cohesion. The system of punishment under these specific social arrangements equates to repressive sanctions expressed as emotion, outrage and vengeance. In other words, criminal behaviour elicits a strong emotional reaction that functions to re-establish and promote social solidarity. Consequently, and this is a significant point, the punitive-passionate response functions to restore the collective conscience, which has been adversely affected by actions designated as criminal. Durkheim (1984 [1893], p 52) puts it like this: 'punishment constitutes essentially a reaction of passionate feelings, graduated in intensity, which society exerts through the mediation of an organised body over those of its members who have violated certain rules of conduct'.

The main function of punishment is not primarily directed at the guilty individual to deter future criminal acts, or even to deter others (it is not philosophically justified on the grounds of either individual or general deterrence). The purpose of punishment should not be understood in terms of its instrumental utility or transformational efficacy to achieve individual correctionalism.[7] Rather, its expressive quality, emotional content and acting-out response culminates in a passionate reaction towards the offender that may contain a vestige of illogicality and irrationality. However, its fundamental sociological purpose is to 'maintain inviolate the cohesion of society by sustaining the common consciousness in all its rigour' (Durkheim, 1984 [1893], p 63). Furthermore, the nature of crime and associated systems of rules, laws and punishments provide important clues to the nature of society and type of social solidarity. We have just considered Durkheim's theorising about crime and punishment under conditions of mechanical solidarity, but what of organic solidarity?

Organic solidarity describes a more advanced and complex form of society contrasted to mechanical solidarity, as the following features exemplify: a larger population; a more complex division of labour, with specialised functions; individuals becoming more dependent upon each other's specialised roles; a society marked more by difference than sameness; legal contracts rather than obligations; individualism and differentiation; and occupations in a more secular society and their differential status. The nature of law and punishment associated with organic solidarity is more restitutive than repressive. Instead of repressively punishing offenders, it restores human relations to what they once were prior to the crime being committed. As Durkheim (1984 [1893], p 68) explained in *The Division of Labour in Society*, the nature of the restitutive sanction is sufficient to demonstrate that the social solidarity to which that law corresponds is of a completely different kind. Therefore, from expiation to restoration constitutes a visible index indicative of a more advanced, specialised, contractually based form of society and corresponding human relations. Arguably, this is constitutive of post-Enlightenment, capitalist and emerging industrialised society in the 19th century, which required relations to be restored between individuals rather than promoting individual–group solidarity, as in more primitive forms of social arrangements. However, and importantly, this ideal-type construction of organic solidarity and its constituent elements may not be possible under conditions of a dysfunctional and anomic division of labour.

When reflecting on Durkheim's discussion of law, crime and punishment in relation to differential forms of mechanical and organic solidarity, one of the criticisms levelled against him is that he did not sufficiently allow for the existence of restitutive sanctions under former social arrangements or repressive sanctions as a feature of the latter. From a functionalist and consensual perspective, Durkheim considered that crime could be understood as a normal phenomenon in society because it makes a contribution to the promotion of social solidarity and stability. In fact, the benefits of crime, articulated in *The Rules of Sociological Method*, are as follows: it functions to heighten collective sentiments; it functions to integrate the community in opposition to the transgressor; it has an adaptive function in that crime can promote social change, thus preventing social stagnation; and it also has a *boundary maintenance* function in that it reinforces social values and helps to differentiate right from wrong (see Newburn, 2007, p 170).

In summary, it is beneficial to refer to the exposition of Durkheim's sociology of punishment in David Garland (1990). Garland reinforces that Durkheim's sociology is primarily concerned with the nature of social solidarity (see also Coser, 1977, p 133) and those deep moral structures at the heart of social life that have a claim upon the individual, and that elicit a strong reaction when violated. As Durkheim expatiates on crime and punitive responses, it can be viewed as a 'moral phenomenon operating within the circuits of the moral life, as well as carrying out more mundane social and penal functions' (Garland, 1990, p 24). It may well be the case, as Garland argues, that the contemporary nature and forms of penality at work within the criminal justice system can be approached from the standpoint of their utilitarian and instrumental efficacy, and empirically evaluated accordingly. However, Durkheim draws attention to a different set of impulses, which include the moral basis of penality, the involvement of the onlooker beyond the individual offender, the symbolic meaning attached to penal rituals, the relationship between punishment and moral sensibilities, and, importantly, the emotional nature of punishment as the expression of community disapproval through the formal mechanisms of the criminal justice system. Punishment is also a 'communicative device', a language that delivers messages deep into the social body (Wacquant, 2009, p 108). Society may well develop over time from simple to more complex forms that correspond with changes in penality, but punishment continues to communicate emotionally laden passionate responses.

The Two Laws of Penal Evolution

This was an essay written after *The Division of Labour in Society* when Durkheim was at Bordeaux between 1887 and 1902. The essay was originally published as 'Deux lois de l'évolution pénale' in *L'Année Sociologique* (1899–1900, vol IV, pp 65–95). I have utilised the paper translated from French into English located in Traugott's (1978) *Emile Durkheim: On Institutional Analysis*. At the beginning of the paper, the *deux lois* are stated as follows:

The Law of Quantitative Variation

The intensity of punishment is greater as societies belong to a less advanced type and as centralised power has a more absolute character.

The Law of Qualitative Variations

> Punishment consisting in privation of freedom – and freedom alone – for lengths of time varying according to the gravity of the crime, tend more and more to become the normal type of repression.

Where the first law is concerned, Durkheim refers to the form and intensity of punishment being greater in a less advanced type of society. By contrast, as society becomes more advanced, punishment becomes correspondingly more lenient. This restates the basic argument differentiating between mechanical and organic solidarity explicated in *The Division of Labour in Society*. Nevertheless, Durkheim modifies his earlier thesis by introducing an important qualification, which is the absolute character of centralised power (see Lukes, 1973, pp 257–65; Thompson, 1982, p 88; Garland, 1990, pp 35–41). Durkheim argues that both elements – the nature of social arrangements and absolute politico-governmental power – can operate independently of each other. As society passes from a less to a more advanced state, from mechanical to organic solidarity, punishment becomes less repressive. However, the modification is that in 'passing from a lower species to other, more advanced types, we do not see punishment decrease, as could be expected, because at the same time the governmental organisation neutralises the effects of social organisation' (Traugott, 1978, p 175).

Durkheim expands the argument through a historical analysis that explores a number of hideous punishments, beginning with ancient (pre-classical) societies. By way of illustration, Egypt resorted to hanging, beheading and crucifixion, in addition to other physical torments. Assyrian malefactors were thrown to wild beasts or roasted in a basin over a fire. Intriguingly, strangulation and decapitation were considered insufficiently severe. Syrian offenders could be crushed under the feet of animals. When arriving at the Hebrews of the Old Testament, arguably not a more advanced social type in Durkheim's analysis, he makes the assessment that they were in possession of a less severe Mosaic law. Next, he proceeds to consider more advanced city-states, where one may observe a more marked regression of penal law. Rome had a less repressive system of penality, but it became more severe when the Empire became an absolute power. When turning to Christian societies, Durkheim explicates how penal law evolved according to the same law in that 'the facts' indicate that punishment was milder. However, from the 14th century, royal power escalated and penal law strengthened, so that the 'apogee of absolute monarchy also marks the apogee of repression' (Traugott, 1978, p 163). Illustratively, during the 15th–16th centuries, we observe the growth of political absolutism and a centralised state in England under the Tudors. This was complemented by the rise of Spanish absolutism, absolute monarchy in France until its collapse in 1789 and humanitarian protestations against Beccaria's suggested reforms to the *ancien régime* (for an alternative reading, see Foucault later).

The argument is played out throughout this historical excursion that during the course of penal evolution, the *form* of punishment experienced change, yet its essential *function* remained the same. Furthermore, in less advanced societies, the intensity of penal measures was associated with, and can be explained by, the religious and collective permeation of society. Crime constituted an offence against the sacred moral order, which elicited a passionate response marked by vengeance and outrage. By contrast, as societies advanced and became less religious, more morally diverse and more individualistic, the force and passion of punishment was attenuated as the distance between offenders and the offended against reduced. These two types of criminality differ profoundly because 'the collective sentiments which they offend are not of the same nature. As a result repression cannot be the same for both' (Traugott, 1978, p 172).

This quantitative shift in the form of punishment is complimented and accompanied by a qualitative shift as the prison, rather than physical punishment, becomes the normal type of repression. For Durkheim, such a qualitative transformation represents a discernible change in human sensibilities, away from bodily mutilations and tortures and towards the restriction of liberty. In fact, the prison, from being initially a place of detention for those awaiting trial, to assuming its role as a discrete form of punishment within modern penal systems, produced a second historical survey in the *Two Laws*. In more advanced organic societies, it has become necessary to ensure that miscreants do not evade punishment, which was less difficult in primitive societies because of the closer-knit nature of families and communities, who would exercise group-clan oversight responsibilities for the individual. Thus, the prison can be interpreted as a further illustration of the attenuation of severity because of the change in the collective conscience and corresponding social arrangements. Later, I will provide a different perspective on the prison system when turning to Foucault.[8]

Moral Education

Durkheim delivered a course on moral education initially offered at the Sorbonne during 1902–03, yet it appears that the details were sketched earlier at Bordeaux (I have used the Dover edition of the text to explore this theme). In two substantive parts containing a total of 18 chapters, Durkheim addresses 'The elements of morality' and 'How to develop the elements of morality in the child'. Pertinently, in three consecutive chapters (Chapters Eleven, Twelve and Thirteen), he discusses the theme of punishment within the context of education and the role of the school in socialisation: 'The use of punishment in the school' (for additional expositions, see Lukes, 1973, pp 110–19; Garland, 1990, pp 41–6; Giddens, 1972; see also Chapter Three).

In Chapter Eleven, Durkheim poses the question: why do we punish? He answers by saying that to punish a child to prevent misbehaviour, to exact retribution and even atonement are all theoretical possibilities. In fact, to engage in this discussion touches upon the instrumental function of penality in addition to philosophies, theories and justifications of punishment. Nevertheless, for Durkheim, if someone commits an offence, or violates a school rule, this is tantamount to breaching something inviolable. Consequently, the law that has been violated 'must somehow bear witness that despite appearances it remains always itself, that it has lost none of its force or authority despite the act that repudiated it' (Durkheim, 2002, p 166). He continues by arguing that the essential nature of punishment 'is not to make the guilty expiate his crime through suffering or to intimidate possible imitators through threats, but to buttress those consciences which violations of a rule can and must necessarily disturb in their faith' (Durkheim, 2002, p 177). By doing so, he reinforces the position contained in earlier intellectual contributions to the subject. Once again, Durkheim advances the proposition that the real purpose of punishment should not be conceived in terms of its instrumental efficacy directed at individual perpetrators. Rather, its expressive nature is directed towards restoring the sacred moral order that has been violated and for the benefit of the law-abiding. Punishment remains preoccupied with the expression of feeling as it is 'a notation, a language, through which either the general social conscience or that of the school teacher expresses the feeling inspired by the disapproved behaviour' (Durkheim, 2002, p 176). A breach of social morality elicits a passionate reaction that restores the sacred socio-moral order, which is deemed to exist independently of the child in the classroom, and this position can be extended to the individual appearing in court.

Durkheim summation

Durkheim draws attention to a number of themes within the orbit of crime and punishment that are of interest in themselves, but that are easily overlooked by approaching the phenomenon through a narrow lens of utilitarian and instrumental efficacy. It is suggested, in anticipation of a later discussion, that Durkheimian themes have a contemporary relevance when excavating the complex and multifaceted nature of probation practice within the modernised criminal justice system. It is the Durkheimian sociological corpus, as Garland insightfully elucidates, which draws attention to a troubling dilemma illustrated by the outpouring of punitive passions deemed politically necessary or useful – expressive nature contained in the politics of punishment – yet, at the same time, penologically inefficacious and, to some extent, irrational as a means for controlling crime. There is no shortage of punitive impulses; there appears no diminution in the punitive instinct; futility has the quality of sheer persistence. For Garland (1990, p 80), this constitutes an illustration of punishment's 'tragic quality'. Essentially, the Durkheimian corpus embodies crime and punishment within a consensual sociology, where the latter functions to restore social solidarity. Later, Marx confronts us with radical conflict, not the comforts of consensus. After considering a number of Durkheimian themes, we now turn to different ideas located within a different sociological tradition, but that are just as relevant for our excavatory purposes.

Max Weber, 1864–1920

Introduction and some biographical references

In marked contrast to Durkheim, Foucault (see later) and to some extent Marx, Weber did not apply himself to the systematic study of crime and punishment. A close scrutiny of the extensive index to *Economy and Society* (Weber, 1968 [1922]) provides evidence to support this claim. Nevertheless, there are a number of Weberian themes, more theoretically abstract than Durkheim, which are undoubtedly relevant when excavating developments in probation and criminal justice. This perspective constitutes another conceptual lens that brings into focus certain facets that belong to the multifaceted modernised domain of probation. There are two areas of interest pertinent to this chapter. Prior to expatiating upon these, the following biographical references are worth pursuing: Bendix (1960), MacRae (1987), Gerth and Mills (1948) and Allen (2004).

Some key sources – primary
- *The Protestant Ethic and the Spirit of Capitalism* (Weber, 1958 [1904–05]).
- *Economy and Society* (three volumes) (Weber, 1968 [1922]).
- 'Selections from Weber', in Gerth and Mills (1948).

Secondary sources
- Albrow (1970).
- Giddens (1971).
- Coser (1977).
- Garland (1990).
- Sayer (1991).
- Whimster (2004).
- Löwith (1993).
- Morrison (1995).
- Ritzer and Goodman (1997).
- Hudson (2003).
- Allen (2004).

Some themes in Weber

In the three-volume edition of *Economy and Society* (Weber, 1968 [1922]), Weber addresses numerous sociological themes. He examines the types of social institutions that best serve the interests of a modern capitalist state (Hudson, 2003, p 105; Whimster, 2004, p 300). In Volume One, he refers to sociological terms and provides a definition of sociology, types of legitimate domination, status groups and classes. In Volume Two, he turns to religion, the sociology of law and political communities. In Volume Three, domination and legitimacy, bureaucracy, patriarchalism, feudalism, charisma and the city are subjected to rigorous analysis. There are other thematic points of interest: *verstehen*, ideal types, zeitgeist of the modern world, rationalisation and how the spirit of Protestantism was conducive to the emergence of capitalist modernity.

Where the conceptual orientation of this book is concerned, I want to foreground two specific Weberian themes that are relevant for an analysis and critique of contemporary probation, and the excavation of the criminal justice system. The first is Weber's concept of *verstehen*, located within the context of his understanding of sociology (Weber, 1968 [1922], vol 1, pp 4–24); the second is *bureaucracy* (Weber, 1968 [1922], vol 3, pp 941–1003). It may be suggested that the notion of *verstehen* is particularly relevant when thinking about the rationale of probation practice, and pertinent to the division between the natural and social sciences. The following questions may be posed at this stage: should the organisation of probation, in conjunction with the 21 Community Rehabilitation Companies since 2014, have a definitive role to play in excavating, analysing, understanding and then explaining offending behaviours to the courts? Or, is the primary task on the platform of neoliberal capitalism the bureaucratic management, punishment and control of offenders? The following discussion bears down upon these two questions through the lens of Weberian social theory.

Verstehen and debates on the natural and social sciences

Verstehen, a German word meaning *human understanding*, draws attention to human subjectivity, including the inner states and motivations of individual human actors. Outhwaite (1975) explains that its origins can be traced to theological hermeneutics that appertain to the meaning of written texts. Weber, influenced by Wilhelm Windelband and Heinrich Rickert on *methodenstreit* (controversy over methods in the social sciences during the 1880s), focused upon the unique individual rather than forms of knowledge 'afforded by the physical sciences, which was abstract, general and capable of being stated in the form of invariable natural laws' (MacRae, 1987, p 63). This is supported by Gerth and Mills (1948, p 46) when they state that it was within the context of conflicting intellectual currents that Weber worked out his distinctive orientation, in which the individual was the primary unit of analysis. Consequently, there is a discernible point of contrast between Weber's focus upon the individual human actor, an Enlightenment theme, and the Comtean-Durkheimian sociological approach that elevated social structures acting upon, constraining and sociologically constructing the individual.

Following Rickert, Weber expressed the view that the sociological domain should concern itself with the interpretation of social action and the concept of values because acts of evaluation and judgement are a precondition of social action (Morrison, 1995, p 274). Moreover, social action has four main concepts, one being *verstehen*, which embraces how human actors assign meaning to their own and others' behaviours. In the first volume of *Economy and Society*, Weber says that there are two types of understanding appertaining to the context of social action. One is direct and the other is exploratory or interpretive. Direct understanding addresses the level of comprehension based upon the direct observation of an act. If we observe someone chopping wood, or being angry, it should be clear what action is occurring.

Alternatively, when turning to exploratory understanding, the emphasis shifts from *what* is occurring to an interpretation of *why*. In other words, we may observe and clearly understand *what* someone is doing by their presenting actions, but this is different to understanding *why* the action is being performed. For example, $2 + 2 = 4$ is being used to demonstrate a mathematical formula, and someone is chopping wood to use as fuel in winter. Exploratory understanding proceeds to put the '*what*' of an action into a framework of meanings and motives. This is a more complex form of understanding because it requires additional work to explain the link between the activity being observed and its meaning for the actor (and observer). For Giddens (1971, p 148), it involves elucidating the motivational link between the observer observing the behaviour and understanding what it means to the actor. Barbara Hudson (2003, p 107) says that human beings constantly interpret each other's actions and from this they build 'patterns of identity, behaviour and meaning which become generalised within their own lives and within society. These stable patterns become the customs, social roles, laws and institutions that we call culture'. This means that, for Weber and those sociologists who followed in the *verstehen* tradition, the route to studying culture is through observing the actions of individuals. This is a salient point to extrapolate within the Weberian tradition, the social or human sciences have as their orbit of concern empathic understanding – the actions, motives, meanings and consequences of individual human action. Accordingly, a necessary distinction is required between *understanding* and the *interpretation* of individual behavioural inner states (human science) and *prediction* (associated with the domain of the natural sciences).

It is possible, at this stage, to drop the unsubtle hint that such a distinction has relevance when considering the rationale of probation and clarifying its discrete contribution to the competing professional logics operating within the institutions of the criminal justice system. For those organisations that purport to work with people within the context of humane–professional relationships, the future could never assume the status of an exact science. Accurately predicting future events from previous behavioural repertoires, while not dismissing the possibility of anticipating future possibilities from previous occurrences, does not operate within an uncontentious epistemological context. It is necessary to distinguish conceptually between *inferentially predicting* the future based upon the totality of evidence at our disposal inductively, and *knowing* what will occur, which is beyond our epistemological compass (Buchdahl, 1969, p 339). This is a distinction that should be clarified in light of inflated positivistic claims attached to risk technologies, such as the efficacy of the Offender Assessment System (OASys). Furthermore, operating within the human science of *verstehen*, in *Economy and Society*, Weber (1968 [1922], vol 1, pp 21–2), expressed the view that it could well be the case that the vast majority of human beings behave in a state of half-consciousness. They do not act in full self-knowledge of what they do or even why they do it. Rather, behaviour can be a consequence of impulse, force of habit and conscious-rational or unthinking response. It becomes difficult for the probation officer, social worker or youth worker to engage in an interpretation of the 'other's' behaviour to understand and predict future events in the contingent social world.

The human sciences are more concerned with hermeneutics, elucidating the complex meanings and interpretations of human action, than the causal, predictive and invariant laws associated with the natural sciences, which was at the centre of the *methodenstreit* debate. Morrison develops the point by stating that Weber came to the conclusion that the natural and social sciences operate within different domains of knowledge. In the natural sciences, knowledge is of the external world, which is accounted for by valid laws, whereas within the social sciences, knowledge must be internal or subjective in the sense that 'human beings have an inner nature that must be understood in order to explain outward events' (Morrison, 1995, p 337; see also Morrison, 1995, p 276). Turner (1996, p 43) stated that Weber 'reintroduced the discussion of meaning to the analysis of human action, thereby serving as a major, though by no means comprehensive, resource for later schools of interpretative sociology'. This constituted an epistemological challenge to the positivistic domain of science, offering a more substantive inspiration to study the meaningful viewpoints of human actors and the consequences for action.

Coser (1977, p 217) contributed to this discussion by saying that Weber did not follow the Durkheimian schema in applying the methodology of the natural sciences to the newly emerging social sciences. Consequently, there is no unity of the sciences, no consistent methodological approach uniting both disciplines. Coser supports the view that the natural and social sciences are ontologically and epistemologically distinct. What they have in common is that neither can claim to provide a total explanation of the phenomena under investigation. The world is too rich, complex and unpredictable, both in the realm of nature and history, so that even in physics and medicine, it is not possible to predict with certainty what will happen in the future (Coser, 1977, p 219). Gerth and Mills (1948, p 57) say that in drawing a clear distinction between understanding and interpreting people, and the natural sciences, Weber draws the line between his interpretive sociology and the 'physique sociale in the tradition of Condorcet, which Comte called sociologie and Durkheim worked out in such an eminent manner'. Due to the centrality of this theme, in addition to preparing the ground for a later discussion, it is necessary to penetrate the matter more searchingly at this point.

There is a long scientific tradition that, particularly since the 15th-century European Renaissance, has employed mathematics to explain the world (Hall, 1954). By manipulating combinations of numbers, it was thought possible to predict the movement and future positions of the planets. Copernicus advanced the heliocentric principle, Newton discovered the laws of motion and gravity, and Galileo thought that mathematics was the key to unlocking the mysteries of the universe. It was as though numbers were imbued with revelatory ontological and epistemological properties. This impulse to use numbers to measure the world, that mathematics could account for things as they are 'in reality', continued into the 1700s, with Alexander von Humbolt and Carl Frederick Gauss. It was Von Humbolt who accumulated various measuring instruments, from barometers for measuring air pressure and hypsometers to measure the boiling point of water, to theodolites for measuring the land and Leyden jars to capture electrical charges. Everything must be measured to explain it (Kehlmann, 2007, p 29). Concurrently, Gauss was pursuing his own research, and in Kehlmann's (2007, p 73) book on *Measuring the World*, we read that:

> Again and again he laid his quill aside, popped his head in his hands, and wondered whether there was a proscription against what he was doing. Was he digging too deep? At the base of physics were rules, at the base of rules there were laws, at the base of laws there were numbers; if one looked at them intently, one could recognise relationships between them, repulsions or attractions.

Additionally, the French tradition encompassing Montesquieu, Condorcet, Turgot, St Simon, Comte and Durkheim approached social facts as thing-like objects in nature to establish the scientific and predictive laws of society. What Humbolt and Gauss did for measuring objects in the natural world, Comte and Durkheim attempted for the social world, as we noted earlier.

By contrast, the alternative German tradition, to which Weber belongs, questioned that the methodology of the natural sciences could seamlessly be extended to the social, historico-centric world of human beings. This is the tradition which acknowledges that human beings are complex actors, with ambiguous histories, who cannot be reduced to passive objects being acted upon by the world's forces, its repulsions and attractions. Nor is it possible to reduce human beings to combinations of numbers or measurement scales. Rather, individuals possess the capacity to act upon the world, to alter their immediate environment and to change themselves and the course of events that pits agency over structure (see Frayn, 2006). Objects, things and mechanistic events in the natural world are not of the same ontological or epistemological order as the social world of individual human beings, with their social actions and differential meanings attached to actions. Therefore, one encounters rich debates on the differences between the domains of the natural and social sciences in the scholarly literature (Giddens, 1978, 1982; Bryant, 1985). Giddens drives home the point that neither the formulation of laws nor causal analysis has any place in social science. This is precisely because social science is a hermeneutical endeavour and, as such, 'a logical gulf separates such an endeavour from the logic and methods of the natural sciences' (Giddens, 1982, p 4).

It is pertinent to suggest at this early stage that probation work should be fundamentally engaged with the language of human events, behaviours, meanings, nuanced understandings and interpretations, in other words, the Weberian concept of *verstehen*. This is in marked contrast – ontologically, epistemologically and axiologically – to an aggregately based and positive science of risk prediction supported by a fusillade of numbers (Whitehead, 2007). The tradition and application of *verstehen*, as Giddens (1978, p 277) concedes, does not provide a basis for scientific research. Nevertheless, it does provide a basis for empathic understanding, which is required when working with people in what is self-evidently a people-facing organisation.

Positivist orthodoxy, with its deadly scientific embrace, adopts a specific posture towards the natural and social world. This view, replete with the claim of objectivity and theoretical and value neutrality, proceeds on the basis of observation, induction, the collection of 'facts' and, of course, the assumed certainties of quantitative measurements to reveal the nature of 'objective' reality. However, it does not exist unchallenged because the positivist-scientific approach to the world, purported to exist outside our minds, is ontologically and epistemologically complex. In other words, it is extremely difficult to disentangle those features that belong to material objects and those imposed by the Kantian active mind of the human observer (German idealism). Therefore, it is possible to advance the position that the world does not have an innate meaning, a given essence, which can be discovered by assiduous scientific endeavour and revealed by numbers. Rather, reality, and the presumed knowledge that purportedly supports it, is to some extent constructed and imposed by our cognitive faculties. There are many realities created out of the subjective experiences of different individuals. There is no objective social reality 'out there', but a bewildering collection of interpretations and opinions that get projected onto the world (Tarnas, 1991).

This anti-positivist and pro-humanistic perspective, which arguably resonates with the organisational rationale of probation, with its people orientation, should be required to understand clients' lives from the standpoint not of the expert practitioner, but of clients themselves in all their complexity and nuanced meanings. This is a form of *verstehen* that is conducive to an emotionally empathic and imaginative level of understanding of the person; it has an appreciative quality; it is more art than science, qualitative than quantitative. This is not so much a calculated or even definitive description of human action, but a holistic exploration, excavation and interpretation of the human condition; not scientific prediction based upon aggregated data sets, but a rich, nuanced and *de profundis* understanding of the individual located within the broadest parameters; not measurement by well-tuned instruments producing systems and combinations of numbers, but ambiguous meanings that defy the neat classification system of risk scales. However, this is not an account of the place that the probation service inhabits within the criminal justice system by 2015. However, this recounts pertinent themes that can be developed within a Weberian framework consistent with *verstehen*, to which we return later.

Bureaucracy

If *verstehen* is a Weberian concept with pertinent applicability to the functioning of the criminal justice system that foregrounds the qualitative understanding it brings to people who offend, equally applicable is Weberian bureaucracy. Martin Albrow (1970) explains that the word 'bureaucracy' is of 18th-century origin and means rule by officials within organisations. In an interesting aside, Albrow refers to Von Humbolt in 1792, the same Von Humbolt who appears in Kehlmann's book alluded to earlier, who made reference to the mechanisation of human life. Nevertheless, when turning to Weber, Albrow establishes the point that the idea of bureaucracy was associated with changes in German administration during the 19th century, and links are forged between bureaucracy, administration, organisations, modernity and power. The argument is advanced that bureaucracy constitutes the most efficient form of organisation, exemplified by precision, continuity, discipline, strictness and reliability. According to Weber, bureaucracy is an inevitable process in the modern, post-18th-century Enlightenment world, and gathers pace and power as it develops. However, as Albrow (1970, p 47) clarifies, the problem that Weber addressed was how the inherent tendency of bureaucracy to accumulate power 'could be prevented from reaching the point where it controlled the policy and action of the organisation it was supposed to serve'.

Albrow explores seven modern conceptualisations of bureaucracy: rational organisation; organisational inefficiency; rule by officials; public administration; administration by officials; the organisation; and modern society. Bureaucracy has been employed in a wide variety of theories about modern society. It has been linked 'with the growth of tertiary occupations, with the differentiation of social functions, with the alienation of man from work, with the growth of oligarchy and with a general process of rationalisation' (Albrow, 1970, p 85). From *Economy and Society*, the defining characteristics of the Weberian ideal-type bureaucracy can be summarised as follows:

- a specialised division of labour, where different individuals-officials undertake specialised tasks in pursuit of organisational goals;
- a hierarchical chain of command and offices, with higher offices supervising lower ones;
- actions of officials governed by rules and administrative regulations, so there is little scope for individual initiative, discretion, autonomy, even human feeling;
- appointment to office is based upon merit;
- there is a clear separation of public role and private life; and
- a uniform organisation replete with documents, files and knowledge contained in technical experts. Additionally, the Weberian analysis of bureaucracy takes place within types of domination that correspond to three types of legitimation:
  - rationally regulated with a structure of domination that is bureaucratic;
  - traditionally prescribed social action is represented by patriarchalism; and
  - charismatic, based upon the authority of the individual.

Weber advanced the position that a central feature of the modern capitalist world is the trend towards rationalisation. It is planned, technical, calculable and rigorously efficient, but correspondingly depersonalised and lacking in human feeling, which can be described as the *disenchantment of the world*. Bureaucracy is an illustration of the modern trend by which law, rules and prescriptive regulations displace charismatic and affective elements. Bureaucracy may well be the most technically efficient form of domination in a capitalist, industrial society. However, there is a price to pay because of its discernible dehumanising tendencies. It may be stated that Weber, with Nietzsche lurking in the background (Tarnas, 1991; Safranski, 2003), was concerned with the way in which, during the 19th century, those human values associated with the affections of the human heart were being damaged by the cold penetrating light of reason and science. On the one hand, rational and bureaucratic tendencies produce a technically efficient organisation and society; on the other, they create an oppressive *iron cage*, where human beings are reduced to cogs in a vast impersonal machine from which there is no escape. As Weber (1968 [1922], vol 3, p 975) said: 'Bureaucracy develops the more perfectly, the more it is "dehumanised", the more completely it succeeds in eliminating from official business love, hatred, and all purely personal, irrational, and emotional elements which escape calculation'. We must never forget that the acme of bureaucracy found a cogent and disturbing manifestation in the timetables that organised trains hurtling towards the Nazi death camps. It is within this context of Weberian thinking on bureaucracy that, in previous work on modernising trends within probation, I resorted to distinguishing the notion of *bureaucratic technician* from *therapeutic imagination* (Whitehead, 2007). Consequently, *verstehen* and bureaucracy, rationality and rationalisation, constitute a complimentary set of critical tools for exploring and explaining what probation has become within the modernised criminal justice system, particularly since 1997. If modernity equates to a disenchanted world in Weberian social theory, modernisation and transformation exemplify the disenchantment of probation practice.

Karl Marx, 1818–86

Introduction and some biographical references

It bears repeating that the Durkheimian perspective emphasises how punishment functions to maintain social order and promote the bonds of social solidarity. Punishment buttresses the collective conscience, the moral basis of society, the prevailing social consensus. Zedner (2004, p 77) succinctly summarises Durkheim by saying that the function of punishment is less concerned with controlling crime than with providing a vehicle for the 'expression of outrage when crime is committed and thus to reaffirm the social value transgressed. The subject of punishment is, therefore, less the offender than society as a whole'. Next, Weber does not, as Durkheim clearly does, address the themes of crime and punishment directly. Arguably, though, there are Weberian themes that resonate with, and can be developed within, the organisational domain of probation work, namely, *verstehen*, bureaucracy and technical rationality. It will be suggested in more detail later that both of these perspectives can be put to work as functioning explanatory theories to draw attention to contemporary, modernising and transformational features affecting probation and criminal justice.

When turning to Marx, he, like Weber, but in marked contrast to Durkheim, had little to say directly about crime and punishment (Tierney, 2006, p 186; Cowling, 2008).[9] Nevertheless, it is possible to identify a discernible Marxist tradition that explicates crime and punishment. This is a body of social theory that advances the proposition that material, economic and technological change, specifically appertaining to the mode of production, is a necessary condition of socio-cultural and moral transformation. This, in turn, has implications for the operational logic of punitive responses (McLellan, 1976). Therefore (this point was raised when exploring the Durkheimian position), law, crime and methodologies of punishment should be understood as relative phenomena. They constitute a distinctive compendium of institutional forms and expressions that change over time as the economic and material platform transmutes. Notwithstanding criticisms of the Marxist tradition,[10] one can turn again to Zedner (2004, p 80), who alludes to the enduring nature of Marxist analysis to provide a framework for thinking about the nature of punishment as a government strategy 'inherently linked with power relations, economic struggle, and social conflict'. Accordingly, it incorporates the analytical category of class-based justice in the way that the existence of rules and laws promote the interests of the rich over the poor, the strong over the weak, thus maintaining the vested interests of the few over the many (see Reiman, 1998). In doing so, we proceed from Durkheimian consensus to Marxist conflict. Helpful biographical texts for consultation are McLellan (1976) *Karl Marx: His Life and Thought* and McLellan (1986) *Marx*.

Some key sources – primary
- *The Economic and Philosophic Manuscripts of 1844* (Marx, 1964 [1932]).
- *The Communist Manifesto* (Marx and Engels, 1967 [1848]).
- *The German Ideology* (Marx and Engels, 1947 [1845]).
- *Capital: A Critique of Political Economy Volume 1* (Marx, 1976 [1867]).

Secondary sources
- Rusche and Kirchheimer (1968 [1939]).
- Giddens (1971).
- Taylor et al (1973).
- Bailey and Brake (1975).
- Coser (1977).
- Hall et al (1978).
- Walker and Beaumont (1981).
- Wacquant (2009).
- Garland (1990).
- George and Wilding (1991).
- Sayer (1991).
- Löwith (1993).
- Morrison (1995).
- Hudson (2003).
- Cowling (2008).

Themes in the Marxist tradition

Morrison (1995) provides a succinct overview of key themes in the Marxist corpus, which constitutes a voluminous literature. These pertinent thematics are: alienation (which resonates with rationalisation in Weber); the industrial capitalism of the 19th century and how the newly emerging mode of production structured class relations in the post-feudal period; the dialectical idealism of Hegel transformed into the dialectical materialism of Marx (Morrison, 1995, p 316) – this is history with a teleological purpose and the law of historical development; political economy; surplus value; and the salient base and superstructure metaphor.

McLellan, a biographer of Marx, expands upon these themes by reminding us that Marx was influenced by German-Hegelian idealism, French political theory and English classical economics. McLellan (1986, p 24) clarifies that the intellectual background of Marx's home and school was the 'rationalism of the Enlightenment, a pale Protestantism incorporating the virtues of reason, moderation and hard work'. For Hegel, who followed but reacted against Kantian idealism, with its postulation of an active rather than passive mind in the construction of reality, advocated a view of history as unfolding according to a plan. In other words, through a dialectical process of thesis, antithesis and synthesis, what is referred to as Reason–Spirit–Absolute is unfolding itself within the historical and evolutionary process.[11] Moreover, the entire Hegelian philosophic edifice is raised upon the assumption that the nature of reality is *ideal* or mental in content and that 'human reason as part of that reality, of the Ideal whole, is capable of direct, intuitive knowledge of the world in which it operates' (Sampson, 1956, p 191). By contrast, Marx eventually emerged from Hegel's metaphysical abstract system to reconstruct a *materialist* rather than *idealist* conception of reality and the historical process. Rather than beginning with the ideal before moving towards the material world, Marx inverted the Hegelian conception and, in the process, turned it the right way round. Mazlish elucidates that Hegel's emphasis on consciousness, on what was inside the human mind, was correct. However, what was erroneous was the attribution of consciousness to ideal rather than material forces and movements (Mazlish, 1968, p 225; see also Chadwick, 1990).

According to Marx, it was the economic system – the way in which societies are founded upon the basic requirement to produce in order to sustain life itself – which was determinative of the socio-ethical system, as well as being the locus of power. This is the *base–superstructure* metaphor as the fundamental economic base and the dependent non-economic superstructure. The latter includes, for example, a society's legal and political institutions. We can also add the education system, family, religion and the criminal justice system, conditioned by, but also reflecting and reproducing, the demands of the economic system and promoting the interests of those who own and control the means of production, distribution and exchange. Morrison takes this further by saying that in resorting to the concepts of base and superstructure, Marx demonstrated that the system of economic production shapes social relations and therefore the very structure of society. The economic system shapes the class structure and the corresponding ideas that are related to the roles that people perform in production (Morrison, 1995, p 313). The base–superstructure relationship has been interpreted in terms of a crude economic determinism, with recourse to causal terminology. McLellan (1986, p 41) questions this by saying that the most that can be said is that, for Marx, 'technological change was a necessary, though not sufficient, condition of social change'. Therefore, with these preliminary thematics in mind, I want to continue the discussion by exploring a number of perspectives that are located within the Marxist tradition. I begin with a criminologist during the early years of the 20th century, and conclude with a probation commentator in the 1980s.

Marxist tradition from Bonger to a reference in McWilliams

During the early years of the 20th century, Willem Bonger (1969 [1916]), according to Reiner's (2007b, p 352) re-evaluation, was one of the first criminologists to construct a Marxist analysis of crime. Even though Taylor, Walton and Young (1973, pp 222–36) were critical of Bonger, Reiner supports a more charitable encomium by saying that such criticisms signally fail to acknowledge Bonger's position as a pioneer of the political economy of crime. According to Bonger's analysis, crime should not be understood as a fixed or absolute concept, following Durkheim and Marx. It has no ontological reality but constitutes a variable phenomenon. Additionally, it was the structure of capitalist organisation itself that generated conflict and exploitation, and was criminogenic in the stimulation of egoism and avarice. It was precisely this destructive melange of capitalism and egoism that accounted for motivation towards crime throughout the whole class structure, that is, the working class, sub-proletarian criminality and the crimes of the powerful. One of the central perspectives within the Marxist tradition is that the phenomenon of crime is rooted within the politico-material organisation of capitalist society, rather than individual pathology.

In *Punishment and Social Structure*, Rusche and Kirchheimer (1968 [1939]) examine the relationship between the economic system, labour markets and punishment. These authors, within the broad context of unfolding a historical analysis commencing in the mediaeval period, demonstrate that penality is shaped by prevailing productive relations and labour market conditions. As changes occur within the economy, so changes correspondingly occur in the nature of penality, a thesis advanced to support the contestation that economic forces determine punishment. In other words, one should talk about punishment in not general terms, but rather as a specific form of punishment structured by, and functional to, the prevailing means of production. Accordingly, when labour is in plentiful supply, penal responses can be harsh and reckless with human life, as exemplified in the late Middle Ages, when capital punishment was prevalent. By contrast, when the demand for labour in the economy exceeds supply, the state is less disposed to exercise excessive punishments. Consequently, the labour market determines the social value placed upon human life. Rusche and Kirchheimer (1968 [1939], p 5) elucidate that 'Every system of production tends to discover punishments which correspond to its productive relationships'. According to this analysis, *there is no direct or unambiguous relationship between crime and punishment. Rather, the system of penality is involved, beyond the narrow crime–punishment nexus, in controlling surplus populations (always the poor) under specific economic conditions.* Rusche says that criminal laws and the daily work of the criminal courts are 'directly almost exclusively against those people whose class background, poverty, neglected education, or demoralisation drove them to crime' (quoted in Garland, 1990, p 91). Laffargue and Godefroy (1989) established a correlation between unemployment and imprisonment. Chiricos and Delone (1992) reviewed evidence which demonstrated that labour surplus was associated with prison populations. Additionally, De Giorgi (2006), in *Re-Thinking the Political Economy of Punishment*, summarised studies from the US, UK and Australia that gave support to the thesis of Rusche and Kirchheimer on the theoretical and empirical linkages between labour market conditions, unemployment and punishment.

Garland (1990) and Hudson (2003) remind us that there are diverse perspectives within the Marxist tradition, more nuanced than the economic determinism of Rusche and Kirchheimer. Pashukanis (1978), Hay (1975) and Ignatieff (1978) explain punishment within the politics and ideologies of conflicts and struggles between classes, and as a way of maintaining and promoting the power of the state and hegemony of the ruling class. Correspondingly, the argument is advanced that the operation of the criminal justice system, of which probation and social work are constituent elements, functions as a component part of the state's repressive strategy for controlling the poor located at the material hinterland of society, sub-proletarian populations who lack the rudiments of socio-economic security and who form the backbone of probation and Community Rehabilitation Company caseloads. Under capitalism and its neoliberal variant (Harvey, 2005; Reiner, 2007a), certain layers of society are rendered economic casualties, relegated to the status of surplus requirement, veritable social junk (Box, 1987), sand in the machine (Mathiesen, 2006) and deregulated populations (Parenti, 1999), which the state, through its penal agents both in prison and the community, manage, control and contain, but also punish, discipline and exclude. Therefore, there is some veracity attached to the claim that the rich get richer and the poor get prison, or other penal dispositions, in a criminal justice system that neutralises the threat of crime represented by the recalcitrant poor under neoliberal capitalist arrangements (Reiman, 1998).

It was during the late 1960s that criminological perspectives, influenced by Marxist theory, surfaced in the US. Subsequently, an outbreak of radical Marxist theorising appeared in Taylor, Walton and Young (1973), who contested the prevailing orthodox consensus of functionalist perspectives, scientific positivism, determinism and predominantly individualistic explanations of, and responses to, crime. They engaged in a ground-clearing critique of major criminological theories – classicism and positivist paradigms; Durkheimian anomie and Mertonian strain; the Chicagoans; Marx, Engels and Bonger – before making a case for their *fully social theory* of deviance, which, they argued, must take account of the class-based political, social and economic structures of capitalism. The authors argued for a politics of social reform in contradistinction to the traditional panoply of positivism, quantification, measurement and prediction, which are associated with a criminal justice system predominantly in pursuit of correcting the pathological and maladjusted individual, understood as embodying an essential 'otherness'. Consequently, to do otherwise than to work for the collapse of capitalism and the transformation of society to one of socialist diversity is to become implicated in correctionalism. In other words, there is a problem with 'the coercive use of the criminal sanction to "correct" behaviour on a personal basis when its roots lie in social structural inequalities of wealth and power' (quoted in Downes and Rock, 1988, p 247). This criminological perspective embraces the following themes: human action is meaningful and voluntarily chosen rather than being positivistically determined; a conflict rather than a Durkheimian consensus view of society; socio-economic arrangements must be factored into an analysis of crime, which can be interpreted as a legitimate and rational response to these arrangements; the state, through the criminal justice system, draws attention to certain forms of behaviour (working-class benefit fraud) rather than other, more serious, social harms (tax evasion), such as white-collar crimes and the crimes of the powerful. Finally, moral panics (but see Hall, 2012) are generated by the media in conjunction with the politics of power, which serve to mystify the real source of people's problems located within the political economy.

Policing the Crisis (Hall et al, 1978) provides a good illustration of what a fully social theory of deviance looks like. Within the historical context of exploring the phenomenon of mugging during the 1970s, and the associated moral panics generated by the media, the argument advanced is that it is not possible to detach human behaviour and repertoires of offending from wider political, socio-economic, macro-structural and cultural variables. Consequently, Hall and his Birmingham colleagues during the *crisis decade* of the 1970s analyse mugging and crimes of violence connected to a number of factors, including the role played by the media in fabricating rather than reporting the news. The state, faced with turbulent socio-economic dislocations during the 1970s (a crisis of hegemony), engenders moral panics, which divert attention away from the real source of problems located in class relations and fundamental crises within the capitalist system. Crime was utilised by the state as a 'symbolic source of unity in an increasingly divided class society at a time when traditional modes of providing consensus were diminishing' (Valier, 2002, p 122). A veil of ideological mystification is thrown over the real source of the problem; capitalism is restructured at the expense of the working class to maintain profitability for the economic elite; and problems that are fundamentally rooted within class conflict are shifted onto authority relations as crime and politics are separated. During a crisis of hegemony, the theory was advanced that the crime card is cunningly dealt by a state supportive of capitalism to restore its hegemony at the expense of the working class and its youth.

It was also around this time that the National Deviancy Conference (NDC) was airing its intellectual grievances (Zedner, 2003). Beginning in 1968 and associated with Stanley Cohen, David Downes, Ian Taylor, Jock Young, Paul Rock and so on, objections were raised against a criminological orthodoxy in league with positivism that, among other things, denied meanings to human actions. It should be noted, as an aside, that Leon Radzinowicz (1999, pp 229–30), when pondering the activities of the NDC and its radical Marxist orientation, referred to its advocates as naughty schoolboys. Furthermore, during the early 1970s, a group of radical social workers published their Case Con manifesto. After reflecting upon the creation of the welfare state, a combination of altruism and political expediency, it also constituted a strategic-political response to the threats posed by the militant working class. It was theorised that the welfare state was a concession made by the capitalist state during the 20th century in the interests of stability and social order, as well as contributing to the provision of a fit and efficient workforce that would facilitate a capitalist economy. The radical critique of Case Con draws attention to the practices of casework, which can be seen as a *con* in the way that it ascribes blame to the individual for problems that are largely rooted in capitalist structures, such as poverty, inequality, homelessness, economic exploitation and differential life chances. Indeed, the professionalisation of social work encouraged by Seebohm in the 1960s (Whitehead and Statham, 2006) resorted to casework as a tool that pathologises behaviours, demanding individual responsibility within conditions of socio-economic inequalities. Consequently:

> Case Con believes that the problems of our 'clients' are rooted in the society in which we live, not in supposed inadequacies. Until this society, based upon private

ownership, profit and the needs of the minority ruling class, is replaced by a workers' state, based on the interests of the vast majority of the population, the fundamental causes of social problems will remain. (Case Con manifesto, quoted in Bailey and Brake, 1975, p 147)

Case Con's emblematic status for radical social work was complemented in probation circles by the publication of *Probation Work: Critical Theory and Socialist Practice* (Walker and Beaumont, 1981). This text, after exploring the state of probation practice – court work, prison-based work and the assimilation of new developments – proceeded to pick up on themes alluded to earlier as they worked out their radical critique of probation within a Marxist analytical framework. By doing so, they theorised that the organisation is involved in the reproduction of capitalist social relations, individualising crime and promoting consensus within society, which is basically conflictual. During the course of their exposition, they arrived at the point that 'A fundamental conclusion of our analysis is that Probation Officers are paid to do a particular job for the state and that this role is generally supportive of capitalism' (Walker and Beaumont, 1981, p 160). Accordingly, they advocated a form of socialist practice, which is characterised by the following elements:

- Defend clients from the worst forms of punitive excess within the criminal justice system, and minimise the use of custody and recourse to breach proceedings as a last resort.
- The provision of help consistent with the position taken by Bottoms and McWilliams (1979) in their explication of the non-treatment paradigm (see Chapter Three).
- Educational work and the provision of useful services to meet the varied and complex needs of clients.
- Community involvement in addition to campaigning action for social change and also changes within the criminal justice system.

It is of paramount importance for Walker and Beaumont that there are probation officers prepared to state publicly that prison is indubitably destructive, laws can be unjust, law enforcement is discriminatory and the probation service 'cannot cope with the poverty and hardship our work uncovers' (Walker and Beaumont, 1981, p 169). They also invited magistrates, police officers and prison staff to share responsibility with probation officers in articulating dissent at the system they describe (a very different slant to the concept of multi-agency arrangements that subsequently gathered pace).

Finally, Bill McWilliams, in a quartet of papers published in the *Howard Journal* during the 1980s (McWilliams, 1983, 1985, 1986, 1987), analysed the history of changing ideas in probation since the period of the police court missionaries towards the end of the 19th century. He was an important thinker within, and contributor to, the literature on probation, as a practitioner, researcher and academic at the Cambridge Institute of Criminology. In the paper published in 1987, he identified three significant ideologies underpinning practice during the 1980s. These are explained as: *personalism* (see Chapter Three); *managerialism*; and a *radical-Marxist* approach mainly represented by the work of Walker and Beaumont. McWilliams argued that all three approaches, notwithstanding clear philosophical differences, located people who offend within a framework of government policy and that they were united in pursuing alternatives to custody within a decade committed to this objective. In fact, it can be suggested that the 1980s were thematically emblematic of alternatives to custody, rather than rehabilitative optimism, an objective politically supported until the events of 1993 put the policy into reverse gear under Howardian reactionism for political rather than penological reasons.

After reflecting upon various perspectives within, and numerous illustrations of, the Marxist tradition, I have concluded this overview by alluding to its presence within probation in the 1980s. Valier summarises the perspective by reminding us that three main claims emerged from this tradition in the 1960s: criminalisation is a central feature for maintaining capitalism; criminals can be seen as proto-revolutionaries who see through the injustices generated by their class position (Left idealism); and a focus upon working-class crime rather than ruling-class, white-collar crimes and the crimes of the powerful. Furthermore, Barbara Hudson (2003, p 115) ties these elements together within the Marxist perspective by stating that the functions served by social institutions are described by Marxists as:

> regulatory (mechanisms to keep the system working), repressive (penalties for workers who do not accept the rules of capitalist production), and ideological (making workers believe that social arrangements which in fact serve the interests of the capitalists, are in the interests of all.

It is suggested that probation is implicated in these functions as it comes into contact with some of the poorest individuals within society, illustrated as follows: problems within the family home; underachieving educationally; unemployment; low income; and impoverished life chances. If supporting evidence is required, beyond perusing statistics produced by the Ministry of Justice, then an ethnographic visit to a local magistrates' court can be instructive. These are the individuals who predominantly make up the supervisory caseloads of probation, particularly within inner-city areas, in addition to occupying prison cells. These are the people who are currently subjected to regimes of punitive responses towards offending behaviours but were also, in turn, at the receiving end of additional punishments in the form of the erstwhile benefit sanction and rigorous enforcement policies (Whitehead and Statham, 2006).

The argument can be advanced, located within a radical theoretical frame of reference, that the criminal justice system has been modernised (see Chapter One) to crack down mainly on deregulated populations from whom probation and prison derive, but also recycle, the majority of their clients. The argument is further advanced in the US, UK and France, for example, that the police, prisons and probation have been restructured to deal with the crisis created by the pursuit of neoliberal-capitalist economics (Parenti, 1999; Young, 1999, 2007; Harvey, 2005; Reiner, 2007a; Wacquant, 2009; Whitehead, 2015b). The neoliberal order is conducive to hardening attitudes towards the urban poor under conditions of advanced marginality, culminating in structural violence imposed 'from above' by the repressive state apparatus (Wacquant, 2008, 2009). The criminal justice apparatus is functional for the capitalist order. This is the modernised context within which a much reduced probation system, and 21 Community Rehabilitation Companies, operate following the rehabilitation revolution.

Michel Foucault, 1926–84

Introduction and a biographical reference

We cannot unproblematically graft Foucault onto the aforementioned triumvirate of classical social theorists to construct a seamless quartet. Nevertheless, he should be afforded his rightful place at this juncture. Some of his work facilitates exploring modern probation and theorising the criminal justice system. In the first manifestation of this book, in 2010, I attempted to situate Foucault within the Western intellectual and philosophical tradition (see Russell, 1946). Through excavating the turning point of Renaissance science, continental rationalism, British empiricism, and the Copernican revolution in knowledge contained in

Kant's *Critiques*, followed by the Hegelian reaction, we picked our way towards Foucault in the 20th century. Hegel's death in 1831 signalled the 'collapse of absolute idealism and the emergence of other lines of thought' (Copleston, 2003 [1963], p 2; see also Copleston 2003 [1953], 2003 [1959], 2003 [1960]). We encounter the decline of grand metaphysical system building and the rise of positivism during the 19th century, whose antecedents were mentioned earlier.

To reiterate positivism, associated with Comte in the 19th century (Simon, 1963), it is asserted that positive science constitutes the only reliable source of knowledge about the world. Comte, indebted as we saw earlier to the tradition of Renaissance science – Bacon, Turgot, Condorcet, Montesquieu and St Simon – stated that knowledge progressed through the law of three stages, from theological, then metaphysical, to the positive sciences. Moreover, just as laws govern the world of nature, there were those who similarly claimed that the social realm of human activity is also governed by discoverable laws. Later, in the 20th century, logical positivism was defined by a number of reductionist features, which included that: statements claiming to be factual have meaning only if it can be shown how they can be verified; metaphysical speculation is questionable because it is unverifiable; and statements about moral, aesthetic and religious values, which are not scientifically verifiable, are basically meaningless (Simon, 1963). Nevertheless, the exalted claims made by science, as the only reliable route to truth and epistemological certainty, have themselves been questioned. In other words, the viewpoint is expressed that the nature of reality, knowledge and truth are just too complex to be encapsulated within any one intellectual paradigm. Perhaps another way of putting it is that all human understanding is provisional and therefore perspectival rather than unalterably fixed, and that no one single interpretation can be definitively final, which even includes the scientific paradigm (Tarnas, 1991, p 397).

One such interpretation during the 20th century brings us circuitously to Michel Foucault. We have witnessed how, notwithstanding the bold assertions of science to describe the world *as it is in itself*, Kant (see Kuehn 2001) questioned whether it is possible for the human mind to acquire this kind of knowledge. Furthermore, the *second* Enlightenment during the 18th century and its modernist project, with its faith in science and humanity, believed in rational progress and the power of human reason to establish truth and certainty. By contrast, since the 1970s, late or postmodernity has expressed disenchantment with the modernist project by drawing attention to a series of interconnected impulses: globalisation; post-industrialisation; consumerism; and the contingent nature of what is real and what can be known. There is no longer any overarching master narrative, but a plethora of competing opinions, interpretations and relativities. The ground has shifted beneath our feet, solidity turned to quicksand (Belsey, 2002). Meaning does not inhere within or is naturally given up by the world itself (essentialism), but is existentially contested and constructed. Although it is extremely difficult to categorise the multifaceted intellectual contributions of Foucault, it is argued that his contribution is located within a postmodern reaction to the tenets of Enlightenment modernism (Tarnas, 1991, pp 351, 418).[12] This is a position that questions the scientific and progressive assumptions underpinning the Age of Reason, particularly human beings as autonomous and rational subjects. One biographical text that can be alluded to before proceeding further is the helpful introductory text by Didier Eribon (1989).

Some key sources – primary
- *The Order of Things: An Archaeology of the Human Sciences* (Foucault, 1970).
- *Discipline and Punish: The Birth of the Prison* (Foucault, 1977).

Secondary sources
- Garland and Young (1983).
- Cousins and Hussain (1984).
- Merquior (1985, 1986).
- Garland (1990).
- Macey (1993).
- McLellan (1976).
- McNay (1994).
- Gutting (1994, 2005).
- Hudson (2003).
- Scheurich and McKenzie (2005).
- Schwan and Shapiro (2011).

Some themes in Foucault

Garry Gutting (1994, 2005) warns of the danger of distorting the Foucauldian corpus because of its many complexities. The main reason for this is that he produced such a diverse body of work, which defies categorisation. This warning indubitably applies to *Les Mots et les Choses* (*The Order of Things*), the first of two texts I draw attention to shortly because of their relevance for theorising probation. According to Didier Eribon (1989, p 156), *Les Mots et les Choses* is an extremely complex work, as well as a masterpiece (Merquior, 1986). Eribon assists with the book's interpretation when he says that it addresses the point at which man became an object of knowledge within the context of Western culture, with the appearance of the human sciences. The argument is advanced that every period is characterised by an 'underground configuration that delineates its culture, a grid of knowledge making possible every scientific discourse, every production of statements' (Eribon, 1989, p 158). In other words, Foucault suggests that a historical *a priori* exists that constitutes an episteme governing the parameters of knowledge and thought, so much so that human agency becomes a fanciful concept. Additionally, Foucault should be located within the intellectual tradition of *continental philosophy* (see Solomon, 1988). Other themes to note are: the centrality of language in constructing and understanding social practices; the illusion of autonomous discourse; the oppression of people by taxonomic classification systems and confinement; technologies of power presented as scientific knowledge; and the discontinuity of history rather than Hegelian and Marxist teleological progress.

The Order of Things (Les Mots et les Choses)

One should not rush past the revealing subtitle to Foucault's work: *An Archaeology of the Human Sciences*. Scheurich and McKenzie (2005) address Foucault's archaeological methodology (see also Merquior, 1986; Gutting, 2005) by explaining that it is predominantly qualitative because of its interest in texts and archive material. These authors elucidate that Foucault was indebted to Georges Canguilhem, Gaston Bachelard and the theme of discontinuity (caesuralism = epistemological break or rupture). Discontinuity, along with disorder and non-linear development, constitutes a postmodern perspective that opposes the optimistic-modernist position of the linear development of history with a purpose (eg Hegelian, Marxist and Christian teleologies, and the Comtean idea of progress). The archaeological method encapsulates the way numerous elements in a society at a given period, from philosophical ideas to everyday opinions, as well as institutional practices, determine its prevailing knowledge base. It is the epistemological unconscious of a given era. Scheurich and McKenzie (2005, p 845) proceed to explain that Foucault's archaeology is a complex set of concepts including '*savoir, connaissance*, positivity, enunciations, statements, archive, discursive formations, enunciative regularities, correlative spaces, enveloping theory, level, limit, periodisation, division, event, discontinuity, and discursive practices'. Archaeologically, this approach has affinities with a structuralist perspective (Piaget, 1971; Merquior, 1986; Gutting, 2005). *The Order of Things* subjects four historical periods to critical analysis:

- pre-classical – up to the end of the 16th century (Renaissance);
- classical – up to the end of the 18th century (Enlightenment);
- the modern period of the 19th century; and
- the contemporary age since 1950.

First, the 16th–17th-century pre-classical period is described by Foucault in the language of correspondence, similitude or resemblance between language and the thing it names. This is a unity or mirror-like image between words, ideas and objects. By unpacking the following terms – convenientia, aemulatio, analogy and sympathy – Foucault elucidates that this episteme and draws all things together in one continuous chain of being, thus providing a knowledge of things that is unmediated. Furthermore, Merquior (1985, p 43) refers to this episteme as 'the prose of the world defined by unity of words and things'. This is one of the Foucauldian constructions for ordering things that was stimulated by his chance encounter of Borges's discussion of a Chinese encyclopaedia.

Second, Don Quixote's adventures mark the end of the Renaissance and the beginning of the classical episteme because words and things no longer resemble one another (Foucault, 1970, p 48). The excavation is advanced that there was a discernible cultural and epistemological disruption (caesurae) because within the space of a few years, 'a culture sometimes ceases to think as it has been thinking until then and begins to think other things in a new way' (Foucault, 1970, p 50). Accordingly, the pre-classical age of resemblance is coming to an end in that classical knowledge excludes mirror-like resemblance (similitude) and a new, discontinuous approach based upon representation, comparison, measurement and order emerges. Foucault elucidates the differences between the two epistemes by stating that the mind's activity no longer consists:

> in *drawing things together*, in setting out on a quest for everything that might reveal some sort of kinship, attraction, or secretly shared nature within them, but, on the contrary, in *discriminating*, that is, in establishing their identities, then the inevitability of the connections with all the successive degrees of a series. (Foucault, 1970, p 55, emphases in original)

Additionally, mathesis is the basis of a science of measurement and order in order to render phenomena calculable. Foucault (1970, p 120) proceeds to suggest that the fundamental task of classical discourse is to 'ascribe a name to things, and in that name to name their being. For two centuries, Western discourse was the locus of ontology'. Cousins and Hussain (1984, p 33) illuminate the discussion by stating that a radical change has occurred because interpretation 'has been replaced by analysis. Resemblance has been replaced by the representation of identity and difference. The entire mode of knowledge had changed'. Even though Foucault describes different historical epistemes, he does not say how or why one is replaced by another.

Next, according to this Foucauldian schema, is the modern 19th century and beyond, from the natural and physical sciences to the rise of the social and human sciences. Foucault suggests that prior to the emergence of the human sciences in the 19th century, 'man' did not exist as an object of scientific knowledge. Nevertheless, they made their appearance – biology, economics and philology, and one may add psychology, sociology and criminology – occasioned by the demands of an industrial-capitalist society and the attendant norms of order and normality required. This created a new episteme associated with the demands of capitalism as opposed to former feudal arrangements. Therefore, it can be argued that systems of thought, the production of knowledge, discourse and language, from a postmodernist perspective, constitute the products of power relations. As Foucault himself (1970, p 353) explains, the human sciences are not:

> an analysis of what man is by nature (essence); but rather an analysis that extends from what man is in his positivity (living, speaking, labouring being) to what enables the same being to know (or seek to know) what life is, in what the essence of labour and its laws consist, and in what way he is able to speak.

The concept of discourse is important because it constitutes an institutionalised way of thinking, imposing limits upon what can be said about a subject. Accordingly, forms of discourse are involved not in revealing or *discovering* 'truth', but rather in the *production* of what constitutes 'truth'.

The subject matter of *The Order of Things* is how *fundamental cultural codes* impose order upon experience (Merquior, 1985, p 35), which change over time and are discontinuous with previous manifestations. In other words, the existence of a mental infrastructure, or conceptual grid, which functions as a historical a priori, "almost a historical form of Kant's categories" (Merquior, 1985, p 38). Significantly, these discontinuous blocks of knowledge, or epistemes, do not advance human beings in some Comtean-linear or progressive fashion nearer absolute truth or indisputable forms of knowledge of themselves or their world. Accordingly, the human subject is not the sole origin of meaning, which means for McNay (1994, p 5) that 'the subject is in fact a secondary effect or by product of discursive formations'. This perspective not only takes issue with the assumption that meaning inheres within the human subject, but also calls into question associated notions of truth applied to human beings, and what constitutes knowledge and progress. This can be constructed as a clash between modernist and postmodernist ways of thinking about the nature of human beings, reality and knowledge, thus raising profoundly complex issues surrounding ontology, epistemology and particularly language (Belsey, 2002) in relation to conflicting perspectives on *discovered* contrasted with *imposed* meanings. For Foucault, knowledge is geared not towards the truth, 'but to the everlasting skepsis of endless random interpretations – and his Nietzchean soul refuses to be depressed by it' (Merquior, 1985, p 75).

As a corrective to this Foucauldian-structuralist and anti-humanist thesis, Giddens (1982) contests the notion of epistemic blocks or periodisations, interpreted as human affairs being determined by unconscious *a priori* forces that they are not aware of and can do little to change (again, the tension between structure and human agency, determinism and free will, being played out sociologically and philosophically). Consequently, how do we accommodate the notion of freedom of thought and the capacity of human beings for autonomous action, including the efficacy to change given situations, within this Foucauldian framework? It appears that there is little room for human agency in this text. Notwithstanding the troublesome nature of such questions raised by Foucault's treatment of structure and the epistemological unconscious of a given era contained in the complex material laid out for us in *The Order of Things*, the second text for consideration also deals with the theme of discontinuity. This is Foucault's treatment of the transition from public punishments directed at the body to the birth of the prison. Also, by doing this, we continue to reflect on the relationship between the status of the sciences, knowledge, power, domination and socio-economic relations that resonates with Weber and Marx.

Discipline and Punish (Surveiller et Punir)

Foucault begins his analysis by describing in graphic detail the execution of Robert Francois Damiens in Paris in 1757, following his attempt to assassinate King Louis XV. This was an expression of monarchical power under the *ancien régime*. By contrast, the birth of the prison, several decades later, should not be assumed to illustrate the humanisation of punishment according to Enlightenment principles of reason and Comtean progress. Rather, the prison – with its timetable for the regulation of bodies, deprivation of liberty, tutelary supervision and programmes that focus upon the offender's mind and soul – reflects a new form of Nietzchean will to power. Not so much to punish less, but rather to punish better by penetrating more deeply into the individual offender and then outwards from the institution of the prison into the wider social body. Monarchical power, with its assemblages of physical punishments, tortures and executions, is replaced with a form of positive disciplinary power that constitutes a different technology of power and punishment.

Early on in the text (Foucault, 1977, pp 24, 54), Foucault refers to Rusche and Kirchheimer to support the position that differential forms of punishment are related to prevailing economic and productive arrangements. Nevertheless, Giddens (1982, p 221) suggests that, for Foucault, it is the prison and asylum, rather than the factory or place of production in Marx, which delineates the modern age (more Nietzsche than Marx). Foucault makes several references to Marx in *Discipline and Punish* and it should be reiterated that the late 18th century witnessed the emergence of industrial capitalism, contrasted with previous feudal arrangements and corresponding mode of production. This, in turn, produced an expansion of towns and cities on the back of a transition from a mediaeval to capitalist mode of production, so that 'the economy of illegalities was restructured with the development of capitalist society' (Foucault, 1977, p 87). It is argued that the birth of the prison, and its expansion in the 19th century, is connected with problems created by, and the needs of, an industrial society under capitalist arrangements. This was the pressing need to discipline and control those who constituted a threat to the emerging form of social order and the vested interests of the few over the many. The prison constituted a new form of power, a new technology of punishment, which enabled the institution to create new forms of knowledge of the individual based upon close observation. It was also the aim of the reformers, through the institution of the prison, to re-establish the delinquent as an obedient subject: the individual subjected to habits, rules, routines, and the demand for order (Foucault, 1977, p 128). Accordingly, the power to punish is reconfigured. The methods that make control of body and mind possible are also found in the disciplinary methods utilised in monasteries, armies, workshops and schools: exercise, training, manipulation by hierarchical power and authority conducive to obedience.

Control over minds and bodies is illustrated by turning to a more contemporary illustration, located outside the total institution of the prison, in Wacquant's (2004) sociological exploration of the pugilistic arts in *Body and Soul*. During his period of study at Chicago University in the 1980s, Wacquant produced an ethnographic account of boxing being practised in a gym not far from the university. When examining the meanings, regimen and ethics of training (in fact, 'Busy Louie' acquired first-hand knowledge and experience of boxing), he describes how:

> the gym functions in the manner of a quasi-total institution that purports to regiment the whole existence of the fighter – his use of time and space, the management of his body, his state of mind, and his most intimate desires. So much so that pugilists often compare working out in the gym to entering the military. (Wacquant, 2004, p 56)

This has a Foucauldian resonance. There is even a further reference to the 'monastic devotion' of the boxer (Wacquant, 2004, p 60).

Discipline and Punish proceeds from what is going on inside the prison to the wider social body, symbolised by the panopticon. As mentioned earlier, the creation of disciplined, trained and obedient bodies was a necessary requirement for the capitalist industrial machine. It should also be acknowledged that the techniques for examining the individual inside the institution – hierarchical observation and normalising judgement – turn the delinquent into a 'case', the observation of whom becomes an object of knowledge linked to a regime of power. This is the individual malefactor rendered measurable and then amenable to control and classification, who is eventually normalised. It can also be seen how the prison operates in a realm located beyond legal infraction, the sphere regulated by codified law. In other words, normalising judgements are made about forms of conduct that are not necessarily in breach of the prevailing legal code. It has therefore been pointed out that numerous judges of morality exist – teachers, doctors, educators, social workers, judges, even probation officers – who operate in spheres that regulate and control behavioural norms (Cousins and Hussain, 1984, p 137) in what is an extended carceral continuum and archipelago.

Towards the end of the book, Foucault (1977, p 264) intriguingly argues that the prison, since its inception, has always been a 'failure'. What he means is that it does not ostensibly reduce recidivism or diminish the crime rate. By contrast, it actively encourages a milieu of delinquency that, at first sight, is the opposite of the assumed rationale of the prison system. Furthermore, the conditions to which inmates are released condemn them to recidivism and adversely affect prisoners' families. One can safely arrive at the conclusion based upon numerous criteria that the institution fails, and yet it continues to exist, expand and even thrive. It has become the politician's institutional friend since 1992–93. Indubitably, there is plenty of money for prisons (imperialistic wars and exercises in state violence), which is a relatively expensive mechanism for maintaining law and order. Why should this be the case?

Paradoxically, argues Foucault, even though the prison ostensibly fails, it is nonetheless *useful*. Useful because it produces, as a deliberate political strategy, a specific delinquent class by a deliberate process of criminalisation. In so doing: it creates a body of 'knowledge' that is useful for power; it turns the spotlight upon one group of fabricated delinquents and directs attention away from other social or state-inflicted harms; it justifies the existence of the police; and, in what seems to be of critical importance, the political construction of a delinquent class separates *crime* from *politics*. Where the last point is concerned, it is implied that crime is constructed as a problem for the criminal, just as poverty can be constructed as a problem for the poor, so that the 'problem' is individualised. Consequently, crime becomes detached from the politics of power under capitalist socio-economic arrangements, which diverts attention away from the real source of the problem (see, eg, the earlier analysis of Hall et al, 1978; see also Simon, 2007). Beirne (1993, p 68) advances the intriguing argument that, for Foucault, positivist criminology emerged in France 'as a calculated response to the need for an official and comprehensive discourse which could justify these new strategies of penality' and thus obfuscate the differences between crime and politics. Furthermore, the creation of delinquency divides the working class against itself and enhances the fear of the prison in working class communities.

The prison is a failure penologically, yet useful for politically tactical and strategic reasons. David Garland (1990, p 150) pursues this point when he says that 'the prison does not control the criminal so much as control the working class by creating the criminal', and this seems to be, for Foucault, the unspoken rationale for its stubborn persistence. According to the Foucauldian schema, it is an institution inextricably associated with the politics of power, discipline and the subjugation of recalcitrant populations. He provides an alternative account of the modern world that resonates with Nietzsche and Weber. The Foucauldian thesis is, on the one hand, supported by Cohen's (1985) dispersal of discipline thesis; yet, on the other, it has been challenged by the analysis of Tony Bottoms (1983).[13] As a retort to the positivist enterprise, Foucault (1977, pp 288–9) says the following:

> There is not, therefore, a criminal nature, but a play of forces which, according to the class to which individuals belong, will lead them to power or to prison: if born poor, today's magistrates would no doubt be in the convict ships; and the convicts, if they had been well born, would be presiding in the courts and dispensing justice.

There is an echo of Foucault in a novel written by Eric Arthur Blair when we read:

> Fear of the mob is a superstitious fear. It is based on the idea that there is some mysterious, fundamental difference between rich and poor, as though they were two different races, like Negroes and the white man. But in reality there is no such difference. The mass of the rich and poor are differentiated by their incomes and nothing else, and the average millionaire is only the average dishwasher dressed in a new suit. Change places, and handy dandy, which is the justice, which is the thief. (Orwell, 1933, p 107)

After exploring bodies of classical social theory with Durkheim, Weber and Marx, before proceeding to Foucault, it is now necessary to expand our conceptual grid and theoretical framework by turning to Lacan and Žižek.

Lacan and Žižek – from psychoanalysis to radical politics

Introduction

For a relatively short span of historico-political time in the history of capitalism between 1945 and the late-1970s, public sector organisations were essential components of the post-war social-democratic settlement. The rationale of the Keynesian polity was to put an 'end to the hell on earth' (Driver and Martell, 1998, p 8) of liberal capitalism through manipulating the levers of economic management that facilitated the welfare-social state, the stabilisation of markets and a collective-universal morality that functioned in the national interest. This polity also included the aspirational pursuit of equality, justice and full employment. This state complex and its accompanying organisations did not establish some blessed utopia (Townsend, 1979), but organisational structures mediated between the state and public, which were put under pressure by the inundation of neoliberalism during the 1980s. Subsequently, the electoral phenomenon of New Labour moved to the right to solidify the formation of a new political consensus manifested in the ditching of 'old' Labour politics and its commitment to the Keynesian polity, state–public ownership and tax and spend collective-assistantial welfarism. The argument is advanced that the organisational pillars that buttressed the post-war settlement encoded a symbolic order comprising health, education, welfare and a criminal justice system that provided rehabilitative services, the normative signifiers of integrated citizenship within the bonds of social solidarity. This was the symbolic order that mitigated the harsher extremes of the capitalist order and its potential for social disruption.

However, beginning in the 1980s with the initial spate of privatisation, qualified continuity after 1997 and the upsurge between 2010 and 2015, these organisational supports are experiencing coercive expulsion from what remains of the symbolic order at the hands of the obscene capitalist *Real*. These organisations are rapidly becoming the ethico-cultural and symbolic relics of a former dispensation, relegated to historical texts describing a former misguided age as they assume the form of a more robust capitalist-neoliberal hue after the tumults of 2007–08. These are the political, socio-economic and organisational transformations that can be explicated by recourse to a Lacanian-Žižekian conceptual framework that legitimates the following detour into psychoanalysis and radical politics through the categories of the *Imaginary*, *Symbolic* and *Real*.[14] Although the primary focus of this conceptual detour is the distinction between the *Symbolic* and the *Real* which has the efficacy to enhance organisational analysis, it is of academic interest to begin with the *Imaginary* (to extrapolate from human subjectivity to organisational critique).

Some key sources – primary
• Lacan (2001).
• Žižek (1992, 2006, 2009, 2010, 2014).

Secondary sources
• Myers (2003).
• Elliott (2005).
• Homer (2005).
• Eagleton (2009).
• Hall (2012).
• Winlow and Hall (2013) (see excellent Lacanian glossary).
• Roudinesco (2014).

Lacanian-Žižekian conceptual framework

The Lacanian *Imaginary* is complex, complicated by competing analyses of the human condition. For example, Stevenson and Haberman (1998) explore the ontology of the subject through the philosophical lenses of: Confucianism; Hinduism; Biblical (Augustinian – *you made us for yourself*) essentialism; Platonic and Kantian perspectives; Marxist materialism; Freudian unconscious; Sartrean existentialism; Skinner's behavioural conditioning; and Lorenzan aggression. There is no space in this schematic formulation to accommodate Lacan, who utilises phenomenology, psychology and ethology to theorise the human psyche, which exists at the intersections of disharmony, fragmentation and conflicting drives. Lacan is not the first to explore the turmoil of anthropological subjectivity, as ancient Greek texts containing Pauline theological-anthropology reveal: 'I do not understand my own actions. For I do not do what I want, but do the very thing I hate' (Romans 7v15 RSV).[15] Lacan differentiates between the *ego* and *subject*, elucidated by Homer (2005, p 25) when explaining that the ego function is one of misrecognition by refusing to accept fragmentation and alienation. Moreover, and importantly, 'The ego is an "imaginary function" formed primarily through the subject's relationship to their own body. The subject, on the other hand, is constituted in the symbolic order and is determined by language' (Homer, 2005, p 44). For Lacan, as well as Žižek, it is the *Imaginary* order that presents a serious problem because postmodernity, in conjunction with capitalist excess, is indicative of narcissistic self-obsession at the expense of the interests of the *other*. While it is relevant to refer to the *Imaginary* to present a fully rounded picture of the psychic categories, particularly its relationship to the *Symbolic* and *Real*, it is the latter that require careful attention.

When turning to the symbolic order, Lacan draws upon the work of Lévi-Strauss and Saussure, who argue that the subject is the product of, and constituted by, language (Saussure on language as an all-embracing *system*; Lévi-Strauss on *structure*; Lacan on the *symbolic*). This implies that human subjectivity is the product of a signification system, where language comprises a set of signs or signifiers that do not correspond to how things exist in the world, thus inverting the working assumption of the linguistic function to name things accurately (see Foucault earlier). In other words, there is an arbitrary rather than transparent link between language and reality, a problematic that stretches back to Plato's *Cratylus* and Aristotle's *De Interpretatione* (Merquior, 1986, p 12). Accordingly, the correspondence between word and object (or signifier and signified) is undermined when language is differentiated between its referential and differential functions, elucidated when Belsey (2002, pp 8–9) explains that:

> Meaning, Saussure proposed, did not depend on reference to the world, or even to ideas. On the contrary. He argued that, if the things or concepts language named already existed outside language, words would have exact equivalents from one language to another, and translation would be easy.

Extrapolated to human subjects, this line of enquiry conveys that they cannot be evaluated primarily in and of themselves, as free-floating rational agents, thus forcing again to the surface of critical enquiry the sociological conflict between the efficacy of agency and structure. In other words, the ontology of the subject can be conceptualised as reflecting and reproducing the signification system in which the human subject is inescapably located. Importantly, though, if the fragmented and alienated Lacanian subject is the product of an arbitrary signification-language system, then the symbolic order is not a permanently fixed structure, but open to manipulation (Myers, 2003, p 24). Change the system-structure and you transform the subject.

Third, the Lacanian *Real* is not synonymous with reality. If, what we assume to be, and understand by, reality consists of symbols as the constituent elements of a socio-linguistically constructed signification system arbitrarily imposed on the world rather than essentially given, then the 'Real is the unknown that exists at the limits of this socio-symbolic universe and is in constant tension with it' (Homer, 2005, p 81). If the *Imaginary* can be summarised as alienation, deception, fragmentation and the order of narcissistic identification, the *Symbolic* as the order of language, law, culture and the Big Other (opposed to nature, red in tooth and claw), and the *Real* located outside the *Symbolic* that resists signification, it is the latter that is inexpressibly beyond language and the symbolic. The *Real* is the experiential enigmatic and traumatic at the heart of the subject and, according to Eagleton (2009, p 141), is the disruptive 'gash in our being where we were torn loose from the maternal body, and from which desire flows unstaunchably'. It is both vacuous and 'horrifically enjoyable' (Eagleton, 2009, p 143).

From psychoanalysis to politics

When transposing Lacanian psychoanalytical categories into a political register, Žižek proceeds by utilising Hegel's dialectical methodology,

Marx's critique of capitalism and Lacanian psychoanalytical insights (Myers, 2003). Harrington summarises that 'Žižek's writing, stranded somewhere between high modernism and postmodern pastiche, can be viewed as an attempt to develop a psychosocial diagnosis of the self in its dealings with the global capitalist economy' (Harrington, 2005, p 184 – *the attempt to develop a politico-psychological diagnosis of organisational transformation under neoliberalism*). Žižek (1992) provides his own introduction to Lacan and psychoanalysis, specifically the categories of the *Symbolic* and *Real*, which are explicated through popular culture and a critique of postmodernism. For Žižek, postmodernism has fashioned a subject riddled with doubt, ontologically anxious and insecure, a fragmented self detached from fixed universal anchoring points. Additionally, postmodernity signals the decline of the symbolic order as the framework of collective meanings, intersubjectivity and mutuality, essential if human beings are not to be reduced to self-indulgence at the expense of the other, through the eruption of the obscene *Real*. The postmodern subject is preoccupied with narcissistic identification, ego-obsessed, pursuing stupid pleasures at the expense of substantive meanings and values, and, in doing so, reflects and reproduces the capitalist-neoliberal order so that 'When symbolic efficiency is suspended, the Imaginary falls into the Real' (Žižek, 2009, p 374).

The response, inspired by Marxist critique, is a political act that adopts a revolutionary stance that would dislodge a world order in thrall to capitalism in order to replace it with a symbolic order of intersubjectivity and interpersonal relations of mutual benefit premised on cooperation rather than conflict. To put the matter differently, it is the critical shift from raw nature to human culture that constitutes the symbolic order 'which allows the creation of social life to take place within its structure of communicable meanings and committed relations' (Winlow and Hall, 2013, p 153). This is where Žižek positions the discussion on subjectivity, informed by the Cartesian cogito and reflections on the transcendental materialist subject (Hall, 2012). Here, the subject is not pure agency, a model of humanity complying with Sartrean existentialism as the fully free and responsible subject burdened with existential choices, nor, at the other extreme, the Durkheimian subject penetrated by structures or the Foucauldian subject devoid of agency as it is obliterated by structure in *The Order of Things* (Foucault, 1970). Instead, the subject is hard-wired yet malleable,[16] as are organisational structures.

To repeat, the *Imaginary* is an acute problem under neoliberal capitalism because of the promotion of, and identification with, narcissistic obsessions, the release of libidinal energies and compliance with dominant material signifiers (see Myers, 2003; see also Homer, 2005). Alternatively, the *Symbolic* is the socio-ethical domain we enter when taking the step from self to other. It can be described as the locus where we play our part in the wider community of fellow human beings, a significant challenge since the Agricultural Revolution (Harari, 2014). The *Symbolic* is constituted by language, which self-evidently appertains to the social dimension of existence. It is the sphere of: social relations and dialogic engagement; rules and regulations; and the law of prohibition to prevent actions that cause injury to others. Furthermore, the *Symbolic* contains the verbal and non-verbal conventions of daily encounters, socially constructed customs and practices, and normative codes of conduct and unwritten rules that comprise the expectations we place on each other without which social relations would be problematic, as they sometimes are. Just as a word is comprised of a combination of letters or marks on a page that acquire meaning in its usage by its precise location in a sentence, so, by extrapolation, the individual human subject acquires meaning and value through having and playing a role in the socio-*Symbolic* order. We must make the transition from self to other, ego to social, state of nature to state of culture to become a person alongside other persons. Eagleton (2009, p 6) clarifies that Lacan derived his thought from Hegel, for whom 'the transition from one state to another has an ethical dimension'. Furthermore, Winlow and Hall (2013, p 153) insightfully explain that it is the 'passage' from the 'state of nature' to the 'state of culture' that Žižek positions subjectivity. For him, subjectivity remains forever tied to the sense of loss and profound negativity that defines the transition. Once we arrive in a 'state of culture' we are presented with the substance we can use to 'fill up the void of subjectivity'. By contrast, for Žižek, the *Real*, as the pre-*Symbolic*, is associated with capitalism and postmodernism, which has wreaked havoc on the *Symbolic* order, ethico-cultural conditions and moral and social regulation.

This conceptual framework constructs a set of intellectual and ethical coordinates by which to analyse our present condition and steer a course out of it, out of an absurd present and into an open future for which we alone are responsible and that can be different to current arrangements. Žižek (2010: 180), establishing the role of atheistic theologian, states 'I think this is the legacy of Christianity – this legacy of God not as a big Other or guarantee but God as the ultimate ethical agency who puts the burden on us to organize ourselves'. Some of these theologically pertinent references will be developed in Chapter Three. Although the burden of this discussion is the nature of subjectivity under late-modern capitalism, the Lacanian-Žižekian conceptual framework can be advanced to facilitate organisational analysis and critique. In other words, when politico-ethical symbolic efficiency is interrupted or suspended, as it assuredly has been in the transition from Keynesian to neoliberal conventions, organisations are ditched into the realm of the *Real*. We will return to this in Chapter Four.

Table 2.1 concludes this chapter by summarising these disparate bodies of classical social theory, Foucault, Lacan and Žižek. Later, they will be put to work to explore and explain the modernised form of probation within a politically induced and transformed criminal justice system.

Table 2.1: Summarising bodies of social theory

Durkheim	*The Division of Labour in Society; Two Laws of Penal Evolution; Moral Education* Crime disturbs society's moral consciousness, which elicits a punitive response characterised by passionate outrage, denunciation and vengeance. Law, crime and punishment constitute a visible index of the nature of society, social type and culture, strength of collective conscience, acting as a barometer of social change. Punishment is less concerned with correcting or deterring the offender than with reaffirming the moral sensibilities of the law-abiding community, promoting social solidarity and bolstering the collective conscience. Durkheimian consensual sociology is where punishment functions within the moral circuits of society.
Weber	*Economy and Society; verstehen,* natural and social sciences, bureaucracy, rationality and rationalisation *Verstehen* is concerned with human understanding, and the meanings human actors attach to their own and others' behaviours. The social science discipline of hermeneutics addresses the complex meanings and interpretations of human action, not predictive and invariant laws. The natural and social sciences inhabit different ontological and epistemological domains, dealing with objects, things and people, respectively. Also, themes of *bureaucracy*, managerialism, rationalisation and rationality; modernity as an 'iron cage' under industrial capitalism.
Marx	**The Marxist tradition** The substructure–superstructure metaphor of economic base and dependent non-economic superstructure. The latter includes legal and political institutions, education, family, and criminal justice, conditioned by the demands of the productive system, which supports the interests of those who own and control the means of production, distribution and exchange. Class-based nature of capitalism; punitive exclusion of surplus populations, who, as the subordinate class, constitute a threat to social order under neoliberal capitalism. From Durkheimian consensus to Marxist conflict sociology.
Foucault	*The Order of Things; Discipline and Punish* Epistemological disruptions; radical changes in social unconscious, thinking and institutional practices. 'Man' becomes an 'object' of knowledge for the social sciences, which do not discover some essential 'truth', but rather construct forms of knowledge useful for power. Next, from monarchical to disciplinary power and new technologies of punishment. The prison transforms people into objects of knowledge, useful for a Nietzschean politics of will to power. Post-Enlightenment social order as dystopian; Benthamite panopticon – surveillance, discipline, regulation; the all-seeing gaze of state authorities cast over individuals and families. Normalisation, control of minds and bodies to render them docile under industrial capitalism. The separation of *crime* from *politics*.
Lacan and Žižek	**Winlow and Hall's Lacanian glossary; Roudinesco; Myers on** Žižek The excavatory significance of the tripartite *Imaginary, Symbolic* and *Real* in Lacan. For Roudinesco these terms encapsulate Lacan's psychic topography. From psychoanalysis to radical politics in Žižek to interpret the modern-postmodern condition. From Keynesian conventions to the transformational order of neoliberal capitalism. Hegel's dialectical methodology, Marxist critique and Lacanian psychoanalysis have profound interpretive meaning for understanding human subjectivity and organisational transformations.

Notes

[1]   Beirne (1993) explains how Quetelet and Guerry are the forerunners of the ecology of crime school that emerged in Chicago in the 1930s. Quetelet contributed to the rise of positivist criminology in that he 'attempted to reveal that the same law-like, mechanical regularity that had been determined to exist in the mechanics of the heavens and in the world of nature also existed in the world of social facts' (Beirne, 1993, p 77).

[2]   For additional references on positivism and the natural and social sciences, see Giddens (1978), Garland (1985), Bryant (1985) and Beirne (1993).

[3]   For an extended discussion on classical and positivist criminology, see Garland (1985) and Roshier (1989).

[4]   Merquior (1986, p 38) alludes to Durkheim and Descartes, and suggests that Levi-Strauss turned Durkheim on his head in the following way. Durkheimian sociology moved from the mental to the social, from the content of ideas in the mind to the external world, so that the mind mirrored society. However, for Levi-Strauss and structuralism, the movement is from the social to the mental, from social relations or cultural constructs to intellectual structures.

[5]   See Durkheim and Merton on their understanding of anomie. There are a plethora of sociological and criminological texts on anomie, but probation staff may want to consult Whitehead (2007, p 68f) for an introductory summary of key themes prior to looking at more detailed work.

[6]   The labelling perspective is summarised briefly in Whitehead (2007, p 73).

[7]   For additional material on philosophies, theories and *justifications* of punishment, see Bean (1981), Duff and Garland (1994), Hudson (2003) and Easton and Piper (2005). By contrast, on sociological *explanations* of punishment, see Garland (1990), Hudson (2003) and Cavadino and Dignan (2002).

[8]   For a very helpful paper on Durkheim's theory of penal evolution, see Steven Spitzer's (1975) paper: 'Punishment and social organisation: a study of Durkheim's theory of penal evolution'.

[9]   Radzinowicz and Hood (1990), considering socialist writers towards the end of the 19th century, argue that, for them, law was an instrument that benefited the ruling class. Engels said more about crime than Marx but it is suggested that Marx's position was that law benefited property-owners; he attacked the bourgeois concept of law and crime; following Quetelet, crime is a social phenomenon and punishment exists to defend vital interests; he criticised England for its brutal criminal justice system; he was more discriminating than Engels in his interpretation of criminal statistics; and the criminal is productive and he seems to echo Durkheim that crime is inevitable and beneficial (Radzinowicz and Hood, 1990, p 40).

[10]   For criticisms of the Marxist tradition, see the helpful summaries in Garland (1990, chs 4, 5) and Hudson (2003, ch 7).

[11]   Post-Kantian philosophy witnessed the attempt to produce a more unified and coherent interpretation of reality. Previously, Kant bifurcated reality into phenomena and noumena, and, by doing so, imposed limits on knowledge. Subsequently, Hegel suggested that the purpose of philosophy is to overcome divisions between phenomena and noumena, body and soul, subject and object, finite and infinite, to achieve a more unified approach. Furthermore, for Hegel, the task is to understand reality as a rational process that can be known by the philosopher. By contrast, the task of the philosopher for Marx is not so much to understand the world as the unfolding of the Absolute/Spirit, but rather to

change it via social action. The materialism of Marx conceptualises human beings as alienated from work, which socio-economic changes are required to overcome.

[12] or some additional help in understanding Foucault, see Lois McNay (1994, pp 52–66), the chapter by Canguilhem in Gutting (1994, pp 71–91), Merquior (1985, p 56; 1986, p 208) and Piaget (1971, p 128).

[13] For a discussion and critique of Foucault's thesis, see Garland (1990) and Hudson (2003). One should also include Matthews (1999, p 64) on Foucault and Weber, when it is stated that: 'Foucault's approach is similar to Weber's in a number of ways. Like Weber, Foucault examines in detail how bureaucratic and administrative processes operate within these segregative institutions and how they sustain order and secure compliance. Foucault also focuses on the way in which a bureaucratic institution can become an iron cage which eventually constrains its creators'. Here, Matthews is quoting from Gerth and Mills (1948).

[14] See Lacan (2001) Écrits. A useful place to look is: seminar II (1978) and the early formulation of the symbolic order and how the subject is constituted by and within a chain of signification; seminar VII (1986), which is important for the social sciences and humanities; and seminar XI (1973), which is indubitably complex. For an explanation, see Homer (2005).

[15] See also Davis (2010, pp 100–1): 'Paul's sensitivity to his own interior fragmentation is what Lacan identifies as the break with the Mother (that is, a primordial oneness) that introduces into the world an insatiable desire that longs to overcome the lack (created in the very break with the Mother) in an ultimate return to a point where desire is totally neutralized'.

[16] See Žižek on the insights of Descartes, where the 'I' of the cogito is a void deprived of content, alive in the Lacanian *Real*, devoid of culture, out of which we must create a symbolic order to confront the horror of nothingness.

THREE

The religious and personalist tradition: or, reflections on the moral economy of criminal justice

Introduction

A developing theme in this updated and revised edition is that probation's organisational rationale, explicated within the operational dynamics of the modernised criminal justice system sketched in Chapter One, has become analytically complex. It is a multifaceted phenomenon that demands an explanatory approach that assimilates various theoretical standpoints. This is why Chapter Two established the position that it is necessary to summon the excavatory support provided by Durkheim, Weber, Marx, Foucault, Lacan and Žižek to facilitate this task. No one approach, represented by any single body of social theory, can adequately capture the organisational complexity of the probation domain between 2010 and 2015. Accordingly, all those perspectives in Chapter Two bring into view a clearer image that would immediately become distorted if any one of them were neglected.

Furthermore, it is not intellectually permissible to remain content with the combined weight of theoretical propositions contained in Chapter Two. We have started the process of theorising the probation domain and accompanying transformations in criminal justice, but it is necessary to extend this theoretical platform. The argument is advanced that there has existed, for a considerable period of time, another significant element within probation that has influenced the judgements and decisions of the criminal justice system for over 100 years in England and Wales. Not so much a classical social theory, as a discernible set of values, an ethico-social sensibility, which has had recourse to the following lexicography: religion, humanitarianism, philanthropy, religious and secular forms of personalism, social work help, mercy, and benevolence.

Notwithstanding a politically driven and centrally imposed process of modernisation and cultural change that has launched probation into the orbit of punishment, personalist sensibilities have not been eradicated from the operational dynamics of the criminal justice system.

In other words, one can plot historically, and continue to uncover traces of, footprints left by personalist influences that are resonant of moral economy (Whitehead, 2015b; see also Mawby and Worrall, 2013; Deering and Feilzer, 2015). This may no longer represent a set of dominant social work values for the reason that they have been heavily compromised by the politics of punishment – not that there ever was a period when they solely dominated the scene, but they are less evident now than formerly. It is also clear that these humane impulses and sensibilities have been diluted coercively from *without* (the political impositions discussed in Chapter One), and colluded with from *within* by organisational representatives who, only two or three decades ago, operated within a very different system of axiological coordinates. In fact, the 'leadership' of probation has allowed itself to be mugged by the politics of power and disavowal, particularly since 1997, when other courses of action were possible, including resistance. All discourses have their day, a perspective that contains some veracity when reflecting on the place and space occupied by social work values within criminal justice during a discrete period of its history. Moreover, fashions come and go, as, apparently, do values and moral commitments within organisations.

This chapter draws attention to a religious, humanitarian and moral perspective within the probation service, but also the wider context of penal reform. Its longevity should be explored lest we forget that we did things differently in the past. This task is necessary prior to putting bodies of social theory, personalist impulses and moral sensibilities to work in Chapter Four. It is urgent and vitally necessary for probation, and the 21 Community Rehabilitation Companies, to rediscover their intellectual and ideological heritage that differentiated them from other criminal justice organisations.

Some relevant sources

- Howard (1973 [1777]).
- Leeson (1914).
- Le Mesurier (1935).
- Hinde (1951).
- Glover (1956).
- Rose (1961).
- Clay (1969).
- Ignatieff (1978).
- Bottoms and McWilliams (1979).
- McWilliams (1983, 1985, 1986, 1987).
- Garland (1985, 1990).
- Rose (1994).
- Whitehead (2015b).

Religious and humanitarian impulses associated with prison reform

Michael Ignatieff (1978), in his nuanced exposition of the penitentiary during the Industrial Revolution (1750–1850), affirms, as does Foucault (1977) in his graphic overture to *Discipline and Punish*, that during the 18th century, the system of punishment was predominantly a public spectacle. Until around 1776, a system of transportation operated from England to the 13 American colonies, but when it abruptly ceased following the War of Independence, administrative difficulties were caused for the prevailing system of justice. Subsequently, a temporary solution was found in superannuated warships – hulks – prior to the commencement of the second wave of transportation to Botany Bay in Australia after 1787 (Hughes,1987). This second wave of expulsions continued for a period of 80 years, until the last transport ship left England in 1867. Ignatieff continues the story by reminding us that we had to wait until the 19th century for the system of imprisonment to be firmly embedded within the piecemeal emergence of the criminal justice system. He develops the analysis by stating that during the 19th century, prisons were in the grip of a complex combination of forces. These forces should be located and disentangled within the wider political, social and economic context of evolving capitalist social relations. Nevertheless, one should be reminded that these forces included measures for reform that can be traced to an earlier period, prior to the 19th century, in the work of John Howard (1726–790), and later Elizabeth Fry (1780–1845). These reforming measures constituted a set of impulses that blended religious and humanitarian elements with political expedience. This was not so much a set of alternative impulses that threatened the emerging order of capitalism, or that represented a radical challenge to the authority invested in the state, but reforming and humane gestures running alongside class politics, the will to power and the perennial quest for social order – in other words, religious reform, philanthropy, humanitarianism and personalism, circumscribed and mediated by political imperatives.

According to Ignatieff, it is possible to trace a melange of nonconformist religiosity, philanthropy and humanitarianism in the reforming zeal of Howard, who wanted to improve the physical and mental health of prisoners. Howard's religious sensibilities did not so much apply the balm of comfort and warmth to the miscreant's soul; rather, they were a stern, unyielding and demanding influence. This was an impulse for reform and human brotherhood, working in conjunction with the discipline and regimentation of the poor in spirit, heart and pocket. Within the confines of an 18th- and 19th-century episteme that constructed crime as a disease, a symptom of moral weakness, the offender was categorised as a sinner who required the awakening of conscience by the divine light. Later, when reflecting on the work of Elizabeth Fry, Ignatieff (1978, p 143) draws attention to philanthropy, benevolence and religiosity, connected with evangelicalism and quietism (Quaker influences), providing a theological basis for the salvation and moral reform of reclaimable individuals. As a Christian philanthropist, Fry was concerned not only about the poor conditions she discovered at Newgate, but also with the plight of the homeless. Therefore, there is some evidence to advance the view that the penal system in the 18th and 19th centuries, and particularly impulses contributing to prison reform, had their roots in religion and moral sensibilities manifested in philanthropy and humanitarianism. Foucault rejects this interpretation, as explained in Chapter Two, as benevolence masks the will to, and deposits of, political power (see Garland, 1990, p 168).

In establishing this position, one must not lose sight of the sophisticated analysis of Ignatieff, which he expounds by saying that 'whilst the reformers liked to characterise Prison reform as a neutral philanthropic crusade "above politics", they were, of necessity, drawn into the tactics and strategy of class rule in a time of conflicts' (Ignatieff, 1978, p 162). In other words, any analysis of reform must be located within the political parameters of the period in question: its class relations under emerging capitalism; the institutions of prison, workhouse and industrial and reformatory schools; the management and control of the recalcitrant poor constituting a threat to social order; in addition to the inevitable fallout from an economic system conducive to inequality and injustice, particularly for those on the downside of class relations under industrial capitalism. Nevertheless, the importance of Ignatieff's approach is that he accommodates a melange of impulses into his account of prison reform that take the reader beyond an account rooted solely in Marxist theory considered earlier.[1]

We must penetrate some of these matters more expansively through the work of Hinde (1951). His little-read and -referenced book on *The British Penal System 1773–1950* is more descriptive than theoretical, analytical or critical, yet it contains instructive materials worth alluding to within the context of this chapter. During the reign of George III in the 18th century, Hinde refers to four pieces of legislation that gave power to the Justices of the Peace to appoint chaplains to local gaols.[2] In fact, Howard discovered chaplains in most county gaols when pursuing his own enquiries (Hinde, 1951, pp 17, 238). It should also be acknowledged, when exploring the influence of religion on the penal system during the 18th century, that this was the period that experienced the Wesleyan evangelical revival initiated from within the Church of England. Additionally, Hinde draws attention to the work of George Whitfield in Bristol in 1737, then Abel Dagge, who, as the Keeper of Newgate, was converted to Christianity, which animated his spirit towards prison reform. This apparent metanoia enabled Hinde to state that these 'humanitarian reforms, inspired as they were by deep religious convictions were also recognised the following year' (Hinde, 1951, p 20) in the Annual Register of 1761. Consequently, as indicated earlier, the lives, behaviours and deficits of prisoners could be interpreted within a theological framework as sinners in need of moral reform through the agency of God's saving grace (Hinde, 1951, p 44). It was the same store of metaphysical grace that kindled the hearts of those who worked with prisoners in the direction of reform. Another example of the latter is Sarah Martin, born in 1791, who stated that 'In the same year (1810) whilst frequently passing the gaol, I felt a strong desire to obtain admission to the prisoners to read scriptures to them, for I thought much of their condition and of their sin before God' (quoted in Hinde, 1951, p 71).

It is of interest, before proceeding to other related matters, to remain with the theme of prison chaplains. Radzinowicz and Hood (1990, pp 511, 541–42), at two specific points in their book on *The Emergence of Penal Policy in Victorian and Edwardian England*, consider the work of the chaplain. It is suggested that they played only a minor role in the 19th-century convict prisons and that governors had the upper hand in terms of power and influence. Therefore, one should be careful not to exaggerate their spiritual influence, or any other form of influence, on prison regimes. It is suggested that chaplains 'seemed to be more like tired functionaries, expected to discharge difficult duties in a hostile environment' (Radzinowicz and Hood, 1990, p 541). Initially, they were drawn from the Church of England, but from 1864, Roman Catholic priests were appointed. Also, Jews and nonconformists were allowed their own religious representatives, in addition to which there were facilities for Hindus. It should also be acknowledged, for the sake of completeness, that the ideological basis of the Victorian era clustered around the salient features of evangelical religion, individualism, laissez-faire liberal economics and post-Benthamite and post-Beccarian utilitarianism (Garland, 1985). Towards the end of the 19th century, it was the Gladstone Report (Home Office, 1895) which recommended that outside preachers should attend chapel services in prison.

Prior to completing this introductory section, one should not overlook the situation appertaining to young offenders within the context of personalist impulses and moral sensibilities, notwithstanding the reference to Platt's research in the following. During the 19th century, it is possible to trace the emergence of a separate system of juvenile justice in industrial schools for the perishing classes and reformatory schools for the dangerous classes. By the early 20th century, the borstal system consolidated these separate provisions, as did the creation of a separate juvenile court established by the Children Act 1908. There was further consolidation in the Children and Young Persons Act 1933, which affirmed the welfare principle when working with young offenders. Even though it can be argued that the history of juvenile justice is one of tension between the oscillating demands of care and control, punishment and welfare, justice and treatment, the 1960s stand out as the acme (with hindsight, perhaps one should say *aberration*) of the welfare approach. If the Children and Young Person's Act 1969 had been fully implemented, this would have signalled a victory of the welfare approach over the attractions of punishment and custody for young people who are involved in offending behaviour (Thorpe et al, 1980). However, because of a changing political situation from the summer of 1970, the following decade witnessed a doubling of punitive custody for juveniles; the 1980s saw a move in the opposite direction; until the 1990s witnessed a shift towards punitiveness rather than welfare. There have been, and continue to be, many competing discourses in youth justice, as well as adult criminal justice – welfare, justice, managerialism, punishment, restorative justice, authoritarianism. The welfare impulse has not been totally eradicated, but nor has it completely seized the day (Brown, 2005; Muncie, 2009).

To summarise, if the influence of religion is an inescapable factor in analysing and understanding the history of the prison, as well as being associated with reforming impulses after the 1700s in connection with Howard, Fry and many others, it was also a significant factor in the emergence of what became the probation system during the 20th century. Writing in 1958, Radzinowicz (1958, Preface) stated that 'If I were asked what was the most significant contribution made by this country to the new penological theory and practice which struck root in the twentieth century … my answer would be Probation'. It is to this that we now turn.

Probation orthodoxy tempered with revisionism

With its roots in the 19th-century practices of bail, judicial reprieve and the recognisance, the example of significant individuals including Matthew Davenport Hill and Edward Cox, in addition to what was happening in other countries such as the US and New Zealand (Leeson, 1914; Rose, 1961; Raynor and Vanstone, 2002), probation work emerged from the Police Court Mission of the Church of England Temperance Society (Whitehead and Statham, 2006; Nellis, 2007). Probation was not conceived as a punishment, but rather constituted as an alternative to punishment and imprisonment, containing elements of mercy, advice, assistance, friendship and practical help, mediated through a relationship with a missionary after 1876 and then appointed officer of the court from 1907/08. Again, we must exercise care when analysing the origins of probation. Raynor and Vanstone (2002) argue that it is legitimate to resort to the language of mercy and help when excavating the early history of the probation system within the context of late-Victorian philanthropy, evangelical religion and benevolence. Nellis (2007) utilises the language of 'humanising justice' when analysing probation history until the early 1970s. Radzinowicz and Hood (1990, p 49) explain that during the 19th century, individual moral reform in conjunction with social amelioration were important features, often motivated by 'deep religious convictions, and philanthropic zeal and was thus a true reflection of the dominant ethos of Victorian society'. The motivation of the missionaries was deeply religious, articulated in the language of saving sinners to bring them to salvation. Accordingly, the orthodox account is assembled. Nevertheless, a necessary injection of revisionism into this explanatory account after 1876 must incorporate the fact that police court missionaries were not extending God's mercy and benevolence to *all* lost offenders' souls when they appeared before the London Police Courts. The Victorian categories of deserving and undeserving invaded the probation system, and the work of the missionaries oriented towards a middle-class perspective. With this in mind, it is of critical interest to turn to the following empirical corrections.

In a critically challenging paper by Peter Young (1976), published 100 years after the first appearance of the Police Court Mission, it is correctly acknowledged that reformist impulses in the process of penal developments were explained by the efficacy of the religious, philanthropic and humanitarian spirit during the 19th century (Young and Ashton, 1956). Nevertheless, it is Young's contention that this analysis omits certain ingredients that he rectifies in presenting a more rounded sociological analysis of the early history of probation. In other words, he provides a more nuanced reading of events. Young's central thesis is that the probation service has its roots in the relationship between the classes towards the end of the 19th century. This thesis is consistent with a version of social work in that it functioned from within the orbit of the middle class as an attempt to stabilise what was then a rapidly changing social order by extending its largesse towards the working class. Young's position is similar to this. Additionally, Young sees the existence of social work not as a mechanism for the liberalisation and democratisation of society, but rather as a mechanism to *drain away* and *neutralise* working-class demands, potential agitation and threats to social order generated by, albeit modified, capitalist social relations.

On the one hand, it can be argued that probation work constituted: a clear alternative to the Victorian prison system; an alternative to punishment (punishment was, in fact, suspended and conditional upon future behaviour); and an act of mercy within a supervisory relationship delivering advice, assistance and friendship. By contrast, after 1907, it functioned as part of a reformed capitalist state, its focus on the individual's soul did not threaten the existing social order and theological doctrines of salvation and moral reform were conducive to ensuring compliance and order. Young's analysis is sympathetic to the position that the class position of probation officers, in forming relationships with working-class offenders, was conducive to stabilising the existing social structure under a modified form of capitalism that had been emerging since the 1880s (Garland, 1985). Therefore, it had a political dimension and constituted more than religious, philanthropic, humanitarian compassion for a specific socio-economically disadvantaged group within society. Probation work was implicated from the beginning in complex class relations, even though Young rejects a class-based conspiracy theory that probation and social work solely existed to promote and maintain ruling-class interests. A similar point is advanced in the thesis of Anthony Platt (1977) on young offenders in the US. The emergence of a separate juvenile justice system in the US is not an example of humanitarian and liberal developments, argues Platt. Rather, the story recounted is one of more intrusive supervision, control and the labelling of working-class young people (resonant of Foucault earlier). Consequently, political issues, engendered by US capitalism, are transformed into problems of personal adjustment and, as with Foucault, crime is separated from politics. In other words, juvenile justice can be understood by malign politico-economic developments, rather than by benign ethico-cultural challenges.[3]

Even though it is necessary to inject a note of revisionism into the orthodox account, the McWilliams quartet (1983, 1985, 1986, 1987) returns to the view that police court missionaries were possessed of a religious philosophy. The increased power awarded to the justices attendant on the Summary Jurisdiction Act 1879, then the Probation of First Offenders Act 1887, enabled the missionaries to inject mercy and leniency into the proceedings of the lower courts. When unravelling missionary work, McWilliams (1983, p 134) states that its vision was relatively clear in that it would 'rescue individual drunkards, render them susceptible to the influence of the spirit of God and their souls would be saved'. After 1876, the magistrates utilised the police court missionaries on an informal basis to supervise offenders released on recognisance under existing legislation, prior to the legislative supports of the probation system under the terms of the Probation of Offenders Act 1907. Significantly, argues McWilliams (1983, p 138), for a period of 60 years after 1876, the rationale for the mission to the courts was the saving of offenders' souls through divine grace. Subsequently, the gradual decline of the missionary spirit after the 1930s, but not its total extinction, was occasioned by the emergence of a more secular and scientific social work discourse in its application to the recalcitrant (Whitehead and Statham, 2006).

Cecil Leeson (1914), of whom there are numerous references in the research of McWilliams, had worked as a probation officer, as well as spending two years studying probation systems abroad, mainly in the US. He refers to probation work in theological terms, as the following illustrates: a system for the reclamation and reformation of offenders (Leeson, 1914, p 3) and 'essentially constructive and redemptive in character' (Leeson, 1914, p 42). He also made it clear that the probationer required the guidance of a probation officer rather than punishment. Leeson (1914, p 114) expands by saying that it was possible that social and religious agencies could facilitate reclamation, and that the attitude of the officer should be as a 'sensible friend; for the essence of Probation is constructive friendship'. Before developing the theme under consideration in this chapter, it is of interest to allude to a number of additional points raised by Leeson in what is one of the earliest books to have been written on probation in the UK. First, his work has a contemporary applicability when it is stated that: probation work is involved in the protection of the community; offending is analysed more at an individual than social level; and the offender's swift return to court is necessary if the probationer breaches a court order (which could then activate the suspension of punishment). Second, and by contrast to those bonds that unite 1907 with the organisation's centenary in 2007, there are marked discontinuities. According to Leeson: probation is about reform and not punishment; an emphasis is placed upon religious influence; the probation officer is a friend encapsulated in the legislative adage to assist, not a bully or dictator; and the officer must operate with discretion. Therefore, there are continuous and discontinuous elements in his account.

If Leeson provides an important resource for understanding probation work during the early years after 1907, this is complemented by the evidence contained in four Home Office Departmental Committee Reports (Home Office, 1909, 1922, 1936, 1962). These documents, particularly the first three, constitute a rich resource on those impulses under review and contrast markedly with modernising developments since the 1990s. The Departmental Committee of 1909 also underlines the rationale of the inchoate probation system as an alternative to punishment, custodial institutions and financial penalties, and that it is suitable for youths as an alternative to the Victorian industrial and reformatory schools. Moreover, the personal influence of the officer is considered an essential component in the realigned system of justice that was taking shape during the early years of the 20th century under a reforming Liberal government. However, the threat of punishment remained for those whose conduct constituted a breach of the court order, which would result in a return to the sentencing court. We should remind ourselves that the first probation officers, appointed after 1907, were gleaned from the pool of missionaries that had been accruing since 1876, and by the 1922 report, the religious convictions of probation officers remained an essential ingredient. In fact, the notion of probation work as a religious vocation was very much in evidence (Home Office, 1922, p 9). Interestingly, the second Departmental Committee report arrived at the conclusion that 'Many qualities were mentioned to us as desirable in a good Probation Officer – sympathy, tact, common sense, firmness, are but a few – but there was general agreement that a keen missionary spirit, based on religious conviction, is essential' (Home Office, 1922, p 13).

Part of the third and more detailed report of 1936 provides a detailed historical survey of the contribution made by former missionaries. These forerunners of the probation system exemplified a 'humaner spirit' operating within the penal system. Incidentally, the document cites the influence of Howard and Fry during the 18th and 19th centuries. It is confirmed that: probation officers should avail themselves of religious agencies in their work with offenders (Home

Office, 1936, p 64); the probation officer is constructed as a social worker of the courts (Home Office, 1936, p 77); and, to reiterate, the pioneering work of the police court missionaries is given due recognition: 'The example they gave of devotion and self-sacrifice has inspired the work of successive Probation Officers in later years' (Home Office, 1936, p 102). Nevertheless, following the recommendation that the system should evolve into a wholly public service, thus bringing to an end the potential for divided loyalties between the courts and religious associations, religious influences were attenuated over subsequent decades. By the 1960s, social casework eclipsed theological constructions and justifications for probation practice (Home Office, 1962). During a period of change that started to gather momentum from the 1960s and 1970s (Whitehead and Statham, 2006), it is appropriate to turn to various academic and practitioner voices that offered support to the impulses and sensibilities that have thematic resonance in this chapter.[4]

Academic and practitioner responses to political incursions

Robert Harris

In two papers by Robert Harris (1977, 1980) that remain worthy of consultation, the argument is advanced that since the mid-1960s, probation has experienced rapid change and expansion, resulting in the service being drawn increasingly towards the centre of penal policy. Dissonance had emerged at three levels, which Harris explained as follows: first, *moral dissonance* is the gap between the justice ideology of society and the welfare ideology of social work; second, *technical dissonance* is the gap between the task of reducing crime and the failure to do so, illustrated by numerous research studies (Brody, 1976); and, third, *operational dissonance* alludes to the complex relationship between care and control, a distinctive conundrum during the period under review. Therefore, a central argument in response to this predicament is that the care and control functions within probation work should be distinctly separated. This would result in probation no longer being entrusted to carry out the statutory orders imposed by the courts, which would become the responsibility of a new and separate agency. This would leave the probation service to become a court-based social work service:

> to provide a highly trained, caring and effective social work service to a disadvantaged section of the community: the offender. It can help him with accommodation, social security, jobs; it can give him counselling with many personal problems; it can teach him social skills; it can help him with marital or family difficulties. (Harris, 1977, p 436; see also Harris, 1980, pp 180–1)

In the climate of the late 1970s, Robert Harris was keen to clarify the practical problems involved in implementing such a bifurcated model, but he was more concerned with its theoretical and ethical efficacy than practicability. The theological lexicography may well have declined, but Harris advocated a distinctive configuration of axiological impulses within probation work with offenders, consistent with personalist sensibilities.

Malcolm Bryant et al

Bryant et al (1978), and other practitioners, *were* concerned with matters of practicability when, after accepting the critique of Harris and also empirical research that seriously questioned the efficacy of supervision to reduce reoffending, they proposed their two contract model. The primary contract would be made between the court and offender to ensure that the latter complied with all the requirements the court imposed. Additionally, the subsidiary contract would be established between the probation officer and probationer, which would consist in the offer of social work assistance, but at the request of the client and not imposed as treatment. Consequently, a failure to comply with the subsidiary contract would not constitute a breach of the primary contract between the court and offender. Interestingly, the rationale underpinning this approach was that social work help would not be forced onto unwilling clients. Instead, a range of welfare services would be made available: counselling, help with family problems, group work, education, welfare rights and employment skills. Bryant et al intended that this approach would encourage clients to deal with their problems, treat them as responsible people and encourage self-determination. The authors also advanced the view that magistrates would have more faith in probation orders if they could determine the length and frequency of reporting under the terms of the primary contract. Accordingly, it addressed some of the criticisms levelled at Harris's thesis, for whereas he argued for a clear separation of care and control, Bryant et al advocated preserving both care and control but on the platform of redefining their parameters, how they would be delivered and by whom. Probation would become a punishment on the tariff of court disposals according to clear legal requirements, but social work assistance would also be available. It was concluded: 'In short, offenders would be supervised in the community with opportunities for personal development rather than being "sentenced to social work" as at present' (Bryant et al, 1978, p 114).

Tony Bottoms and Bill McWilliams

Perhaps the best known and most often cited re-conceptualisation of probation practice from the period under discussion is the non-treatment paradigm of Bottoms and McWilliams (1979). These thinkers explicitly stated their purpose:

> We believe there is a need for a new paradigm of Probation practice which is theoretically rigorous; which takes seriously the exposed limitations of the treatment model, but which seeks to redirect the Probation service's traditional aims and values in the new penal and social context. (Bottoms and McWilliams, 1979, p 167)

The authors discussed the main elements of practice by claiming that the four basic aims have been and should remain as:

- the provision of appropriate help to offenders;
- the statutory supervision of offenders;
- diverting appropriate offenders from custodial sentences; and
- the reduction of crime.

Where the first aim is concerned, Bottoms and McWilliams argued against the medical/treatment model provided by so-called social work experts if this was understood as something forced onto offenders without proper consultation, and paternalistically delivered after a one-sided process of assessment and diagnosis. Consequently, the word 'help' constituted an important corrective to treatment, and the rationale of practice based upon help is that it faces up to the collapse of the rehabilitative ideal while retaining the values of respect for persons and hope for the future. Therefore, treatment becomes help, diagnosis becomes shared assessment and the client's dependent need leading to social work intervention becomes a collaborative task.

Next, when turning to the second aim, Bottoms and McWilliams said that probation officers should accept that probation involves elements of control and surveillance (as it did in 1907). However, the client should be made aware of the demands of the order consistent with the offences committed. Furthermore, and here is an echo of Bryant et al, the court should determine the length and frequency of reporting when clients are made the subject of probation orders. Clients should also be able to accept or reject social work help.

The third aim, diverting offenders from custody, can be achieved by social enquiry reports providing social information to facilitate this objective. It is important to keep this aim in mind when we turn to the research findings and changing nature of court documents in Chapter Five. The final aim is concerned with discussing the elusive goal of reducing crime, and consistent with their critique of the treatment model, the authors contend that measures directed primarily at individuals are destined to fail. As crime is a social problem rather than a consequence of individual pathology, the argument is advanced that it is possible to reduce crime by 'microstructural and socially integrative ameliorations within communities' (Bottoms and McWilliams, 1979, p 188). This model, in addition to other contributions being discussed here, must be seen as a response to what was referred to as the collapse of the rehabilitative ideal, which had a major impact during the 1970s, precipitating a range of responses.[5]

David Haxby

By the end of the 1970s, the probation service was at a crucial stage of development. Many changes had occurred and more were anticipated, and in this situation, Haxby advanced the argument for the ongoing development of a separate community correctional service (separate, that is, to assimilation within reorganised social services departments, which was a real possibility and that actually occurred in Scotland; see McIvor and McNeill, 2007). Haxby's (1978) notion of a community correctional service would continue to provide alternatives to custody, it would be involved in crime prevention, it would also have to diversify its one-to-one casework methods by providing group work, and it would remain involved in penal institutions, after-care and hostels. This was a case for a reconceptualised probation service that had changed much since the last Departmental Committee report of 1962. What is of interest, notwithstanding change afflicting the service and a corresponding case for change being advanced by Haxby, is the following comment: 'It is my hope that the twentieth century will be able to devise a durable, but rather more flexible and humane, system for dealing with offenders in the community, reflecting a different set of values' (Haxby, 1978, p 299). If Bottoms and McWilliams retained a place for a helping impulse, Haxby wanted to retain humane responses.

Peter Raynor

During the mid-1980s, Peter Raynor (1985) made his contribution to a re-conceptualised probation service. If rehabilitation via casework was a redundant ideology, how could one begin to rethink probation? While accepting the critique of Bottoms and McWilliams (1979), Raynor wanted to retain a philosophy of respect for persons, in addition to client responsibility and informed choice, rather than diagnosis and coercion. Raynor recasts probation as a participatory, problem-solving, dispute management model, in which negotiated and agreed outcomes to the problems created by crime are preferred to imposed goals and one-sided procedures. Importantly, this approach would enable probation officers to involve themselves in the criminal justice system, which includes offenders, victims and the community. The aim is not to eliminate crime, which is not feasible, but rather to contribute more to satisfactory ways of living with its consequences. Presciently, he warned back in 1985 that because the service was being pushed in the direction of more social control, humane and social work values are important features of probation practice and should remain.

Bill McWilliams

At this point, I would like to return to the McWilliams quartet, specifically, the final contribution published in 1987. Nearly 10 years after Haxby's book was published, McWilliams began his paper by summarising the three main phases of probation work previously analysed. The first phase, from 1876 to the 1930s, contained the theologico-metaphysical impulse of saving souls by God's grace. It was the phase of special pleading. The second phase of 'scientific' diagnosis lasted from the 1930s into the 1970s, prior to the collapse of the rehabilitative ideal. Then, according to McWilliams, the third phase began in the 1970s, which provided the context within which he completed his quartet during the 1980s. By this time, the religious mission was a distant memory as the offender became increasingly situated within a framework of secular government policy. Consequently, three main schools of thought are identified: emerging *managerialism*; the radical *Marxist* perspective associated with Walker and Beaumont (1981); and *personalism*. Previously, in Chapter Two, I alluded to the first two, but at this point, I need to expand on the doctrine of personalism.

If we approach the rationale of probation practice from the standpoint of a social work, people-oriented profession, it may be suggested that it is the doctrine of personalism that locates the individual and salience of personal relationships at the centre of theory and practice. The concept has a long and distinguished history within the Western philosophical tradition and constitutes a corrective to what has become an increasingly scientific, technological, computerised, bureaucratic and impersonal predicament for human beings. This echoes the Weberian image of rationalisation associated with the post-Enlightenment modern world as a technicist 'iron cage' from which there is no escape. Accordingly, the personalist ethic emphasises personal and human categories, which are set against the drift towards the forces of impersonalism (Mounier, 1952).

Personalism conveys the axiological position that human beings have innate and irreducible meaning and value. The individual is deemed worthy of respect, and as a rational being, should be treated as a Kantian end, rather than manipulated as a means to an end. Nor should people be approached as an object, thing or 'it' as they are always 'subjects'. Within the probation tradition, there is an identifiable personalist bibliography: Biestek (1961), Hugman (1977), Millard (1979), Bailey (1980), Stelman (1980) and Raynor (1985). Some of my own work (Whitehead, 2007, 2015b) is also written from within a personalist-radical, ethical realist, tradition that argues the case for probation as a social work organisation in clear opposition to an impersonal, risk-obsessed, politicised, computerised and technicised bureaucracy. It also resists probation officers being reduced to the role of bureaucratic technician by endorsing the notion of therapeutic imagination. Arguably, the language of personalism can be seen as the contemporary and secular manifestation of those religious impulses that can be traced to the penal system since the 18th century. In other words, the ethic of personalism encapsulates humanitarian social work help directed towards needy people, without a commitment to theological orthodoxy. This chapter contends that probation work within the criminal justice system is not currently, nor has it ever, solely consisted of expressive forms of punishment (Durkheim), class-based justice (Marx), impersonal bureaucratic responses (Weber) or strategies of discipline and control (Foucault). The reason for this is that evidence exists to support the view, from missionary endeavours to secular social work, that there have been employees who have been vocationally motivated by the impulse to care, understand, befriend, help and provide humanitarian forms of assistance even to people who offend. Nevertheless, both the religious and secular impulse to understand and care for people in difficulty can be encapsulated within a personalist ethic.

Additional contributions

During the late 1980s, I researched various aspects of probation practice in the north-east of England (Whitehead, 1990). On this occasion, a total of 11 in-depth interviews were conducted with probation officers in two probation teams. After analysing a number of social enquiry reports where a probation order was made by the courts, then later discussed in detail with respondents, content analysis revealed how officers included the following terminology when working with their probationers: help, support, advice and guidance. This was tantamount to providing a predominantly welfare-oriented service to clients who had a variety of personal and social problems in the areas of accommodation, finances, depression and stress, alcohol, and unemployment. This research found that out of a total of 132 cases that were included in the study, 79.5% were unemployed and 60% had no educational qualifications. A few years later, research undertaken with young offenders by Lancaster University academics found widespread disadvantage among probation clients. Specifically, 64% were unemployed and there was evidence of impoverished educational experiences (Stewart et al, 1994).

Returning to some of the findings of my own research in the 1980s, when discussing underpinning and sustaining ideologies with respondents, these were articulated as: advise, assist and befriend; care and help; and a social work service that was utilised to pursue the goal of rehabilitation. Punishment hardly featured at all, which is consistent with an organisation whose original rationale was *instead* of punishment and prison and before *punishment in the community* started to reconfigure the organisation. I summarised part of the findings of this study, worth repeating in the modernised and transformed context, by saying that:

> In essence, whilst Probation Officers are engaged in a diverse range of practices, which are sustained, at times, by conflicting ideologies and with an eclectic approach to methods, *the unifying thread weaving its way through all the paradoxes and dilemmas is a commitment to a personalist philosophy concerned with the meeting of human need.* Probation

> work, for these respondents, is primarily about a social work
> service to the disadvantaged and not about social control
> or social action. (Whitehead, 1990, p 152, emphasis added)

During the same decade, Fielding (1984) interviewed 50 probation officers and found that empathy and support were important attitudes towards the clients of the probation service.

Much later, I conducted research on the phenomenon of community chaplaincy, thematically relevant to the earlier discussion (see Whitehead, 2011). Furthermore, it is relevant to refer to: an edited collection of chapters from the *golden age* of probation (Statham, 2014); the insightful reflections of Canton (2011); some recent empirical work undertaken by Mawby and Worrall (2013); in addition to Deering and Feilzer (2015). Cowburn et al expatiate on the theme of values. Finally, I would like to update and refine this chapter by referring to some recent excavations on *reconceptualising the moral economy of criminal justice* (Whitehead, 2015b). This offers a new perspective that assimilates some central themes in this chapter.

Notes on moral economy

The purpose and scope of the aforementioned monograph[6] (Whitehead, 2015b) theorises and reconceptualises, but also refines, the idea of moral economy in its relevance for, and application to, criminal justice in England and Wales, with specific reference to probation. Beginning during the 1980s, then followed by successive New Labour administrations from 1997 and the Transforming Rehabilitation agenda of 2010 to 2015, criminal justice has been seized by the technical requirements of economy and efficiency, value for money, measurable outcomes, retributive punishment, prisons, and bureaucratic rationality. These features have combined to impose a paradigm shift in governmental policies and organisational practices, indexed most notably in probation. The vital contribution of my moral economy perspective advances the argument that it is absurd to reduce criminal justice to an instrumentally driven operation to achieve fiscal efficiencies or provide investment opportunities to the commercial sector. Rather, the starting point is to establish its intellectual and moral foundations, the precepts of which are required to legitimate policy and practice. Accordingly, the concept of moral economy constitutes a point of rupture to the parvenu orthodoxy of criminal and penal policy, its modernising blandishments, and the platform of neoliberal ideological and material interests that it reflects and reproduces. Moral economy is foregrounded as an analytical category conducive to excavating discernible transformations; it functions as a conceptual device; it also makes a serious contribution to the urgent task of reconstruction. Moral economy can bear the weight of these heavy demands placed upon it, as well as constructing a platform on which to plot a different way of thinking about doing justice. What has emerged during the period between 1997 and 2015 has not been inevitable, any more than the future is determined to repeat the past 18 years.

Moral economy is informed by a number of historico-intellectual resources on the moral question: philosophy and theology, personalism, psychoanalysis, the *great transformation* signalled by the Industrial Age, and social theory (see discussion in Whitehead, 2015b, chs 1, 2). This is by no means a comprehensive treatment, but rather selective to facilitate theoretical interrogation. Moral philosophers have reflected on the telos (end) of morality, an exemplar being the good life in Aristotle's (2000) *Nicomachean Ethics*. Additionally, ethical systems address intrinsic worth and value. It is possible to argue that neoliberal capitalism constitutes a politico-economic *and* ethical system concerned with the *end* of human existence. Here, the good life is premised upon the pursuit of personal gain from which everyone in the polis (city) benefits as material wealth trickles down. The doctrinal creed is that greed, egoistically pursued, is so good that it results in beneficence for all. The verifiable and experiential flaw with this model is that how capitalism is supposed to work is not, in fact, how it does work. The evidence from Piketty's (2014; or, if you prefer, Rahman, 2014) monumental edifice that draws on extensive historical and comparative data sources on capitalist organisation is that it demonstrably sucks up wealth more than it cascades down, and self-interest is self-evidently not converted into benevolence. Let us not be churlish and give credit where it is due by acknowledging its exemplary capacity to create material wealth, but the system cannot guarantee that wealth is acquired fairly or distributed equitably. Material benefits can be bestowed at the expense of socio-economic inequality that inflicts damage on all of us (Wilkinson and Pickett, 2009). The material surface that shimmers with its tantalising promise of fiscal bliss masks an underbelly of disturbing unethical outcomes. We seem incapable of learning the lessons imposed by historical experience, evidenced by the economic and ethical catastrophe of 2007–08.

I refer to capitalist organisation to make the case that it is conceptually, materially and ethically *different* to the substance of moral economy. Marquand (2014) puts a different slant on the matter, which I contest, because he employs the concept in looser fashion to argue that British history, over the last 200 years, has manifested *four* different moral economies: first, the period before the great transformation, when moral economy was the ideological property of the crowd (Thompson, 1971); second, 19th-century laissez-faire liberal capitalism; third, Keynesian social democracy, which established the social-welfare state from 1945 until the late 1970s; and, finally, the neoliberal era since the 1980s, which includes the analytical parameter of this book from 1997 to 2015. I am afraid that he mangles moral economy with political economy.

Marquand's schematisation is not consistent with my usage because the operational circuits of capital accumulation and market expansion compete with the circuits of ethico-cultural contestation to produce different conditions of existence, individual subjectivity and organisational rationality. Capitalist exchange relations, the extraction of time and resources from human minds and bodies, exploitation, and barbaric and often violent competition between individuals and nations are fixed in mortal combat with a moral economy of regard for others, the common welfare and equality. A system where it is more blessed to receive than to give (capitalist exchange relations) is diametrically opposed to a system where it is more blessed to give than receive. Both have their historical progenitors, ends and aspirations, ways of organising and prioritising life in the polis, and operating circuits and mechanisms of reproduction that have determinative anthropological and socio-cultural implications. Capitalist political economy is a class project played out through markets, capital flows, investment opportunities, profit, self-interest and fearful competition – a free-for-all of un-freedom exemplified by the unequal distribution of material resources and life opportunities. It privatises state assets (from utilities in the 1980s to probation in 2014), liberalises global trade, deregulates financial institutions and labour, and commercialises human life. It is by nature predatory, taking out more than it puts in. Since its revival in the neoliberal 1980s and paradoxically, but not unexpectedly, the great leap forward after the tremors within the capitalist system after 2007–08, it inflicts social murder (Chernomas and Hudson, 2007) and exacerbates social inequality, which is a 'fundamental feature of capitalism generally, [whose] reproduction is part of the logic of this system' (Duménil and Lévy, 2004, p 137).

By contrast, moral economy asserts the unconditional value of human existence. For example, Schweitzer's (1929) anthropological ethic advanced a life-view where the primary principle of the moral is *reverence for life*. Its inviolable and personalist nature is, in and of itself, self-sufficiently and self-evidently good. This is the platform upon which to conduct human relations, its sphere of interest encapsulating just and right dealings within the organisation of the polis. It is a life-view with micro (individual subjectivity), meso (organisational) and macro (political economy) dimensions. Its content can be further enriched by: the Kantian kingdom of ends, not calculable means; Weberian substantive rationality, not instrumental rationality as the motivation for social action; and benevolence being valued more highly than egoistic self-interest. This requires a decisive yet difficult move from the self to the other to establish intersubjective social relations of mutuality, empathy and trust. Schweitzer (1929) and Bonhoeffer (1955) on civilisation and philosophical ethics, Küngian theology and Christology, Pauline epistolary resources appertaining to political ethics, the Judaeo-Christian inheritance, and entreaties on personalism and the Symbolic order (see Chapter Two on Lacan and Žižek) assert the ethico-cultural significance of being men and women for others as the definitive norm of responsibility and maturity. This requires a transformed politico-ethical order that eradicates socially constructed binaries. It is committed to agapē (love), a veritable scandal because it represents a radical challenge to the organisation of life immersed in self-interest, extracting from others to advance the self. The content of moral economy is enriched by Badiou's (2003) references to Abrahamic and Pauline exemplars, where equality constitutes a material sign of the universal. Indubitably, all citizens in the polis matter, and socially constructed binary distinctions, the extreme differential allocation of material resources, and the signs and symbols of material success and status must be transcended. Transcendence is achieved through commitment to a higher unity, which, for some, is the theologian's God, or Other; for others, it is a *Symbolic* order, or Big Other, which fashions a subjectivity different to that required by the neoliberal capitalist system (see discussion on Lacan and Žižek earlier). Moral economy makes demands, requires existential choices and is sacrificially costly in human resources and time. It functions within the circuits of a value system, where it is preferable to give than receive, agapē not exchange relations, and where humanity is one and not divided by the cult of narcissistic hyper-individualism. It is in marked contrast to politico-economic and social organisation that favours an elite who acquire a surfeit of power and material resources, wielded over others to maintain and reproduce a competitive advantage. Its symbol is a sacrificial and renunciating cross (stauros), not the semiotics of material excess so highly prized by consumer culture and its media outlets. It is dialogic, face-to-face not in your face, and it is as absurdly scandalous as unorthodox. It cuts against the grain by challenging *the way the world is* in arguing for justice, fairness, equality and the virtues of moral excellence and goodness. Moral economy is preoccupied with the requisite content to further the good life in the polis.

James Joyce (see Kiberd, 2009), as literary artist, conveyed the moral vision in *Ulysses* that public spaces, the streets where people come into contact with each other, teach social relations. During the early 20th century, Joyce was aware of much wrongdoing – Dublin subjected to the imperial yoke of the British Empire, the baleful influence of the Roman Catholic Church from birth to death, Irish and Jews as hated peoples, the great weight of history pressing down with force, hatred, racism and bigotry. These were not the components of agapē, this was not life, yet 'Growth is possible, even for settled citizens like Bloom, through openness to the Other, a willingness to talk with those who might seem different' (Kiberd, 2009, p 246). Similarly, for George Eliot in *Middlemarch*, human relationships are unquestionably complex, but if taken seriously, they come with the invitation to grow beyond self-centeredness: 'If I really care for you – if I try to think myself into your position and orientation – then the world is bettered by my effort at understanding and comprehension' (Mead, 2014, p 223 – *this is the social worker's and probation officer's creed*). Empathy and imaginative understanding attenuate egoism, so that human growth is possible through openness to others, in taking the step from self to other, from the closed world of the ego to intersubjective relations. It is the leap from darkness to light, nature to culture, the fusion of imaginary and symbolic, resonating with the injunction that in order to find oneself, one must lose oneself in the *Ethical Life*. Moral economy is doing good not evil, it strengthens the fainthearted, supports the weak, helps the afflicted; it is agapē, service and the capacity for self-sacrifice. Although human beings act from questionable motives, we are nevertheless capable of sympathy and benevolence, and, as Adam Smith (2009 [1759], p 13) deduced, show an interest in the fortune of others. Not to do this is a persistent threat to the stability of the socio-moral order.

Accordingly, probation work, within the criminal justice system, was an integral component of the post-war Keynesian settlement as a public good, delivering a public service, as a public duty, largely to a disadvantaged section of the public called offenders. It belonged to the personal social services that operationalised a personalist ethic until, that is, the profession was trashed by the politics of New Public Management and its supporting musculature of managerial consultants, specifically after 1997. Probation's pioneering mission constructed structural, cultural and biographical analyses of the human condition to understand and explain offending behaviour, an intellectual and moral task on behalf of the state and criminal justice system. However, as we saw earlier, it has been vindictively jettisoned into the circuits of privatisation, marketisation and fearful competition between the sectors, catastrophically pushed out of the *Symbolic* order and into the clutches of the *Real*.

Conclusion

Existing alongside the aforementioned discussion on, and excavation of, what is now presented as a refined and extended grid of theoretical perspectives in Chapter Two, the current chapter established the position that religious beliefs, personalist impulses and ethico-social sensibilities have been woven into the texture of the penal system, criminal justice and particularly the probation service throughout its 100 years of history. To some extent, they remain part of the contemporary service, and could also inform the work of the 21 Community Rehabilitation Companies, receiving qualified support from the literature associated with the National Offender Management Service. However, as recounted in Chapter One, there are contradictory pressures at work within a play of forces that this book is attempting to disentangle and theorise. The main features of Chapter Three are summarised in Table 3.1.

Table 3.1: Summary of the personalist, moral economy perspective

Personalism and moral economy	A series of overlapping personalist impulses and ethico-cultural sensibilities associated with evangelical religion. Humanitarian values, altruism and benevolence; advise, assist and befriend the probationer from 1907. Alternatives to custody and punishment; care and compassion, tolerance and social work assistance; understanding, support and help. The importance of establishing personal relationships between the probation officer and people who offend. This tradition can be incorporated and academically refined within the conceptual device of moral economy.

After introducing an extended theoretical and conceptual grid of social theories in Chapter Two, to which have been added the materials in Chapter Three, the next chapter begins to put these theories and personalist impulses to work to explore and explain what the modernised and culturally transformed probation service has become.

Notes

[1] The chapter on imprisonment by Rod Morgan (1997) considers how 18th-century penal reformers were motivated by a blend of religion and humanitarianism. By contrast, Roger Matthews (1999) marshals his evidence in such a way as to provide a more critical account of penal history – in other words, not so much a story of enlightened reform that attenuated punishment, but rather a different form of punishment, which echoes Foucault's analysis. Additionally, on John Howard, then Elizabeth Fry, Matthews (1999, p 7) states that these two, in addition to other 'evangelically-minded reformers, wanted Prisons to operate as healthy and efficient institutions'. Therefore, a number of factors are relevant when theorising the prison. Finally, it is of interest to refer to Copleston's (2003 [1966]) analysis. When assessing the work of Jeremy Bentham and the doctrine of utilitarianism, he supports the view that in the movement for social reform during the 19th century, humanitarian influences, sometimes rooted in Christian beliefs, played a significant role.

[2] During the 1700s, Hinde (1951, pp 17, 238) confirms that Justices of the Peace had the power to appoint chaplains to gaols and that Howard found chaplains in most county gaols. Moreover, relevant 18th-century legislation is as follows: 13 Geo. III, c.58. This was amended later by: 22 Geo. III, c.64; 55 Geo. III, c.48; 58 Geo. III, c. 32.

[3] Garland's (1985) thesis should be alluded to. One must not overlook the wider context of *change* towards the end of the 19th century, and how these changes precipitated a *crisis* appertaining to the role of the state in socio-economic matters – from laissez-faire to more state intervention – including the most effective means to manage, contain and control the recalcitrant poor, some of whom were offenders. There were many *responses*, at social and penal levels, to these changes and crises, one of which was social work and the beginnings of probation in 1907. Consequently, mercy and benevolence melded with a changing political framework that could employ probation work in the service of a new approach to controlling and exercising discipline over offenders on behalf of a modified capitalist state. Altruism and political expedience were held together in a realigned class-based politics during the early years of the 20th century. From a Marxist perspective, religion functions as ideology to mask the operations of political power in the criminal justice system. This brings religion as benevolence into question.

[4] It should be acknowledged, for the sake of completeness, that B.B. Gilbert (1966) spends some time addressing those humanitarian agencies in Victorian society that were concerned with the souls of individuals. Next, Le Mesurier (1935), writing during the 1930s, included material on the religious influences of the missionaries. Young and Ashton discuss the salience of religion in their excavation of social work in the 18th and 19th centuries. In fact, it is stated that in 'some quarters there existed a belief that if only the poor could be persuaded to read their Bible all would be well' (Young and Ashton, 1956, p 31). Furthermore, and intriguingly, Elizabeth Glover's (1956) book contains a chapter on 'Faith', indicating that the religious impulse remained a feature of the work some 70 years after the first missionary was appointed. Nevertheless, one can express care and concern for people without being committed to a specific religious orientation, which can be described as a secular form of personalism (on community chaplaincy, see Whitehead, 2011).

[5] Reform and rehabilitation are ideas with a long association within the prison and probation systems. For Mathiesen (2006), rehabilitation in prison conveyed the

notion of a return to law-abidingness. Garland argues that it played a prominent role in the 20th-century *penal-welfare* system. In fact, it was the 'hegemonic, organising principle' (Garland, 2001, p 35) whose acme can be found during the 1950s and 1960s, supported by an inclusive welfare state. However, the rehabilitative ideal has taken a battering since the 1970s and is one of Garland's (2001) indices of change in *The Culture of Control*.

Before exploring moral economy and putting it to work, it is necessary to assemble some of the intellectual resources on the moral domain by raiding a number of academic disciplines appertaining to philosophy and theology, personalism, psychoanalysis, the *great transformation* signalled by the Industrial Age, and social theory. This is by no means a comprehensive treatment, but rather selective to facilitate theoretical interrogation. Although these diverse academic disciplines are unquestionably informative, they are assembled in my first chapter (Whitehead, 2015b), preparatory to elucidating the content of, and argument for, moral economy in Chapter Two. I want to explain why it should matter, while being mindful of its complex and contested character. It will then be possible to apply moral economy to events within criminal justice between 1979 and 2010 in Chapter Three, and the rehabilitation revolution between 2010 and 2015 in Chapter Four. Finally, chapter Five reanimates interest in morality following the latest bout of privatising public assets. It is imperative to ask: who is responsible for the moral dynamic in what is an increasingly market-driven criminal justice system when investment opportunities assume greater significance than services to offenders, and when the state has ceded its responsibilities to privatised solutions: the probation residue, the 21 Community Rehabilitation Companies announced on 29 October 2014, restorative justice, community chaplaincy and the voluntary sector? Finding answers to this question is urgent because as Burrow (2009, p 115), when evaluating the evidence of moral decline in classical antiquity, comments: 'The past was unlike the present not only in superficial material terms, but morally and intellectually. They did things differently then, and thought and felt differently'. I think a moral economy perspective has the efficacy to excavate critically recent developments in criminal justice, in addition to re-energising the moral dynamic that is fundamental to criminal and social justice.

FOUR

Putting theories and moral sensibilities to work

Introduction

This chapter puts to work the socio-theoretical tools established in Chapter Two, and the religious and ethico-personalist sensibilities in Chapter Three, to elucidate the contours of probation, criminal justice and penal policy since 1997. I have already considered how probation studies have been presented descriptively, referred to ideological constructions that appertain to discrete historical periods, and also the critical academic task of constructing, refining and applying bodies of social theory. It is the third approach that constitutes the most theoretically attractive when excavating the state of organisational complexity and multifacetedness following the intrusive modernising convulsions associated with New Labour between 1997 and 2010, and then Coalition government transformations from 2010 to 2015.

It is worth repeating that the motif of modernisation has been at the epicentre of the change agenda across the public sector (Cabinet Office, 1999), and probation has been reconstructed by a number of discernible politico-penal features: the heightened attention afforded to punishment talk and realigned responses towards offenders; organisational restructuring associated with the creation of a nationalised service in 2001, expeditiously followed by the National Offender Management Service (NOMS) in 2003; the de-professionalisation and demoralisation associated with computerisation, bureaucratisation and the imposition of an expansive target-audit culture; the launch of accredited programmes; stringent enforcement practices; and new community sentences provided by the Criminal Justice Act 2003. Finally, it is crucial to draw attention to ideological and material transformations manifested in privatisation, marketisation and competition between the public, private and voluntary sectors. This is a veritable feast of extravagance compressed into 18 years.

I now turn to the central academic task of applying the classical theoretical frameworks of Durkheim, Weber and Marx established earlier, proceeding to Foucault, Lacan and Žižek, before finally incorporating religion, personalism and moral economy. In other words, this chapter maps the materials contained in the first three chapters onto a more extensive analysis of probation, criminal justice and penal policy. In doing so, it responds to the charge that the criminal justice system is under-theorised, to which this book is a response. I commence the task by returning to Durkheim.

Politico-organisational knee-jerk reactions

When former Prime Minister Tony Blair was resident at Chequers during the Easter of 2000, there is evidence that he allowed his politico-criminological imagination to stray beyond the bounds of propriety, evidenced by the following memorandum:

> On crime, we need to highlight tough measures.… We should think now of an initiative, e.g. locking up street muggers; something tough with immediate bite which sends a message through the system; maybe the driving licence penalty for young offenders. But this should be done soon and I, personally, should be associated with it. (Quoted in Windlesham, 2001, pp 275–6)

At first sight, it may appear unconventional to juxtapose Durkheimian sociological insights with probation work even though, as we saw earlier, he directly addressed issues of crime and punishment in *The Division of Labour*, *The Two Laws of Penal Evolution* and, to a lesser extent, *Moral Education*. Nevertheless, I advance the proposition that part of the Durkheimian corpus draws attention to identifiable features that contribute to an exploration of the political transformation of probation and criminal justice, that is, from what it was to what it has become since the 1980s. Over recent decades, the probation service has been mesmerised by a more intrusive and politically driven penal policy, one exemplar being the rise of expressive forms of criminal justice responses manifested in the predilection to punish, stimulated by a heightened emotional tone. Lucia Zedner (2004, p 77) succinctly summarised the Durkheimian position by saying that the function of punishment is less concerned to control crime than it is to be a vehicle for expressing outrage when a crime is committed, to reaffirm the social value transgressed. In other words, the subject of punishment is not the offender, but rather the powerful message being communicated throughout the whole social body in response to crime events to bolster the law-abiding in their law-abidingness.

David Garland (2001) propounds that the late-modern crime complex (the one that has emerged since the 1970s mainly in the US and UK) has responded to the predicament posed by an increased sense of insecurity and risk, including rising crime during the 1980s, in three main ways: adaptation, denial and *acting out*. In fact, contemporary crime control policies operate at two distinct levels: instrumental means to an end, directed at offenders; and the expressive-emotional communication of a cogent message throughout the social body. The latter, resonating with retributive punishment, condemnation, denunciation and repudiation, has emerged as a salient feature of populist penal politics. This, in turn, ineluctably draws probation work into a cultural trajectory affecting mental conceptions, sensibilities and individual-organisational behavioural repertoires when responding to people who offend. Additionally, this expressive tonal response is repeatedly fed by a rich diet of injudicious reportage in media outlets, a veritable surfeit of sensationalist headlines responding to the phenomenon of crime that reinforces the punitive direction of governmental policies affecting organisational practices. Even government ministers are not averse to passionate knee-jerk reactions to events, exemplified by emotional rhetoric rather than providing a dispassionately reasoned analysis of personal and social problems (Sen, 2009). I say *even* because it is reasonable to expect elected officials to formulate judgements and make decisions as dispassionately and intelligently as possible rather than surf the wave of, and contribute to, media-driven populist hysteria, which, for example, accompanied the UK riots in August 2011. There is a relentless media-driven pressure to conjure an immediate response to every event and headline, a comment to accompany every occurrence, a tweet for every occasion, rather than formulating measured analyses and responses. Located within a chapter utilising bodies of social theory connected to empirical occurrences, it is possible to identify Durkheimian features within probation practice illustrative of expressivism and acting out.

First, a preliminary foray, one of Garland's (2001) indices of penological change that disrupted the penal-welfarism[1] that prevailed for most of the 20th century is expressive justice, reflecting a heightened emotional tone if not vestige of vindictive populism (Reiner, 2007a). It may be suggested that acting out, manifesting the display of sovereign power, is a response that resonates with the war against crime alluded to earlier and the invasion of a so-called zero-tolerance regime.[2]

Second, George Mair et al (2007) research on the Criminal Justice Act 2003 found problems with the Suspended Sentence Order, which implicated probation in up-tariffing offenders, thus making sentencing more punitive, which was unambiguously acknowledged by Lord Carter's (2007, p 51) report on the state of prisons. In other words, this new sentence, available since 2005, was used as an alternative to community rather than custodial sentences. It also appears that there was some empirical support that probation reports prepared for sentencers contributed to this upward custodial trend. During April/May 2008, the Ministry of Justice invested an additional £40 million into probation to cover the period 2008/09. This injection of cash was allocated to facilitate community rather than short custodial sentences, in addition to improving compliance with community orders and licences to reduce the necessity of initiating breach and recall proceedings, which also stoked custodial inflation. Significantly, the application of this fiscal policy in one local probation area precipitated a business plan for the period 2008/09 that specified how the money would be spent. It is recorded that some of the additional funding would be used to reduce proposals for custodial sentences in court reports. It was found that the Teesside Probation Service proposed custody in a relatively high percentage of pre-sentence reports, at 5.2%. This figure was much higher than the national average of 2.7%, and constituted the fourth highest in the country. This is the same local criminal justice system researched by the author that had indisputable problems overusing custody during the 1980s compared to the national scene, specifically for young people (Whitehead and Macmillan, 1985). Accordingly, each new criminal and youth justice generation needs to be reminded of its primary organisational task to avoid perpetuating previously empirically verifiable and avoidable errors in the use of community and custodial sentences.

Third, inappropriate recommendations in breach reports prepared by probation have serious consequences for offenders.[3] Again, the Carter (2007) review of prisons found that the number recalled to prison for breaching licence conditions increased from 150 in January 1995 to 5,300 in August 2007. The number in prison for breaching (failing to comply with) a community court order increased from 180 in January 1995 to 1,200 in August 2007. These organisational response factors were responsible for swelling the prison population. It may therefore be extrapolated that recommendations contained in breach reports for magistrates' courts should be kept permanently under review, specifically when they can be prepared by probation service officers (PSOs), as well as professionally trained and qualified probation officers. Under the new dispensation of the Transforming Rehabilitation agenda, the probation service will continue to prepare pre-sentence reports. Mark Oldfield (2008) stated that in 2002, there were 4,083 PSOs, rising to 7,247 in 2006, a 77% increase. In other words, qualified probation officers comprise only 47% of probation staff (Haines and Morgan, 2007, p 187).

This remains a significant factor worthy of critical scrutiny within a context where enforcement has received intrusive political attention, if not encouragement, since 1997. This means that 'unqualified' members of staff are involved in writing breach reports (as well as the delivery of accredited programmes), without much attention being given to the consequences for practice outcomes of the former. Furthermore, it is important for the criminal justice system to differentiate between the sanctions available for breaching probation rules that do not involve committing new offences, and reoffending while subject to a community order. The sanctions for the former should arguably be less punitive than the latter because the levels of seriousness are not the same. Yet, both have been subjected to the same heightened punitive emotive discourse in the modernising era. The issue of formulating judgements and making decisions on enforcing orders has assumed greater significance with the creation of 21 Community Rehabilitation Companies (CRCs), and must be subjected to careful review of the public, private and third sectors.

Fourth, it should be recorded how initial proposals by the government on breach of community orders prior to the Criminal Justice Act 2003 included a mandatory prison sentence for a second unacceptable failure to comply. Moreover, there was even an attempt to withdraw state benefits from offenders for a reported failure to comply *even before* a finding of guilt was established by a court by testing out the evidence.[4] It has been stated that, with hindsight, it is difficult to see how government ministers and their advisers failed to appreciate that the imposition of punitive sanctions *before* establishing findings of fact by due process of law not only undermined a fundamental precept of justice, but also amounted to being punished twice (Windlesham, 2003, p 275). This amounted to putting political and punitive imperatives before the demands of justice, individual circumstances and evidential requirements. What other reasons could there be for the introduction of the Benefit Sanction experiment from 2001 to 2009, which allowed a proportion of state benefit to be withdrawn for up to four weeks from an unemployed offender? This was tantamount to an additional punitive tax on the poor, with its questionable morality and efficacy to reduce further offending. The same question can be posed when subjecting to critical scrutiny the introduction of a US-style policy of zero tolerance, the three strikes legislation contained in the Crime (Sentences) Act 1997 and the language of *fight* and *war against crime* (on the war against crime in the US, see Simon, 2007). These illustrations can be framed as, and are constitutive of, politico-organisational responses operating at a heightened visceral level, which taps into an emotional urge to punish wrongdoing. Such responses communicate a powerful message through government and the courts into the whole social body. In fact, it has been argued that such measures promote a 'symbolic spectacle of reassurance' directed at, and for the benefit of, the law-abiding majority (Pratt, 2007, p 30).

Consequently, the application of a Durkheimian theoretical framework to developments over recent decades suggests that probation has been coercively manoeuvred into performing more emotionally expressive practices, rather than adhering to dispassionate professional and organisational logics designed to explain and control crime, provide help and support, and prevent the damaging effects of custody. The organisation has been integrated by the politics of modernisation into the prevailing cultural zeitgeist of punishment for its own sake, doing what is expedient rather than what is morally right, a veritable conduit for the rich and sometimes disturbing symbolism of gesture politics directed towards certain sections of the community for symbolic effect. This represents the dilution of its historic mission as an alternative both to punishment and custody enshrined within the probation ideal (Whitehead, 2015b). Indubitably, the probation service is constantly under considerable pressure to demonstrate credibility with politicians, courts and the wider public by resorting to punitive gestures in response to complex human problems within neoliberal regimes (Harvey, 2005; Wacquant, 2008). Nevertheless, emotive knee-jerk reactions operate more at the level of political expedience, communicating the message that *something* is being done. This can be illustrated by recourse to a more punitive breach policy and the Benefit Sanction, which do not constitute solid evidence of a penologically effective, rational, helpful or even evidence-based policy. Jock Young (2007, p 40) elaborated on the expressivity of crime displacing its instrumentality. This is facilitated by the accentuation of organisational expressivism, fuelled by the politics of outrage and punitive vengeance, largely directed against some of the most vulnerable people within society. The criminal justice system and other public sector people-facing organisations must maintain intellectual and moral integrity. In other words, they must resist the lure of political manipulation and disavowal through radical opposition to the dilution of its primary task and historic mission to the courts to promote criminal and social justice.

The escalating involvement of probation in the political web of punishment is manifested in a much greater preoccupation with risk and harm, public protection, punishing and controlling offenders through tougher and demanding community sentences, and stricter enforcement arrangements. It is a retributive penal agenda, fuelled by punitive populism, which has shifted the rationale of probation from caring control to punitive control over recent decades (Burnett et al, 2007). To repeat, the four tiers of the NOMS Offender Management Model incorporated some measure of punishment. Therefore, from advice, assistance and befriend, to enforcement, rehabilitation and public protection, explicates the message that crime is a key indicator of a deep-seated malaise within society and that the punitive response contributes to reinstituting a fragile politico-social order. Whether it reforms or deters the offender is not the issue, but rather the powerful message communicated throughout the whole social body from the political class, through the media, courts and the reframing of probation practice. Under the new convention, offenders become expendable subjects within a process resonating with Durkheimian themes, where punishment is utilised to bolster the law-abiding through targeted expressions of outrage and vengeance. The system of justice may no longer be involved in the extreme judicial response of hanging and whipping, but there is evidence of a punitively heightened emotive drift that can be evidenced under New Labour after 1997, explicable by recourse to Durkheimian theory. Furthermore, between 2010 and 2015 under Coalition government arrangements, there is little evidence to indicate a radical change of direction from retributive punishment and emotive demonstrations of crime control, towards something more discernibly reasoned and dispassionate.

However, following the organisational truncation of probation services by the construction of 21 CRCs in 2014, it is an opportune moment for both organisations to re-evaluate their responses and underlying rationale to people who offend. There is always conflict between political priorities and organisational integrity, political demands and primary organisational tasks. Nevertheless, probation and the 21 CRCs should collaborate to establish a position to resolve this conflict that eschews extremist and emotive responses for political effect. The dominant message is that *something* is being done about crime through retributive punishment, which resonates with Durkheimian theory. The probation residue and CRCs have an intellectual and moral duty to question the efficacy of such a policy, and to argue for an alternative that distances them from the politics of punishment.

Relentless march of the bureaucratic technicians into the 'iron cage'

It has been suggested that selective Weberian themes have an appealing cachet when excavating what probation has become within the modernised criminal justice system. It is worth repeating that *verstehen* draws attention to an understanding of the individual as the primary unit of sociological analysis, which challenges the contemporary preoccupation with bureaucratically managing aggregates of potential risk through numerically based computer systems (Young, 1999; Whitehead, 2007). Next, the thematic of bureaucracy exemplified in Weber's (1968 [1922]) *Economy and Society* can be reprised as follows: a specialised division of labour, with its hierarchical chain of command; the actions of officials, which operate within the parameters of rules and regulations, leave little room for individual autonomy, initiative and discretion; appointment to office is based upon merit; a clear distinction between public and private life; and a uniformity of organisation, replete with documents, files and the knowledge of technical experts. Weber proceeded to advance the proposition that a major feature of the modern capitalist world is the trend towards rationalisation. In other words, it is planned, technical, calculable, measurable and bureaucratically efficient. The downside to rationalisation is the erosion of humane sensibility, which Weber enunciated as the *disenchantment of the world* (MacRae, 1987, p 86; Turner, 1996, p 62). Bureaucracy may well be the most technically efficient form of domination in a modern, capitalist, industrial society, but it is at the cost of an ethico-personalist ethic accentuated in the following analysis.

As the probation system in its initial theological manifestation transmuted into secularism within an expanding organisation by the 1960s, managerial tendencies began to make and leave their mark (McWilliams, 1987, 1992; Whitehead and Statham, 2006). However, it is necessary to distinguish conceptually between *managerialism* and *bureaucracy*. There are points of overlap but they are not synonymous. First, managerialism can be a positive, creative and arguably necessary construct within complex organisations that purport to work with people who have offended, even within those committed to the principle of *verstehen*. In other words, management can be a creative force, utilised to empower staff to work in a manner committed to understanding and helping individuals with their needs and problems. Indubitably, there is nothing to prevent managerial structures from supporting and complementing an organisational configuration centred on explanatory understanding and the impulse to help. Nevertheless, creative and supportive management is different from, and can slide into, bureaucratic inertia. It is the latter that is often portrayed pejoratively because bureaucratic systems and accompanying stultifying structures, rules and regulations, and impersonal procedures and processes can be prioritised before human-professional relationships and the initial primary purpose of a people-facing organisation. These two approaches should be disentangled from each other, and Weber reminds us that the development of bureaucratic power should be prevented from consuming the values and primary task of the organisation.

On the back of the collapse of the rehabilitative ideal and accompanying social work rationality that supported professional training to establish requisite people skills – building relationships, engaging with individuals and probation officers exercising autonomy and discretion when formulating judgements and making decisions about offenders – organisational rationality during my period of interest since 1997 has been oriented towards the efficient containment and control of risky populations. Consequently, the language supplied by New Public Management[5] has transformed the probation service, with the potential for exercising therapeutic imagination, into a functioning bureaucracy accompanied by: the relentless pursuit of economy, efficiency and effectiveness; achieving value for money; chasing politically imposed objectives and targets; and the auditing of tasks in a more routinised environment. In fact, a public service and people-facing organisation has been modernised and culturally transformed into a *business* controlled not by professionals from within the organisation, but by civil servants and government officials since it was centralised and nationalised in 2001. Importantly, the mechanisms of command and control were imposed by the Home Office and then Ministry of Justice, rather than evolving from within probation. This was also expanded through NOMS after 2003.

Colin Leys (2003) develops the point that the Blair governments after 1997 accepted and continued to build upon the legacy of the Thatcher–Major era. This was the era of pro-business, privatisation and an increasingly marketised public sector that operated as a business in conditions of economic freedom complemented by an authoritarian Leviathan centralised state. What the Conservatives initiated during the 1980s, New Labour bought into after 1997, with its audits, league tables and targets, which undermined professionalism and trust by the 'we know best' approach of central government (O'Neil, 2002). Accordingly, within the probation service, the creation of a business-like, commercial and market-driven operating environment transformed a people-oriented service into commodities and products that can be competed for in the marketplace by public, private and voluntary agencies according to the principles of contestability. These accoutrements of the new conventions achieved their apotheosis between 2010 and 2015, as we recounted in Chapter One. Even though such developments could raise standards of performance within the criminal justice system, bureaucratisation, with its emphasis upon technical and calculative features, contains the efficacy to attenuate the pursuit of social and criminal justice, which had been part of probation's remit for many years. John Pratt says that the 'scientific' assessment of risk, and accompanying panoply of actuarialism, helps to inject legitimacy into the concept of dangerousness. Moreover, it allows bureaucratic organisations to avoid 'the moral consequences of their policies by relying on statistical computations rather than human judgements' (Pratt, 2007, p 134). It keeps people at a distance, prevents meaningful engagement with the individual person as the primary unit of analysis within the context of social work relationships and 'fixes' the category of risk conducive to managing people rather than understanding human action. Within this analytical context, serious questions should be posed concerning the time probation staff, including social workers, spend engaging with their clients compared to sitting in front of computer screens in order to maintain the structures of accountability within bureaucratically controlled public service organisations. Bureaucracy meshes with administrative criminology to construct the politico-organisational logics demanded by neoliberal New Public Management.

It can be argued that a number of these bureaucratic elements, associated with the appearance of NOMS in 2003/04, can be embedded within a Weberian bureaucratic framework. In other words, the modernised business-oriented and commercially driven organisation has become more: *calculable* – a target culture emphasising quantification and measurement; *efficient* – pursuing maximum outputs for minimum inputs; *predictable* – the imposition of a blanket of national standards to curtail local variations; and *controlling of uncertainty* – reducing staff autonomy, discretion and scope for individual judgements and morally informed decisions. While the provision of help and support remain part of what is now a slimmed-down NOMS structure, one of the sustained criticisms is that case management, or offender management, has been perceived as a direct threat to the work of practitioners with offenders. This is because of the additional time needed to undertake bureaucratic tasks and an increased emphasis on referring offenders to other services. Reliance upon the time-sapping computerised Offender Assessment System (OASys), as well as the Offender Management model that was central to NOMS, exacerbates these trends (Mair et al, 2006).

At this point, it is of interest to turn to Michael Barber (2007), Head of the Prime Minister's Delivery Unit from 2001 to 2005, who was directly involved in New Labour's talismanic public service reform. The book he compiled, based upon first-hand experience, is devoted to the intoxicating mix of 'deliverology', with its strategies, planning, objectives, targets, delivery maps, delivery chains, trajectories, stocktakes and league tables.[6] Disturbingly, Barber (2007, p 96) informs the reader that not everyone in the public services likes league tables, but 'I love them'. There is a touch of the obsessive and oppressive about this self-congratulatory text in the way it justifies the expanding net of central government control by resorting to incomprehensible government-speak infected with jargonistic flourishes.

Furthermore, there is a frantic atmosphere of desperation surrounding the narrative, inadvertently containing some rather delicious examples of 'Birtspeak', a feature occasionally located within the *Private Eye* satirical publication. Birtspeak functions as a rival to Orwellian 'Newspeak', which, in *Nineteen Eighty-Four*, was ordained by the Party. One illustration appeared in a June 2008 issue of *Private Eye* (plenty more since then), when a BBC trust report on the BBC website stated: 'Overall, we believe that bbc.co.uk performs very well against all these drivers… Quality metrics demonstrate that approval and other perceptions of bbc.co.uk are high'. With this illustration of Birtspeak sitting before us, it may be observed that its convoluted linguistics has also infected NOMS. In the document on Corporate Performance Responsibilities of March 2008, we read that: *Corporate HR* provides HR transactional services; *Capability and Capacity* ensures effective talent and succession management; *Finance and Commercial* leads zero-based reviews; *Strategic Planning and Performance* provides change and portfolio management and a Project and Programme Management (PPM) centre of excellence in addition to delivering cross-cutting corporate change programmes; and *Communications* (this is the closest we get to a NOMS sense of humour) maintains the departmental stakeholder map. Finally, my all-time favourite is that *Research and Analysis* leads Ministry of Justice horizon scanning and blue sky thinking. It also incubates new strategy and policy issues. If this is not enough, enshrined within the NOMS Offender Management Model (National Offender Management Service, 2006) we stumble across the language of 'brokerage' and how 'each offender's period of engagement is a project'. These are some of the modernised illustrations of invasive jargon, linguistic gibberish, spawned by and used in support of what has become a vast bureaucratic empire cascading down from the Ministry of Justice. It obfuscates more than it elucidates the professional task of working with people in a people-facing organisation, immuring a form of Birtspeak to mire the organisation in vaporous inexplicability. The Ministry of Justice has brilliantly reconstructed itself by the linguistic tools of incomprehensibility, and numbers that are less transparent than assumed. Linguistic and numerical reconfiguration has profoundly impacted upon probation and criminal justice.

The current politically imposed bureaucratic form of organisation has inflicted a heavy price upon local area services and working environments for probation staff, intellectually and morally. Most staff join the probation service (and other people-oriented professions) to work with people, and they value the autonomy to be creative, and exercise imagination, in what is demanding work to make a difference. Nevertheless, they currently find themselves in a more centrally controlled organisational landscape: authoritarian top-down mechanisms of power and control; bureaucratic management rather than charismatic leadership; cogs in an all-enveloping NOMS machine; a marketised and computerised working environment endorsing contestability; and relentlessly pursuing numerical targets in a more routinised organisational culture that has attenuated the personalist dimension and moral judgement. These developments are not unique to probation as they exist throughout the whole of the public sector, including the National Health Service (Crawshaw et al, 2002).

The iron cage of Weberian bureaucracy, which, in turn, has diluted the notion of *verstehen*, offers a theoretical framework to account for what probation has become, in contrast to, for example, a personalist philosophy situating the individual and efficacy of personal relationships at the centre of theory and practice. Probation was once an integral component of the personal and professional social services, but it has become a politically dominated and predominantly office-based bureaucracy in a business-oriented environment. Since 1997, particularly after the creation of the National Probation Service in 2001, quickly followed by the emergence of NOMS after 2003, the bureaucratisation of probation and other public sector services has been in full spate. For those who remain committed to operating within a tradition informed by *verstehen*, and who value the morally informed exercise of autonomy and judgement, this form of modernisation is anathema. It constitutes a distorted operational rationale for probation, which should primarily focus on understanding the individual and the possible meanings attached to behaviours as the fundamental starting point for formulating judgements and making decisions conducive to protecting the public. The task of understanding, and ascribing meaning to, offending behaviours cannot be separated from taking cognisance of wider social and economic structures, family, education, employment opportunities, urban marginality, deprivation, poverty, and increasing inequality. In other words, the politico-economic platform of neoliberal capitalism and the insight offered by the searching lens of Marxist theory.

Punishment of insecure populations in the neoliberal order

It was clarified in Chapter Two that there is a discernible Marxist criminological tradition that is pertinent to exploring crime, punishment and criminal justice. This is a body of theory which explicates that economic change is a necessary condition of social change, which, in turn, has implications for understanding crime and transformations in the nature of punishment (McLellan, 1986, p 41). Lucia Zedner (2004, p 80) refers to the enduring nature of Marxist analysis, primarily because it establishes a framework for thinking about punishment as a government strategy inextricably associated with power relations, economic struggle and ensuing social conflicts. At the core of this approach is the substructure–superstructure metaphor, translated as the foundationally significant economic base and dependent non-economic superstructure. As mentioned earlier when evaluating Rusche and Kirchheimer (1968 [1939], p 5), systems of economic production discover punishments that correspond to productive relationships connected to the supply and demand of labour. There is more to crime and punishment than a simple crime and punishment relationship. Rather, the system of penality is implicated in reflecting labour market conditions, promoting the interests of the rich over the poor, the powerful over the weak and the few over the many to order and control surplus populations under specific politico-economic conditions. Furthermore, a significant text to facilitate thinking about probation within the Marxist theoretical framework has already been sketched (Walker and Beaumont, 1981). My task in this section is to move around within this Marxist explanatory framework to excavate the latest manifestation of capitalism and its neoliberal patina, as well as its implications for offenders within the modernised and culturally transformed probation and criminal justice system.

In the trilogy *Punishment and Welfare*, *Punishment and Modern Society* and *The Culture of Control*, David Garland (1985, 1990, 2001) advances a theory of historico-social change with implications for penal policy and the operational functioning of criminal justice. Beginning in the 1985 text with an analysis of mid- to late-Victorian penality, underpinned by an ideology replete with individualism and a laissez-faire minimalist state, Garland proceeds to explain the emergence of the penal–welfare state complex that took shape during the early years of the 20th century under a reforming Liberal government (1906–14). Accordingly, when excavating the system of penality during the 19th century, then the contours of penal-welfare from the 1900s into the 1970s, concluding with an analysis of developments since the 1980s, it is elucidated that institutions of criminal justice have their own internal dynamics and contain the scope to develop according to internal professional logics, values and institutional responsibilities. However, penal policy and criminal justice are also *state-directed practices*, which are directly implicated in the management of disorderly behaviours, whose practices are shaped by wider social movements located within the constraints of macro-social structures. Accordingly, the Garland thesis draws upon the Marxist concepts of base and superstructure, yet without being obsessively devoted to one theoretical position (Garland, 1990). In other words, he borrows theoretical inspiration from Durkheim, Weber and Foucault, as well as Marx, in the explication of how penal policies and criminal justice practices emerge, develop and change over time.

When turning to the 2001 text, he states that it is not intellectually feasible to explore or explain contemporary crime control strategies in isolation from wider macro-level political, socio-economic and cultural variables. A central argument is that the late-modern crime complex is not solely a response to rising crime rates – which have *allegedly* been falling in the US and UK over recent years (Wacquant, 2009; Hall, 2012). Rather, it is an adaptive response to late-modern conditions, with its preoccupation with crime and associated insecurities, the declining efficacy of rehabilitation, and a less generous attitude towards an inclusivist social-welfare state. Consequently, there is a strategic 'fit' between penal arrangements, the shape of the criminal justice system and transformational responses, and macro-structural factors, ideology, hegemony, class relations and authoritarian powers arrogated by the state. The conditions of existence and surface of emergence for the late-modern criminal justice complex, which includes the *modernised and culturally transformed probation service*, is the 'risky, insecure character of today's social and economic relations' (Garland, 2001, p 194). This complex is more discernibly preoccupied with risk, harm, dangerous predators, rigorous mechanisms of control, maintaining order and public protection. The roots for these transformational contours lie deep within the socio-economic dislocations of the 1970s, since when probation has struggled to find a coherent voice consistent with its original mission. At this point, we need to look at some of these issues in more detail, beginning with the captivating analysis found in the work of historian Eric Hobsbawm.

From the 'golden age' of post-war Keynesian economic management, full employment, rising living standards during the 1950s and 1960s, and the welfare state, to the crisis decades after the tumult of the 1973 oil crisis, when the world lost its bearings and 'slid into instability and crisis' (Hobsbawm, 1994, p 404; see also Clarke, 2004). By utilising this comparative perspective, Hobsbawm delineates the features of the *crisis decades* by alluding to: the massive rise in unemployment during the 1980s; the reappearance of homeless paupers on the streets of relatively wealthy countries; growing social and economic inequality manifested in extremes of wealth and poverty; and the supporting role played by the conservative economic doctrines of Hayek and Friedman, who advocated allowing the hidden hand of Adam Smith to replace Keynesian economic interventionism. It was during the 1980s under Margaret Thatcher, ably supported by the intellectual firepower of Keith Joseph and the right-wing political predilections of Ronald Reagan in the US, that neoliberalism was endorsed as the new uncompromisingly natural order of things. Academic cogency was provided in the UK by the Institute of Economic Affairs (which began in 1955), the Centre for Policy Studies (in 1974) and the Adam Smith Institute (in 1976). The following themes are resonant of the neoliberal coda: expecting individuals to be responsible for their own lives and destinies; the strong rule of law – directed mainly towards the bottom of the social pile; free markets and individual freedoms operating within a strong centralised (and penal) state; privatisation; competition between individuals and organisations as a virtue; and the '3Es' of economy, efficiency and effectiveness, including value for money (for a detailed analysis of the neoliberal coda and its effects, see Wacquant, 2009). Within neoliberal cultures, the failures of individuals are more likely to be blamed upon individuals themselves, rather than the prevailing politico-economic arrangements conducive to inequality and differential opportunity (Piketty, 2014).

Harvey (2005, p 19) explains that from the 1970s, but particularly after the Conservative election victory in 1979, neoliberalism was a political project to 're-establish the conditions of capital accumulation and to restore the power of economic elites'. This involved the pursuit and maintenance of profit for the few at the expense of Fordist industrial solidarity for the many. Unfortunately, neoliberalism shed jobs much faster than it could create them. Free markets and competition put the maximisation of profits before jobs and social security for all. Furthermore, during the 1980s, the trade unions were reduced to a weakened state and rendered unable to resist the developments affecting their members, particularly after the miners' strike in the UK. However, such developments have come at a cost in reduced social security, anomie, the breakdown of informal social controls within communities and the accompanying rise of anti-social behaviour (Harvey, 2005, p 80). According to Wacquant (2009, p 306, emphasis in original), neoliberal doctrine constitutes 'a *transnational political project* aiming to remake the nexus of market, state, and citizenship from above'. In the brave neo-Darwinian world created by neoliberal capitalism, the fittest survive and the most vulnerable, if they resort to offending, receive a graduated dose of punishment to bring them back into line with the prevailing orthodoxy. *This became the prevailing context for transforming probation practice and the emergence of the 21 CRCs during 2010–15.*

Jock Young (1999, 2007) contributes to this analysis by pointing to the cultural upheavals of the 1960s, followed by economic dislocations during the 1970s, which exacerbated relative deprivation among the poorer sections of the community in the US and UK. The same economic anxieties among the better off fostered a sense of growing intolerance for those below them on the social ladder, which had the capacity to fuel punitive impulses (see Wilkinson and Pickett, 2009). Psychosocially, when people feel threatened, psychic conditions are created to lash out and fight back against the *essentialised other*, blamed for the prevailing ills of society (from offenders to trade unions, welfare scroungers and immigrants). Katz (1989, p 5) captures the point when cogently stating that by 'mistaking socially constructed categories for natural distinctions, we reinforce inequality and stigmatise even those we set out to help'.

Therefore, the argument is advanced that crime, insecurity and punishment do not have their roots in some essentialist or positivistic differences between those who offend and those who do not (see again the provocative quotations from Orwell and Foucault at the end of Chapter Two), but are associated with dislocation in the labour market and global structural processes, engendered by support for the neoliberal economic musculature. Late-modern conditions have culminated in mass migration, flexible labour, the breakdown of communities, fluid reference points and a prevailing miasma of instability and insecurity, culminating in the dizzying effects of vertigo (Young, 1999, 2007; Reiner, 2007a). Philippe Bourgois (2003), in his ethnographic research in East Harlem, interprets crime and drugs as manifestations of economic dislocations since the 1970s. While he draws attention to human agency, he also attends to the effects of structural factors (family, school, employment and the economy) upon human behaviours that are conducive to vulnerability, relative deprivation and marginalisation. Importantly, these features are inextricably associated with the punitive turn. Probation work, at its best, assimilated and analysed these structure–culture–biography dimensions in reports for courts, but it has become an organisational casualty of neoliberal orthodoxy and its ideological-material forces.

Wacquant (2008), in his disquieting book *Urban Outcasts*, combines empirical research, sociological theory and materialist analysis of the post-Fordist situation mainly in the US and France. He also alludes to the UK. His analysis is elucidated by recourse to Durkheimian expressivism and Marxist materialism, as well as the conditions created by the neoliberal order since the 1980s: poverty, inequality, insecurity, disadvantage, urban marginality and insecure jobs, which culminated in the economic catastrophe in 2007. The reconstructed and functional response of the state's criminal justice system to control the rising tide of disorder has increasingly relied on punishment through an expanded criminal justice domain – the neoliberal order and its consequences joining forces with penal rigour. The result of restructuring is that the Keynesian-Fordist era of cyclical poverty within working-class communities has assumed a more permanent form 'fixated upon neighbourhoods of relegation enshrouded in a sulphurous aura, within which social isolation and alienation feed upon each other as the chasm between those consigned there and the broader society deepens' (Wacquant, 2008, p 261). It is within this new terrain that the criminal justice system has been expanding, and probation has been reconstructed and repositioned as a punishment in the community. It has been severed, as a deliberate political act, from its former historico-cultural traditions and social work ethos, manifesting the politico-organisational choices exercised within, reflecting and reproducing the neoliberal order.

Over recent decades, we have witnessed the creation of a vast carceral network in the US (*deadly symbiosis*), and an expanding community and custodial criminal justice system in England and Wales. Parenti, reflecting upon these phenomena, explores the adverse effects of neoliberalism and its implications for criminal justice responses. He argues that the criminal justice estate in the US, with particular reference to the prison, is a rational strategy for responding to the fallout from capitalist restructuring (Parenti, 1999, p 169). He suggests that the main function of the prison is to 'terrorise the poor, warehouse social dynamite and social wreckage, and, as Foucault argued, reproduce apolitical forms of criminal deviance' (Parenti, 1999, p 169; see also Reiman, 1998). Further evidence for such links can be found in the comparative analyses advanced by Cavadino and Dignan (2006). This text explores the relationship between different political economies and their penal systems in 12 countries (neoliberal, conservative corporatist, social democracies and oriental corporatism). The thesis is advanced that while they do not support a crude form of economic determinism, nevertheless, neoliberalism, with its potential for egoism, markets, competition, individualism and the decline of the ethico-social, is associated with more crime and punishment. This finding is confirmed by Reiner (2007b, p 373; see also Wilkinson and Pickett, 2009), who, after reviewing relevant empirical evidence, established the links between economic factors, the type of political economy, crime and punishment. Accordingly, accumulated evidence helps to demonstrate that neoliberalism, distinct from social-democratic political economies, tends to have a *dark heart* that embraces serious crimes and cruel punishments.

During the course of their book written in the early 1980s, Walker and Beaumont (1981, p 160; see also Young, 1976) gloomily argued that probation staff are paid to undertake a specific job on behalf of the state supportive of capitalism. The argument refined in my revised edition is that the empirical situation is much more complex and nuanced than the one-dimensional analysis of Walker and Beaumont. The politically imposed process of modernisation that began in the 1980s with punishment in the community, the accompanying displacement of advise, assist and befriend, the ideological and material reconstruction of probation on the neoliberal platform and New Public Management has violated the historical traditions of probation work and its association with social work. It no longer operates within, or is supported by, the social-democratic Keynesian nation-state, but is ineluctably enmeshed in the neoliberal market state that it reflects and reproduces. This is not the result of an organic evolutionary process operating from *within* probation, but was coercively imposed from *without*. The final, or rather latest, act in this reconstructive surgery, of the politics of imposition and disavowal, is privatisation, manifested in the formation of the 21 CRCs. If postmodernism has been described as the cultural logic of neoliberalism (Jameson, 1991), the ideological and material modernisation of probation constitutes the politico-organisational logic of neoliberalism. When probation is required to promote the dialectics of criminal justice, to advance understandings of offenders under conditions of late-modernity, marginality and the production of urban outcasts, it is much less able to undertake this primary task because of coercive state impositions. Fundamental questions should be posed concerning the delivery of criminal and social justice, specifically when the intellectual and moral foundation of justice has been systematically damaged (Whitehead, 2015b) by the demise of probation at the careless hands of the political class.

Probation work has been affected by, and is implicated in, the neoliberal logic of organisational modernisation, a victim of the 'asymmetrical effects of power' (Simon, 2007, p 14). Marxist theoretical analysis directs our attention to: organisational reconstruction on a capitalist platform; the affront to the intellectual and moral coordinates of criminal and social justice; and the realignment of the historico-cultural traditions of probation practice. Marxist theory advances critique, but it also supplies some of the tools to formulate a response. Part of the critique exemplifies the argument that neoliberal restructuring, accompanied by modernisation, has diluted the moral responsibility of probation to convey the lives of offenders, to recount their life stories, to magistrates and judges in order to inform the sentencing task of the courts. Some of these analytical features resonate with the Lacanian and Žižekian conceptual framework, which we will return to shortly. Next, though, we need to build upon Foucauldian insights.

Disciplinary normalisation and regulation

Within the Marxist tradition, prison expansion and probation reconstruction have been transformed into instrumental responses of punitive repression, directed largely against the urban poor. When revisiting Foucault's (1977) *Discipline and Punish*, there is a preoccupation with what is occurring within institutions under capitalist social relations, and how power is being exercised (Hudson, 2003, p 134). Before developing this point, it should be anticipated that a later subsection of this chapter will return to what is a progressively humanitarian explication of probation. Similarly, the argument can be restated that there is a progressively utopian reading of broader historical developments since the 18th-century Enlightenment that endorses the positive march of human reason and progress. These developments are encapsulated within the institutions of liberal democracy, notion of individual rights and the social contract, as well as intellectual contributions made by the social sciences. By contrast, Foucault presents the reader, discussed in some detail in Chapter Two, with a dystopian interpretation of post-Enlightenment events, an anti-Enlightenment and anti-reason analysis. This shunts us into the dark shadows, the gloomy rendition, of Nietzschean will to power, which is redoubtably oppressive and disciplinary, where human beings are subjugated by state power. Moreover, the social-human sciences constitute new forms of 'knowledge' constructed within power relations under specific socio-economic conditions. Rather than the social sciences emerging in the 19th century as a direct response to the human subject conceptualised as the sole origin of meaning (McNay, 1994), this is illusory and suspicious nonsense in the Foucauldian schema because the human subject is a by-product of discursive formations linked to the politics of power and demand for order. This is not so much *discovering* or *describing* human beings as they are in themselves, the essence of being, but rather *producing and constructing* them by systems of words and numbers for overt political purposes. Accordingly, one should wise up and always look for the structures of domination and deposits of power lurking behind the language and numbers generated by the social sciences, political processes and organisational functions. Foucault utilises the Nietzschean thematic of knowledge as an instrument of power relations, not truth; 'knowledge' as will to power to secure mastery over others. This is a schematisation of post-Enlightenment order in which human beings are relegated to normalisation by discursive formations, epistemes and technologies of bio-power.

However, according to Hall (2012, pp 140–5), Foucault dramatically misses the point, he constitutes a 'political catastrophe'. This is because Foucauldian analysis eschews an encounter with the obscene *Real*: 'Foucault eschewed the Real of consumerist envy, class antagonism and exploitation hidden by ideology and had no means of conceptualising the generative core of the socio-symbolic order' (Hall, 2012, p 160). In focusing on discourse, episteme and language, he avoided the Lacanian *Real*, unconscious drives and desires, the *real* world operating outside discourse. Similarly, modernised probation work, a catastrophe for criminal and social justice, shuns the impact of the *Real* on the lives of offenders through the political accentuation of management and discipline. Furthermore, modernised probation work can be situated within a dystopian realm at odds with those humanitarian impulses and personalist sensibilities that we will return to shortly. Accordingly, the probation officer works with individuals and families within a framework of disciplinary regulation and normalisation, the eyes and ears of the regulatory state. A very early review of the inchoate system talked about the provision of help and moral reformation (elements of the orthodox perspective). Nevertheless, there is always the lurking threat of the sanction of the penal law and the knowledge that probation officers function as the ears and eyes of the magistracy.

In fact, the foundational legislation, the Probation of Offenders Act 1907, enabled the probation officer to exercise 'a much stronger hold over the offender than the recognizance that was previously the rule' under the police court missionaries (Home Office, 1909, para 13). This perspective reverberates much later in the Morison Report in that while it is acknowledged that probation officers are concerned with the well-being of individual offenders, they are also the agents of a system directed towards the protection of society on behalf of the state (Home Office, 1962, p 23).

Situated in a place and space beyond the commission of the offence, the officer of the court, formerly the probation officer but now repositioned as the modernised offender manager, who keeps the magistracy informed, casts a disciplinary and normalising gaze over the offender's life. This includes thoughts and feelings, the level of insight and awareness, how the commodity of time is being utilised, behavioural repertoires, recreational interests, friends and associates, hopes and aspirations, employment prospects, and so on. Nothing should be beyond the all-seeing penetrating gaze of the state exercised through the court and dispersed through its probation officials. If punishment under the *ancien régime* could destroy the body of Damiens (Foucault, 1977), it was the prison, and later probation, which could retrain and discipline minds and bodies to reconstruct offenders into compliant and useful citizens. It has been stated at various points earlier that probation was initially configured as an alternative to punishment and imprisonment. Garland adds to the discussion by saying that it was the task of probation officers, and the agents of numerous after-care societies, to produce the same reformative effect as the borstal system, which came into existence during the same decade as probation. To achieve this, a variety of means could be adopted, from detailed surveillance, controls exercised over associations and various interventions in the offender's family life, in addition to personal influence or perhaps religious conversion (Garland, 1985, p 25). Similarly, Roger Matthews (1999, p 23) says that probation was basically a welfare sanction that attempted to normalise behaviours under a form of continuous supervision and surveillance.

Within this Foucauldian theoretical framework, it is possible to suggest that since the late 1990s, accredited programmes attached to supervisory orders (eg 'Think First') have operated as mechanisms to inscribe *normal* thinking, problem solving and social skills into the genome of offenders. Probation, and its accompanying suite of programmes, does not so much address adverse socio-economic factors engendered by neoliberalism as an important explanatory context of offending, so much as engage in cognitive restructuring to inculcate new behavioural drills conducive to docility regardless of the prevailing social circumstances. This is a manifestation of equine dressage, which assimilates 'taming, enskilling, and inuring' (Wacquant, 2009, p 106). Stanley Cohen (1985, p 26), when reflecting on the 19th century, stated that the reform of prisoners, in addition to the instruction of schoolchildren, the confinement of the insane and the supervision of the worker, became 'projects of docility related to the new political and economic order. Hospitals, schools, clinics, asylums, charities, military academies become part of the panoptic world'.

Returning to the present, offenders are inculcated with the requisite skills over the course of several months by participating in various programmes, inducing *cultural capital* (Bourgois, 2003) to foster compliance with what are often unpropitious personal and social circumstances. Through such programmes, offenders become cognitively tooled up to negotiate structures of inequality, disadvantage, lack of opportunity and the threat of prison exclusion if offending persists. On one hand, the teaching of cognitive skills can be deemed a positive attempt to do offenders some good – surely a touch of cognitive enrichment and reprogramming cannot do any harm! On the other hand, the same repertoire of skills teach and establish discipline, self-management and self-control to benefit the poor and vulnerable living with burdensome socio-structural problems imposed from above. Life is unimaginably difficult, the future is bleak after 2007–08, and there are lots of risks out there, *but at least we have acquired the skills to handle it, to negotiate around it!* This could be the position offenders find themselves in at the end of programmes that, on the face of it, are well meaning – new thoughts conducive to orderly control over mind and body – but leave untouched those macro-politico-economic conditions as the constitution of the *Real*, requiring fundamental alteration (Beynon et al, 1994).

Foucault's (1977) *Discipline and Punish* proceeds from what is going on inside the prison, outward into the social body, symbolised by Bentham's panopticon. As mentioned earlier, the creation of disciplined, trained and obedient bodies was a necessary requirement for the capitalist-industrial machine. It should also be acknowledged that the techniques for examining the individual inside the institution – hierarchical observation and normalising judgement – turn the delinquent into a 'case', the observation of whom becomes an object of 'knowledge' linked to a regime of power. Offender managers may well be involved in the provision of much-needed help and advice to offenders, but they are also involved with other institutions in processes of disciplinary regulation and normalisation on behalf of a more authoritarian-penal state. Nevertheless, it is important not to overlook the ongoing provision of assistance within a supportive supervisory environment, which is why we need to turn our attention again to the potential of probation work and CRCs. Foucault asks that we remain on the lookout for the traces of disciplinary power, deposits of command, control and regulation. Even benignity is suspect: 'The ethical values, religious beliefs, and humane sensibilities that others present as contributory causes of penal change are, for Foucault, at best the *incidental music* which accompanies change, at worst, a euphemistic covering device for new forms of power' (Garland, 1990, p 168). Prior to picking up on this theme, and to lighten the Foucauldian gloomy mood, it is time to return to Lacan and Žižek and direct confrontation with the capitalist *Real*.

Lacan and Žižek on the decline of symbolic efficiency

Prior to working with Lacan and Žižek, it is helpful to reiterate the tripartite psychic schema elucidated in Chapter Two. First, the *Imaginary* refers to the early stage of human development that incorporates the formation of the self, identity, ego and consciousness. For Lacan, it is a psychic space of self-estrangement, redolent of how the ego fixes upon some feature of the external world by which it is seduced and manipulated (material priorities, consumer culture). The *Imaginary* is a complex hidden space where it is not 'apparent whether I am myself or another, inside or outside myself, behind or before the mirror' (Eagleton, 2009, p 3). Second, the *Symbolic* order is 'outside' the self, to which the self is related and ordered. It is the locus of social institutions, customs, laws and prohibitions into which individuals are socialised, or perhaps not. Human subjectivity is the product of the *Symbolic* order (the *Big Other* is Lacan's term for the *Symbolic*). Third, the *Real* is the pre-*Symbolic*, inexplicable and beyond language, incorporating human drives (for a detailed exposition of these three Lacanian psychic orders, see Žižek, 1992, 2006; Lacan, 2001; Winlow and Hall, 2013).

A suitable entry point to what is a demanding body of thought in weaving together psychoanalysis and radical politics is *Rethinking Social Exclusion* (Winlow and Hall, 2013; see also Elliott, 2005). Attention is directed towards the nature and content of the social, specifically the association between the formation of individual identity (the *Imaginary*), the *Symbolic* order and the Lacanian *Real*. Winlow and Hall suggest that it is too reductionist to attach the term 'social exclusion' to, for example, the poor or people who offend, which conjures up definable subgroups split off from the rest of us, who are presumed to experience the comforts of socio-moral existence. Rather, neoliberal capitalism, and its concomitant cultural logic of postmodernism, has penetrated so deeply into our bones that *all of us* are being excluded from the socio-ethical by the coercive imposition of a political economy that inculcates the subject with a dystopian state of nature exulting in egoistic self-interest that damages the public interest. This is the disturbing dark night of the world (Sinnerbrink, 2008), not the promotion of intersubjective social relations and dialogic engagement. Lacan expatiates on the three orders of the human psyche through the categories of the *Imaginary*, *Symbolic* and *Real*, which, for Roudinesco (2014), can be described as the three elements in his psychic topography.

The Lacanian-Žižekian conceptual framework can be extrapolated to advance an analysis of organisational transformations shunted onto the payment by results (PbR) material platform, and fragmentation of probation by the CRCs. De Angelis reminds us that the essence of the capitalist system, evolving since the 1780s, is to search for new markets, which has become nothing less than a 'social force that *aspires* to colonise the whole of life practices' (De Angelis, 2007, p 43; see also Sandel, 2012, who makes the same point). Between 2010 and 2015, those organisations previously positioned within and sustained by the Keynesian post-war settlement (social-democratic symbolic efficiency) were integrated into the circuits of capital accumulation and market expansion, signified by the PbR fiscal mechanism. Consequently, PbR is a material signifier of the reconfiguration of organisational structures in the interests of capital as a response to the crisis of 2007–08, but also continuous with developments since the 1980s under successive Conservative and Labour administrations. The acute paradox is that the forces that created the economic turmoil of 2007–08 (and all previous economic eruptions) are now being unleashed with even greater penetrative ferocity through being invited to enter public-social domains where previously they did not exist. The capitalist *Real* is premised on exchange relations, the stimulation of competitive desire, narcissistic self-promotion, marketisation and unfettered consumerism, all of which inflict damage on the *Symbolic* order and the reproductive mechanisms of symbolic efficiency. The canker of the *Real* has been released into the criminal justice system, as well as other organisations, which signals the decline of their symbolic efficiency as they are compelled to compete with each other in a market-driven environment, vying within the realm of the *Real* for fiscal resources and basic economic survival, rather than pursuing the primary value of service and responding to social need.

The *Symbolic* order of language, law, ideology, meanings and values is the human-cultural response to the raw and terrifying nature of the *Real*. If this is where Žižek positions the subject (for a full discussion, see Winlow and Hall, 2013, p 150), it is also the place to undertake organisational analysis. If, within the *Symbolic* sphere, human beings promote interpersonal relations, fashion meanings and cultivate values, they also, organisationally, build historical and ethico-cultural traditions over long periods of time that are transmitted from one generation of employees to the next in health care, educational provision, welfare and criminal justice services. The mythical and illusionary aspect of the *Symbolic* order is that these organisations were created to facilitate a more just society, fostering the bonds of social solidarity and collective citizenship, rather than a reluctant capitalist concession (George and Wilding, 1991). Nevertheless, the post-war generation bought into this fiction to proceed *as if* it were true, an established empirical fact that made a positive difference to how people lived alongside and responded to each other. These organisations constituted cogent symbols, ideologically and materially, of this mythical *Symbolic* order. However, now another myth is marauding across and ripping up the landscape, which is that organisations must be banished from symbolic efficiency into the *Real* to improve their effectiveness and efficiency. The difference is that the first was a positively constructed myth that had the efficacy to enhance the ethico-social; the second is destructive because it plunges them and their employees into a terrifying night of the world, a void of brutal competition and market forces indifferent to historical traditions and ethico-cultural contestation. Nothing is sacred, past organisational commitments and motivations count for nothing, orthodox conventions are inverted in pursuit of a scorched earth policy, which puts everything up for sale. The past is confronted by the terror of the *Real*, starkly exemplified in PbR. Probation is an empirically verifiable casualty of this displacement, and 21 CRCs the material result.

Probation's historical lineage and cultural traditions, forged in the period of *penal-welfare* and supportive of personal social services, and its reformist ideology and discrete but essential role in the dialectics of criminal justice, have been eroded by relegation into a state of nature, the capitalist *Real*. This transmutation, relentlessly progressing since the 1980s, but discernibly more penetrative and expansive during the period 2010–15, as we saw in Chapter One, has dislodged the cultural symbols, historical artefacts, inherited ways of thinking and operating, recognisable meanings, and personalist values. The circuits of ethico-cultural contestation, ethico-social dimensions of rehabilitation and welfare, have been destabilised by privatisation and marketisation, which, in Žižek's language, is the transposition from the *Symbolic* into the *Real*, from a moral economy (Whitehead, 2015b) to capitalist political economy. For organisational staff, it has become the terrifying dark night of the world, of which PbR is the material signifier of the re-energised capitalist dispensation after the economic turbulence of 2007–08. The symbolic efficiency of probation comprised a set of discernible values that congealed into organisational circuits, reproduced by training, staff supervision, the cultural transmission of organisational know-how and the maintenance of professional standards (Whitehead and Thompson, 2004). The tensions, intellectual conflicts generated by probation, moral questions posed and mediating checks and balances in pursuit of criminal and social justice, have been insidiously eroded and undermined since 1997. This is an ideological and material revolution that reflects and reproduces the neoliberal order of things, more than a rehabilitation revolution. Although events since 1997 have roughed up the vision of the good society, and criminal and social justice, there remains a trace of the personalist tradition.

The remaining vestige of personalism and moral economy

The emergence of the probation system over a century ago, based upon an orthodox more than revisionist reading of its entry into the penal system (Raynor and Vanstone, 2002), was associated with positive initiatives under a reforming Liberal government. Probation has been constructed as a progressive, humanitarian, altruistic innovation, and an outbreak of benevolence in opposition to the contours of a harsh Victorian penality. Nellis (2007) cogently analyses how the appearance of probation exemplified the humanisation of justice rather than a cunningly lurking Foucauldian deposit of power. It constituted an alternative to punishment and incarceration, with its ethic of advice, assistance and friendship, mediated by supervisory oversight in the community. It was also marked by religious endeavour in that the Church of England Temperance Society had been providing the inchoate system with police court missionaries since 1876, in addition to which religious organisations facilitated the probation task (McWilliams, 1983; Garland, 1985). The dynamic of religion was also significant within penal reform long before the missionary forerunners of probation officers appeared on the late Victorian scene (in the work of John Howard and Elizabeth Fry) (for a contemporary *religious voice*, see Hinde, 1951; Young and Ashton, 1956; Mawby and Worrall, 2013), as we excavated in Chapter Three.

144

If we peer through the benign lens of modified penal sensibilities underpinned by evangelical theology, a number of features hove into view, which traditionally have been associated with probation. Some of these features can be enumerated as: working with individuals who offend within the context of humane relationships; understanding, mercy and help; offenders as ends in themselves rather than means to an end; respect for persons and the irreducible worth of human beings; and a concern not only for behavioural repertoires (*what* people do), but also an empathic and ineffable *feel* for who they are, which takes cognisance of holistic personal and social needs. Such features represent a distinctive axiological orientation that the organisation of probation has brought to the complex dialectics of the criminal justice system during the 20th century within the warp and woof of care and control, punishment and welfare, justice and treatment. Probation was different and made a difference. Even though the analysis of crime is indubitably complex due to incompatible theoretical perspectives, when it comes to responding to people who offend, there is a body of work that argues for the retention of humanistic values and approaches alongside the advocates of harsher forms of punishment.

Notwithstanding major transformations affecting probation since the 1980s, its dalliance with punishment in the community from the early 1990s and particularly the politics of modernisation since 1997 through to 2010–15 (Nellis, 1999), humanitarian and personalist impulses have been attenuated, not eradicated. Of course, it is difficult to quantify the existence of these sensibilities within the culturally transformed probation domain. Nevertheless, they continue to attract support from other criminal justice organisations, as illustrated by research undertaken with a number of solicitors (Whitehead, 2007) in addition to the research findings presented in Chapter Five. It should be acknowledged that effective practice in the 1990s gives some credence to a personalist axiology in support of working with offenders (Chui and Nellis, 2003; Gelsthorpe and Morgan, 2007). Furthermore, NOMS resorted to the language of support and help to address the underlying causes of offending behaviour, such as inadequate accommodation, lack of educational and employment opportunities, financial problems, and drug and alcohol addictions (Ministry of Justice, 2008a). In fact, the NOMS Strategic Business Plan for the period 2009–11 endorsed values of equality and diversity, and stated that offenders should be treated with respect and decency (Ministry of Justice and NOMS, 2009). Probation has been reconstructed by a narrative of punishment in the community, and has experienced periodic bouts of modernising transformations, even revolutionary activity, but it has been encouraged to promote helping strategies to facilitate rehabilitation.

Academic research invites us to proceed beyond, for example, bureaucratic systems and procedures, to acknowledge the efficacy of humane and engaging social work relationships. It is the quality of the *relationship* between the person of the probation worker and the offender that constitutes a key ingredient of therapeutic success rather than overreliance on theories, methods and organisational constructs (Smith, 2006). This was reinforced by the Ministry of Justice Green Paper *Breaking the Cycle* in December 2010. Similar points have been made by Raynor and Vanstone (2002, p 115) when they comment that indications from Australian research by Trotter suggests that probation officers who have received social work training engage more effectively with the 'What Works' agenda than those who come from other backgrounds. The modernisers of the Ministry of Justice – the assembled coterie of politicos, civil servants and administrators – have struggled to acknowledge this salient feature of probation because they lack first-hand experience of practice.

During 2005–06, a number of retired probation staff were interviewed after a request was made in *NAPO News* and contact made via the Edridge Fund. Interviewees were assembled from probation careers spanning six decades, beginning in the 1940s. Some of the voices heard, which constitute a rich oral history, reflect personalist impulses and sensibilities in *Changing Lives* (NAPO, 2007). It is recorded for posterity that probation was something other than a punishment. Even though the organisation established boundaries, engendered responsibility in offenders, sought to bring about positive change and exercised authority on behalf of the state, nevertheless, 'I think probation reflected the great strength of having an alternative to punishment in our society, because punishment is a dead end' (NAPO, 2007, p 60). Another retired officer joined the service in 1966 and stated 'I think probation bothered about people … I advised, assisted and befriended and brought about change' (NAPO, 2007, p 34). Another respondent said that we gave social work help and 'I advised, assisted and befriended, and I gave them a lot of befriending' (NAPO, 2007, p 50). Yet another commented that 'The biggest tragedy was taking away advise, assist and befriend' from the philosophy of probation (NAPO, 2007, p 68). Additional voices can be heard saying 'I cared about the client' (NAPO, 2007, p 47), and probation offered someone to talk to, a relationship and care, and showed an interest in the person who offends (NAPO, 2007, p 48). Another probation officer, trained in 1969, was an active member of the Probation Officers' Christian

Union (NAPO, 2007, p 62), which forges the long-standing religious association with probation work. Additionally, the importance of relationships is underlined (NAPO, 2007, p 63) when it is clarified that 'I wanted to be in an organisation that was caring' (NAPO, 2007, p 67). Consequently, it was more vocation than just another job (for the views of retired senior managers, see also Statham, 2014).

Also included in this oral history is a sustained lament for what probation work has become: overly managed, bureaucratic, de-professionalised and demoralised, the appearance of National Standards and accompanying loss of autonomy and discretion, in addition to the emergence and debilitating effects of a target culture. Two further quotations are worth including, illustrative of this transformation. First:

> For me, I think the sense of a disciplined independence in using personal discretion. Essentially it was professionalism and not tick boxes. It was forming a judgement, expressing a view, but within a framework of understanding in which you placed the material you had, and then put forward a view about what was the most positive way of dealing with the person given all the circumstances. (NAPO, 2007, p 59)

This is a former probation officer articulating his understanding of the pre-modernised service. Second, and crucially, Rod Morgan states that over recent years, '*The service was cast adrift in a sea of structural uncertainty, incoherent management-speak, ideologically-driven poor leadership and political vacillation*' (Morgan, 1997, p 93, emphasis added because this captures some of the key modernising changes that have occurred).

Therefore, it can be argued that these respondents establish the point that combinations of religious beliefs, personalist impulses and moral sensibilities have been tightly woven into the undulating textures of the probation service throughout its history. This continues into the present in the form of the Probation Service Christian Fellowship, which expresses Christian care and concern within the structures of the criminal justice system. There are other organisations worth noting: Social Workers Christian Fellowship, Evangelical Alliance, Lawyers Christian Fellowship and the Churches Criminal Justice Forum. There is also the Prison Fellowship, which leads neatly onto the next point. During the preparation of the first edition of this book (in 2010), it is worth repeating that I made contact with the Chaplain General of Her Majesty's Prison Service, Reverend William Noblett, who provided the following information. In 2008, it was confirmed by letter that chaplaincy arrangements in the 130 public sector prisons comprise multi-faith teams. These teams comprise employed, fee paid (sessional) and voluntary chaplains who represent the faiths and denominations of inmates at each prison in England and Wales, which embraces Anglican, Roman Catholic, Free Church (eg Methodist), Hindu, Jewish, Muslim and Sikh. At the time of writing the first edition, it was made clear that statistics are held on employed chaplains, a mixture of full- and part-time posts, with a total of 334 staff, giving an equivalent of 268 full-time posts. However, and importantly, the prison system has a further 700 chaplains who work part-time or sessionally. In addition to the public sector prisons, there are a further 11 in the private sector. Where the latter are concerned, chaplains are employed by the respective private company, which means that the Chaplain General is not required to maintain official statistics.

Since the creation of NOMS in 2003–04, the work and potential contribution of faith communities (part of the third sector) within the criminal justice system has been acknowledged and encouraged by central government. Beginning with the Communities and Local Government document on *Working Together* in 2004, there are a number of examples that support this development, which can be cited as follows. A document published by NOMS in 2005 on the faith, voluntary and community sector alliance made it clear that the government is keen to involve the community in achieving its strategic objectives for reducing reoffending, resettling offenders on release from prison and rehabilitation. Accordingly, faith communities are expected to play their part in this initiative, which reaches beyond the statutory organisations comprising the criminal justice system. Next, in a speech to the Prison Reform Trust on 19 September 2005 – *Where Next for Penal Policy?* – Charles Clarke, Home Secretary, referred to the support that can be provided by the voluntary and faith sectors, specifically in the form of *community chaplaincies* (see Whitehead, 2011). This was also mentioned in the rebalancing document (Home Office, 2006b), where it was stated at paragraph 3.23 that reducing crime and reoffending 'should be everyone's business'. Subsequently, a Cabinet Office and HM Treasury (2007) document reinforced the message that central government wants to strengthen consultation with the third sector, which is deemed to have an important role in the transformation of public services. By November 2007, NOMS published a consultation document on 'Believing we can: promoting the contribution faith-based organisations can make to reducing adult and youth re-offending'. It is noted that faith-based organisations currently provide 6,000 volunteers, contributing 16,300 hours every four weeks within the prison estate. Finally, it should be acknowledged that the Offender Management Act 2007 provides the legislative basis for contestability within NOMS. This means that the public, private and voluntary/third sectors can compete for the business to provide offender services. This policy was given further support by the Ministry of Justice (2008b), which wants to see a thriving third sector as part of the criminal justice system, which includes religious communities. This came to fruition in the rehabilitation revolution during 2010–15.

From a much wider perspective, it is of interest to note that a combination of Christian democratic communitarianism, which can be described as a tolerant form of Christianity, in addition to humane paternalism and libertarian social democracy, created the conditions for a discernibly more lenient penality (see Cavadino and Dignan, 2006, p 115, when addressing the situation in the Netherlands). Consequently, at an opportune moment, it will be important to theorise and critically analyse some of these third sector developments beyond 2015. For example, are faith communities going to become a challenging presence within the criminal justice system, thus providing resistance to the punitive and exclusionary drift, or, alternatively, are they being encouraged to get involved to provide legitimacy for the punitive policies of central government but also to reduce costs when the Ministry of Justice had to save £1 billion by 2011? (Foucauldian mask for the deposit of power?) Nevertheless, the widest possible interpretation of personalism conveys a set of ideas, a framework of thought and a distinctive set of dispositions and values that mesh with moral economy (Whitehead, 2015b). These attitudes and values should inform the judgements and decisions of the criminal justice domain of those who endorse them, and they have a considerable history. I have just alluded to community chaplaincy, which requires a further comment at this point.

I conducted empirical research on community chaplaincy in Canada and England and Wales (Whitehead, 2011). The aim was to establish an exploratory understanding of community chaplaincy in the criminal justice system of England and Wales at the end of its first decade (2001–11). Six community chaplaincy projects were visited (Leicester, Low Newton near Durham, Manchester, Leeds, Feltham and Swansea), where 22 interviews were conducted between November 2010 and April 2011. These data reveal a person-centred, theologically informed, value-driven and voluntary-charitable organisation operating within a multi-faith ethos. It offers supportive relationships to men, women and young people when they leave custodial institutions. Even though projects are distinguishable from other organisational domains by their faith ethos, this does not mean that all volunteers who work for the community chaplaincy are people of faith, or that they belong to faith communities. The community chaplaincy does not attempt to proselytise offenders. Rather, supportive relationships are offered unconditionally to people of faith and none when they leave custody. It operates with a person-in-situation mentality to counterbalance those punitive, dehumanising, depersonalising and demoralising tendencies that have colonised criminal justice. Its vision is to walk with marginalised and excluded ex-prisoners on a difficult journey due to accumulated problems compounded since unpropitious childhood experiences: family conflict, insecurity, vulnerability, impoverished education, unstable work record, substance abuse, financial problems and substandard accommodation. To people immured in adverse social circumstances, the community chaplaincy provides support as they return to an uncertain future in the community. Will community chaplaincy projects become assimilated into the third sector food chain of the rehabilitation revolution to ensure survival, or offer an intellectual and moral challenge to established orthodoxy?

There is not much left of the probation system that began in 1907, whose rehabilitative credentials were firmly established by the 1960s (Home Office, 1962), becoming centre stage under the Criminal Justice Act 1991. After the rehabilitation revolution, it continues, in truncated format, to work with high-risk offenders subjected to community orders and licence conditions. It is writing court reports to offer sentencing advice to magistrates and judges, preparing risk assessments, allocating cases, enforcing orders and licences, and undertaking parole board and public protection duties. Lying beneath revolutionary incursions is a worthy history of public service, personalist influences, a commitment to community supervision rather than punishment and custody, and human relationships as the medium of practice. In other words, there is a distinctive intellectual tradition and moral convention submerged beneath modernising and transformational accretions. Contemporary probation staff (Mawby and Worrall, 2013; Deering and Feilzer, 2015) are the inheritors of a cultural tradition whose deposits can be recovered by archaeological excavation. Are they committed to preserving this tradition?

There are currently 21 CRCs working with thousands of low- to medium-risk offenders in the new dispensation: Sodexo Justice Services in partnership with the National Association for the Care and Resettlement of Offenders (NACRO) (six areas); Purple Futures (five areas); Working Links (three areas); The Reducing Reoffending Partnership (two areas); Novo Management and Training Corporation (MTCNovo) (two areas); Achieving Real Change for Communities

(ARCC) (one area); Geo Mercia Willowdene (one area); and Seetec (one area). These CRCs are populated by probation staff who were transferred by April 2014. It is of interest to observe that the Sodexo website alludes to values (see Cowburn et al, 2015) and that MTCNovo wants to embody the best of probation. At this juncture (2015), there is no unifying statement appertaining to the intellectual and moral foundations of the CRCs to shape their work in the criminal justice system. Is this an opportunity to build such a foundation? Should they do this in consultation with the probation residue? Or are CRCs pursuing less noble priorities by putting economic opportunity before ethical commitment? The probation residue and 21 CRCs have an *organisational presence* in the reconfigured criminal justice system. Restorative justice, community chaplaincy and other voluntary sector organisations have an *ideological foothold*. The university sector must maintain its critical role as intellectual facilitator, through theoretical and empirical excavations, to advance thinking on foundational moral principles that transcend the ephemeral politics of contingency and disavowal (Whitehead, 2015b). The personalist and moral tradition must be preserved.

Conclusion

Bodies of social theory, a remaining vestige of religious, personalist and ethico-humanitarian impulses, combine to offer an approach to excavating probation and criminal justice that has analytical merit. One hundred years ago, it was possible to make sense of the emergence of probation by recourse to an orthodox *and* revisionist perspective. The former is associated with religious and philanthropic features encapsulated in the now-redundant and politically unacceptable message to advise, assist and befriend. The latter constructs probation as a state-directed enterprise to discipline, control and normalise the recalcitrant in a class-divided society in such a way as to obfuscate the links between crime and politics. Now that the organisation has arrived at, and proceeded beyond, its centenary year in 2007, through to revolutionary transformations imposed during 2010–15, a combination of philanthropy and the Foucauldian discipline of offending bodies is analytically inadequate. It is necessary to put additional theories to work that take their inspiration from Durkheim, Weber, Marx, Lacan and Žižek. None of the theoretical perspectives explored in Chapter Two and put to work in this chapter adequately explain, in isolation from each other, what probation has become. Instead, the argument is advanced that *all* these perspectives are required to capture the complex undulations of what is now a multifaceted and truncated organisation, operating at different theoretical levels, against the background of New Labour's modernising tendencies after 1997 and ideological and material revolutionary activity after 2010. Accordingly, offender managers in probation and the 21 CRCs can function as the *good guys* of the criminal justice system who represent a distinctive set of anthropological values rooted in personalist ethics, albeit attenuated by the punitive upsurge. However, they could also: be enmeshed within expressive knee-jerk reactions consistent with a heightened emotional notation (Durkheim); function as bureaucratic technicians within the NOMS structure (Weber); punish and exclude (as a conduit to prison) the recalcitrant residuum under neoliberal capitalist conditions (Marxist); or operate as disciplinary regulators and normalisers, the eyes and ears of the courts and the increasingly centralised and authoritarian state (Foucault). Finally, the theoretical grid is extended to incorporate confrontation with the capitalist *Real* in the form of privatisation, marketisation and fearful competition, analytically illustrated by Lacan and Žižek.

If recourse to these disparate perspectives has any analytical cogency when exploring the development of probation during the modernising period since 1997, it may be concluded that a state of confusion has erupted because of the lack of a coherent organisational rationale. Probation has become a theoretically contested site, ideologically diffuse and primarily reconstructed to conform to a political image consistent with New Labour's and the Coalition government's view of the world of order and disorder. In other words, modernising transformations have created a system of criminal justice and a probation institution with multiple identities. This multiplicity has not enriched, but rather coarsened, organisational responses due to the way in which it has bureaucratised, punitised, depersonalised and demoralised problems rooted within the structures of a market-driven society under neoliberal arrangements.

Nevertheless, if the preceding suggests that a nuanced and textured methodological approach is required to elucidate the National Probation Service by 2015–16, the same theories and impulses can be put to work to critique and explore future developments on what the essence of the organisation should be. If this chapter, which concludes the four chapters comprising the first substantive part of the book, has focused on exploring *what probation has become*, the next empirically research-based chapter will look at *what it ought to be* from the standpoint of numerous respondents within one local criminal justice system at one specific period of history. First, a summary of the main elements of this chapter is presented in Table 4.1.

Table 4.1: Summarising putting theories to work

Organisational and political knee-jerk reactions	Probation less concerned to control crime than to express outrage to bolster the law-abiding in the *war* on, and *fight* against, crime. Penal populism, sensational media reporting, injudicious political and criminal justice knee-jerk reactions. Acting out and displays of sovereign power through rigorous enforcement; inappropriate custodial recommendations in reports for magistrates and judges; Benefit Sanction 2001–09. Implicated in the symbolic spectacle of criminal justice practices imposed by the politics of repositioning.
Relentless march of the bureaucratic technicians	From facilitative management to bureaucratic inertia. From the individual offender as the primary unit of analysis, to controlling aggregates of risk via the diminution of therapeutic imagination, autonomy, discretion and initiative, amounting to a de-professionalised workforce. Emphasis on New Public Management, the 3Es, value for money and procedures, processes and systems more than engaging with people. National Standards, business audits, targets, computers. NOMS and marketisation, contestability, not forgetting the new language of jargonistic and Orwellian Birtspeak. From understanding to managing categories of risk that constitute the organisational logic of neoliberalism.
Punishing insecure populations under neoliberalism	Probation part of government's punitive strategy directed against the poor. Neoliberalism produces casualties from among the most economically vulnerable, so that in a neo-Darwinian socio-economic system, only the fittest survive. The criminal justice system, with its reconfigured probation service, is a response to the fallout that follows the pursuit of state-imposed neoliberalism via increased punishment and exclusion. Blame attached to individual failings, rather than social and economic 'violence' inflicted from above. However, offenders can be victims too of structural-material conditions.
Disciplinary normalisation	The offender manager casts a disciplinary and normalising gaze over offenders, as the eyes and ears of the regulatory state that employs them. Deviant populations must have their minds and bodies retrained to establish compliant citizenship. Accredited programmes, Think First, induce *normal* thinking through social and problem-solving skills conducive to docile behavioural drills. Probation and the wider criminal justice system are essential components in a Benthamite panoptic society.
Lacan and Žižek	The Lacanian and Žižekian conceptual framework is advanced to analyse and understand the nature of human subjectivity, crime and harm, as a product of the *Symbolic* order. Furthermore, it can be applied to organisational analysis and critique, illustrated by the single case study of probation. Under the Keynesian dispensation, probation and criminal justice were components of the post-war welfare state and supported a rehabilitative ethic. Under the neoliberal order, probation has been jettisoned out of the *Symbolic* and into the capitalist *Real*, manifested in privatisation, marketisation and competition. Payment by results as material signifier of the new dispensation.

Personalism and moral economy	Religion, personalist impulses and moral sensibilities combine to work with offenders within the context of engaging social work *relationships*. Provision of support and help for personal and social problems, rather than punishment. A distinctive set of attitudes and values that promote respect for persons and treat people as ends not means. Helping strategies to promote rehabilitation remain a feature of NOMS discourse, although less in evidence than formerly.

Notes

[1] In the first chapter of *The Culture of Control*, Garland (2001) explores the contours of the penal-welfare system that had been in operation from the early 1900s to the 1970s, since when certain 'indices of change' can be identified:
- decline of the rehabilitative ideal;
- re-emergence of expressive (Durkheimian) punitive sanctions;
- changes in the tone of crime policy;
- return of the victim;
- public protection;
- politicisation of penal policy;
- reinvention of the prison;
- transformation of criminological thought;
- expanding the infrastructure of crime prevention and community safety;
- commercialisation of crime control (deeper penetration during 2010–15);
- a new managerialism (New Public Management); and
- a perpetual sense of crisis.

[2] The war against crime is constructed in emotive language, which has become crystallised in a powerful political and media image. It resembles the war that is constantly being waged on dirt and germs by household products to maintain cleanliness.

[3] An explanation of breach reports is required. At various points, this book makes it clear that procedures and practices concerning breach and the corresponding enforcement of community orders became more stringent. When the courts impose a community sentence, offenders are expected to comply by maintaining regular contact with their offender manager. If they fail to do so, the offender manager has a duty to return the offender to the original sentencing court, either by summons or warrant, when action will be taken. Either the order will be allowed to continue with an onerous requirement imposed (following the Criminal Justice Act 2003) or the order will be revoked and the offender re-sentenced for the original offence, which could result in imprisonment.

[4] This point is linked to note 3 because unemployed offenders who breach their community order, and who are therefore in receipt of state benefit, could have a proportion of their benefit withdrawn for up to four weeks. For more information on the Benefit Sanction, see Whitehead and Statham (2006, p 201; see also Windlesham, 2001, 2003). For a wider discussion on the politics of withdrawing state benefits, see the discussion in Rodger (2008, p 86). However, it is important to clarify that the Benefit Sanction experiment, which operated in four areas of

the country – Derbyshire, Hertfordshire, West Midlands and Teesside – came to an ignominious end in 2009 after eight years.

5   The phenomenon of New Public Management has been dealt with at length previously (Whitehead, 2007, p 34).

6   The public sector remains in the grip of numerous targets and it is difficult to know who was initially responsible for this development since 1997 – Tony Blair as Prime Minister or Gordon Brown as Chancellor. Therefore, it is interesting to hear what Barber had to say on this subject: 'Blair himself sometimes appeared politically ambivalent about targets. He worried they would generate unnecessary bureaucracy. He always favoured fewer rather than more targets, and rightly worried that the system would take them too literally and hit the target but miss the point' (Barber, 2007, p 81). Perhaps this sheds a little light on helping to resolve the query. On the related theme of *deliverology*, it is of interest to refer to the novel by Zia Haider, *In the Light of What We Know*, an accompaniment to Thomas Piketty (2014) on *Capital*. At one point in the novel, it is stated that outcomes are not about being pleasant or unpleasant: 'The only thing that counts is delivery. You got to deliver' (Piketty, 2014, p 369).

FIVE

Modernisation and cultural change under New Labour: views of solicitors, clerks, magistrates, barristers and judges

Introduction: practitioner research in probation

By the mid–1980s, I was several years into working as a probation officer at 'Northtown' within a rapidly changing organisation (Beynon et al, 1994; Haxby, 1978). The election of a Conservative government in 1979 signalled a discernible shift of direction for criminal justice in England and Wales, from an ostensibly rehabilitative discourse towards a more punishment-oriented tone (but see Whitehead, 2015b, ch 3). Paradoxically, events circa 1983/84 produced a *Statement of National Objectives and Priorities* (SNOP) (Home Office, 1984), which encouraged probation to pursue alternatives to custody. Consequently, the theme of alternatives to custody became emblematic during the 1980s, which culminated in the Criminal Justice Act 1991 and its advocacy of *punishment in the community* to enhance the credibility of community sentences to magistrates and judges.

Within this situation, empirical research was conducted between 1985 and 1989 by a practitioner-researcher (Whitehead, 1990). Its main purpose was to determine whether the probation order was being used as an alternative to custody in the post-SNOP political and local service organisational context. Various methods were utilised: a quantitative recording schedule to collect numerical data on probation orders being proposed by probation officers in their reports on offenders, subsequently imposed by the courts; and a qualitative semi-structured interview schedule and additional unstructured interviews to pursue relevant topics in greater depth. For example, data were collected on the rationale of probation, court sentencing practices, probation ideologies and methods of working with offenders. Individual and focus group interviews comprising probation staff, magistrates, judges, recorders and court clerks amounted to 69 respondents.

During the 1980s, there was a tangible sense of unity between the government and probation at the point both pursued alternatives to custody. One can also recall a land of opportunity for the practitioner-researcher to initiate and undertake research activities in the then 56 probation areas. Once it was decided to research an issue of penological concern, the process was supported by staff at 'Northtown'. Governance arrangements enabled chief probation officers (CPOs) to grant permission to aspiring practitioner-researchers, without Home Office approval, if potential benefits were justified. The office of CPO was imbued with autonomy and authority to make such decisions at the local level. Once permission was secured, then access to data and respondents proceeded uneventfully within circumstances where research was perceived as a valued activity, particularly if it contributed to effective practice outcomes. Durham University provided oversight, which facilitated academic legitimacy. Looking back from 2015 to the 1980s, my findings conjure an air of nostalgia for a discernibly different probation culture. That probation culture no longer exists.

Notwithstanding a changing political and criminal justice context during the 1980s, local probation areas maintained room for manoeuvre facilitated by flexible governance arrangements, the governing class and probation were united in pursuing alternatives to custody, opportunities existed for practitioner-researchers, local support endowed the practitioner-researcher role with legitimacy, the service was interested in research findings that enhanced effectiveness, and there were few issues surrounding access to respondents and data collection. I recall isolated pockets of resistance but they were not insurmountable in pursuit of research objectives.

Further research after 20 years, 2006–07

During the summer of 2006, when I had worked as a probation officer for 25 years, I returned to empirical research in the same probation area. This was a markedly different political and probation climate. I was now employed as a part-time probation officer in a team servicing magistrates' and crown courts, in addition to teaching part-time at a nearby university. Since 1997, New Labour had embarked on a mission to modernise the public sector, including the criminal justice system. This politically induced process culminated in the nationalisation and centralisation of probation areas in 2001 that attenuated local autonomy. Moreover, the imposition of the new central command-and-control structure transformed the role of the CPO, by government dictat, into a chief officer as civil servant. This reconfiguration adversely affected operational relationships between senior managers and other grades of staff (Whitehead and Statham, 2006). One effect was the creation of less propitious circumstances for individual practitioner-researcher initiatives within local probation areas. Research activity existed, but it was strategically controlled by the Ministry of Justice, which reflects discernible shifts in the balance of power.

Therefore, political, cultural and organisational reconfigurations since 2001 (Whitehead, 2007), transformed governance arrangements affecting the work of senior managers, and the observation that not all senior managers had worked as probation practitioners raised questions about their level of experience, knowledge and insight into practice issues and related questions of occupational legitimacy. The imposition of a political orthodoxy that actively promoted a 'can do' culture in the public sector is translated as *just get on with the job*, specified by central government, rather than engage in critical scrutiny via research at the local level.

These were some of the dynamics by 2006 when I formulated my research into the nature and effects of modernisation and accompanying cultural changes at 'Northtown'. I was interested in this theme because of first-hand experience of the cultural effects upon probation since 1997, but especially since 2001, while continuing to work within the organisation. I also surmised that it would be difficult to obtain permission from senior managers to pursue my research interests, particularly if this involved interviewing probation staff. Nevertheless, anticipated obstacles within probation inspired innovation to turn my research gaze from *inside* to *outside* the organisation, to solicitors, court clerks, magistrates, barristers and judges. The theme of modernisation remained intact, but the research angle was of practical necessity, and fortuitously, transformed.

Before discussing matters in greater detail, it should be acknowledged that some of the features confronting the practitioner-researcher just alluded to were intriguingly manifested during the summer of 2007. The data collection stage was well under way when my immediate probation line manager informed me, sotto voce, that questions were being asked by senior managers about my research activities. I was not approached directly by senior managers but disquiet was circuitously communicated. As the research with respondents was undertaken during lunch breaks at the 'Northtown' courts, often interviewing on days when employed by the university, not probation, and respondents willing to take part, it was not necessary to satisfy managerial curiosity. This, in itself, revealed the extent of organisational and cultural transformation that had occurred since the 1980s. What was once understood as legitimate criminal justice research was reframed as snooping around that caused consternation. I was perceived as a negative threat, not positive contribution.

Operational framework

After 10 years of New Labour's modernising agenda, and the approach of probation's centenary (1907–2007), I made the decision to research the meanings and implications attached to the related themes of modernisation and cultural change in the probation service (Hope and Walters, 2006). Formulating a proposal should not be limited to specifying *what* the researcher wants to do; it also benefits from reflections on *why*. The experience of working as a probation officer since 1981, periodically as participant-observer/ethnographer, confronted me with a series of profound cultural effects associated with the politics of modernisation that were worth exploring and explaining.

Next, after consulting with university colleagues, it was decided to select quantitative and qualitative methodologies to collect data on perceptions and understandings of modernisation and cultural change in probation. The quantitative approach comprised two tick boxes to collect numerical data on two specific areas of practice (see later). Where the first tick box is concerned, respondents were invited to consider a total of eight statements illustrative of cultural change in probation, for example: *Are you aware of a change of emphasis within probation from advise, assist and befriend to punishment in the community?* These results are assimilated in Tables 5.1 and 5.2.

The second tick box was used to shed light on their understandings of probation work after considering a set of 14 statements. If, for example, they associated probation work with a social work ethos or, by contrast, with an organisation that exists to provide a robust, tough, punitive approach to offenders – possibly both – again, they ticked the appropriate boxes that corresponded with their views. There was no limit to the number of boxes that they were allowed to tick, and these results are contained in Tables 5.3 and 5.4. The form of words comprising the second tick box was constructed with care to represent contrasting value categories (values of tolerance, care, compassion and decency, contrasted with a robust, tough and punitive approach to offenders). These contrasts represent some of the competing impulses, sensibilities and conflicting rationalities within modernised criminal justice.

The qualitative research instrument was a semi-structured interview schedule that posed the same questions to all respondents, in addition to providing opportunities to pursue points of interest in greater depth in order to yield rich bodies of data. The interviews were taped, and some areas of interest pursued were: the rationale of probation work; tensions between achieving government targets and pursuing justice for individual offenders; the punitisation of reports prepared by the probation service, which included recommendations for custody; the personal and social circumstances of offenders; and contestability, which exposes offender services to competition between the public, private and voluntary sectors within the National Offender Management Service (NOMS). Therefore, I concur with Newburn's (2007, p 899) assessment that some of the most useful research involves combining qualitative and quantitative methodologies.

A combination of personal knowledge of probation and criminal justice accrued since 1979, assistance by university library staff and utilising Google scholar confirmed that there was a paucity of published research on modernisation in the criminal justice domain. It was particularly difficult to track down publications related to solicitors and courts clerks, which made this project innovative. By contrast, there is a literature on magistrates, barristers and judges.[1]

Indubitably, employment as a probation officer (from July 1981 to November 2007) cultivated important contacts with different criminal justice professions. To progress the research, I initially approached as many 'Northtown' magistrates' solicitors as possible on the court landing during the summer of 2006 when working as a part-time probation officer. A preliminary exploration revealed that 36 solicitors appeared regularly before the justices to represent their clients. Subsequently, when data collection began in September 2006, 31 out of the 36 made themselves available for interview. Significantly, it was made clear that unless they had worked with and knew me, thus establishing professional trust accrued over a period of time, interviews would not have occurred. In other words, a letter sent to a solicitor's firm by an unknown practitioner-researcher may not have received a favourable reply. Consequently, my professional status as a probation officer opened doors into spheres of research activity, and most solicitors were enthusiastic as well as intrigued about participating. Consent was generously provided in writing and interviews were completed by December 2006.[2]

When expanding the research to court clerks and magistrates, it was necessary to obtain permission from the clerk to the justices, with whom I discussed the interview schedule and clarified that interviews could last up to 45 minutes. Permission was quickly obtained, which facilitated the cooperation of 22 out of a total contingent of 30 clerks, in addition to 20 magistrates who responded to the invitation for interview between February and July 2007. There were over 300 magistrates at 'Northtown' and time constraints could only accommodate 20. However, it became manageable for 101 magistrates to complete the two quantitative tick boxes, which took approximately 15 minutes to complete before they went into court at 10am. Only one magistrate declined to be interviewed because of a reluctance to be recorded on tape, notwithstanding assurances of confidentiality.

It should be confirmed that this research did not claim scientific rigor in terms of being nationally representative, nor could parity be achieved between groups of respondents. I did not have complete control over how many respondents would agree to, and be available for, interview. In other words, the following findings are the result of what became possible during the time allocated and opportunities presented. Most of my time as a practitioner-researcher was spent at the magistrates' courts. Consequently, I made a virtue out of necessity by completing interviews with solicitors, clerks and magistrates before approaching crown court barristers and judges, who operated in a different location. There are identifiable issues of time management when working as a practitioner-researcher, particularly when combining part-time probation work with university teaching. Nevertheless, it was possible to be creative when undertaking this research to ensure the completion of data collection between late summer 2006 and autumn 2007.

It is also worth reflecting on differential experiences at magistrates' compared to the crown court that were not anticipated. The different phases of the research process proceeded smoothly with solicitors, clerks and magistrates. By contrast, when approaching barristers at the 'Northtown' Crown Court, a central issue that emerged was not securing permission to undertake the research, but rather creating space to conduct interviews. Friday was the busiest sentencing day, when barristers attended court en masse. The demands associated with defending clients were such that 45-minute research interviews were untenable. Moreover, after approaching the resident judge, professional proprieties would have been breached if I had conducted interviews with 'the brothers', even after guaranteeing confidentiality. Again, reaping virtue from necessity, 20 barristers and 10 judges agreed to complete the two quantitative tick box documents. In the circumstances of prevailing political sensibilities, including time constraints, I could not have expected any more from the higher court. Either tick-box data or nothing at all was the decision that this practitioner-researcher had to make. The former was gratefully accepted, even though this imposed limitations on my initial data collection expectations, which will become clearer in the following.

As the research was conducted with the support of the local university, the proposal was scrutinised by the ethics committee. However, as an *insider* who had established working relationships with respondents from different organisations (since 1981), I could have been indicted on the charge of using them to put academic research before sensibilities prevailing within the probation service. Additionally, the epistemological privileges inherent within the practitioner-researcher role could benefit some organisations within the criminal justice system at the expense of others. There is always a price to pay for knowledge.[3]

It is eight years since I completed this research (by 2015), but it is included in my revised edition because it provides insights into perceptions of probation under New Labour. It is a slice of history that can be accessed by other criminal justice researchers. Therefore, I now turn to the quantitative data gleaned from respondents, briefly embellished by a handful of qualitative contributions when some respondents made unsolicited comments.

Table 5.1: Evidence of modernisation and cultural change at 'Northtown' Magistrates' Court

	Defence solicitors (*n*=31)	Clerks (*n*=22)	Magistrates (*n*=101)
	Number (%)	Number (%)	Number (%)
Rigorous enforcement	21 (67.7)	18 (81.8)	44 (43.6)
From advise, assist and befriend to punishment in the community	20 (64.5)	19 (86.4)	49 (48.5)
Target-driven organisation	18 (58.1)	13 (59.1)	49 (48.5)
From social work help to a law enforcement agency	17 (54.8)	10 (45.5)	34 (33.7)
Focus on managing the risk of reoffending and harm	17 (54.8)	18 (81.8)	72 (71.3)
Public protection	14 (45.2)	11 (50.0)	45 (44.6)
Benefit sanction	11 (35.5)	19 (86.4)	50 (49.5)
More concerned with victims than offenders	6 (19.4)	4 (18.2)	14 (13.9)

Rigorous enforcement procedures

If offenders do not comply with the requirements of court orders by, for example, absenting themselves from appointments with probation and Community Rehabilitation Companies (CRCs) without valid reason, they can expect to be returned to court in enforcement proceedings. According to the 1995 edition of the National Standards, offenders could receive two final warnings before probation proceeded to 'intention to breach', which resulted in a return to court after a third failure to cooperate with the requirements of supervision. However, by the 2000–02 version of the National Standards, this was reduced to one final warning, followed by intention to breach at the second absence – from three to two strikes and then back to court, which remains the legal position. Additionally, the Criminal Justice Act 2003 introduced the practice of more onerous requirements as the sanction for breach if the sentencing court allows the order to continue, thus eliminating the more liberal regime contained under the 1991 Act, which allowed for discretionary verbal warnings (a ticking off could suffice).

Therefore, there has been a tightening up of procedures, corresponding to a diminution of probation officer and court discretion, one of many factors that has contributed to the rise in the prison population (see Ministry of Justice, 2013e). Previously, the *Review of Prisons* undertaken by Carter (2007) stated that the number of people in prison for breaching an order of the court (this did not include recalls on licence, which constitutes another area of difficulty) had increased from 180 in 1995 to 1,200 by August 2007. Consequently, a number of respondents were aware of these changes, as the first variable of Table 5.1 elucidates – 67.7% of solicitors, 81.8% of clerks and 43.6% of magistrates. One court clerk deduced that probation is no longer a "benevolent organisation.... For example, in the breach courts, there are extremely tight rules about non-compliance and there is no discretion and that seems to be a backward step".

From advise, assist and befriend to punishment in the community

Section 4 of the Probation of Offenders Act 1907 stated that one duty of the probation officer was to advise, assist and befriend the probationer. This was when the probation order constituted an alternative to punishment and custody within the remains of the Victorian prison system. By contrast, from the mid-1980s, culminating in the Criminal Justice Act 1991, the organisation was reconfigured as *punishment in the community*. Accordingly, the duty to advise, assist and befriend was deleted from the legislation. This was part of the government's strategy to make community sentences more credible to magistrates and judges due to growing concerns over a steadily escalating prison population, including worrying future predictions (see Windlesham, 1993; Ministry of Justice, 2014). From advise, assist and befriend to punishment in the community constitutes a significant cultural shift, which 64.5% of solicitors, 86.4% of clerks and 48.5% of magistrates were aware of. One magistrate said that the:

> "shift to punishment I think was mainly as a result of the public perception that we were too soft on offenders and so that came down to harsher management of offenders and you had to set aside whatever they had experienced in their life and some young people were particularly damaged and it was as if they had to take total responsibility for whatever happened. I'm not altogether accepting of that myself. We have to take heed of what life experiences are given to some people."

Another magistrate stated that "I feel the word 'befriend' is inappropriate; it belongs in the voluntary sector". Furthermore, a district judge commented that there has been "a move away from advise, assist and befriend culture, which is where I came into probation 25–30 years ago, to managing risk, managing harm, both to the offender and those offended against, and public protection".

Target-driven organisation

The development of managerial objectives in probation can be traced to the early 1980s, followed by the introduction of a regime of numerical targets from the 1990s, which expanded after 1997. The introduction of targets is an integral component of central government strategic thinking for enhancing performance levels within organisations and demonstrating greater accountability (see Barber, 2007). It should also be acknowledged that NOMS operates within this auditable framework, indicative that probation has acquired the accoutrements of a quantitative business mentality that is ill at ease with a professional culture that exercises discretion. Tim Newburn (2007, p 553) stated that 'the setting of explicit targets and performance indicators enables the auditing of efficiency and effectiveness' within a more business-oriented environment (for a fuller discussion of these developments and their implications within the public sector, see Whitehead, 2007).

Similar proportions of my respondents were aware of a cultural shift towards targets, as Table 5.1 reveals – 58.1%, 59.1% and 48.5%. It is of interest to note that one clerk stated that:

"Unfortunately all organisations have statistics and sometimes it is better for things to take slightly longer to be done properly rather than thinking that we have to get things done to reach targets. I think that's in our organisation as well".

Moreover, the chair of the 'Northtown' Bench asserted that:

"I feel that the probation service should not be a target-driven organisation. Having attended a NOMS conference with ministers, both myself and many of the magistrates and judges attending were shocked by what we heard that you are going to be given targets for the number of drink drive courses, the number of various other courses that you can provide are going to be target-driven. We expressed concern about what happens when you have reached your target and there is no more money for others and if you haven't reached your target for those orders, are probation reports going to be, as it were, influenced by this and perhaps recommend that we adopt a sentence for some of the targets you haven't reached in order to meet those targets? So, certainly, my understanding is that the judiciary are not happy about a target-driven probation service and personally I am not."

Another magistrate said that "I think it's becoming increasingly target-driven and I think that is very frustrating for magistrates but we live in a target-driven society, I guess, and we're all very concerned with ticking the boxes".

From social work help to a law enforcement agency

For decades, probation was conceptualised as part of the helping professions in the inclusivist post-war welfare state, and probation officers were defined as social workers of the criminal justice system (Home Office, 1962). In fact, probation officers were trained social workers who addressed complex personal and social problems associated with the diverse repertoires of offending behaviour. However, there was a discernible shift towards a law enforcement rationale, which means that the implementation and enforcement of criminal laws (including organisational procedures such as achieving central government targets) have taken precedence over pursuing a deeper understanding of those factors that are deemed to be associated with, and underlying, presenting behaviours, then fully explaining them to magistrates and judges. Moreover, within a more neoliberal political and neo-classical criminological context, greater emphasis is placed upon *what* offenders have done – their rational choices – including future risks, rather than exploring, interpreting and explaining *why*. It should also be acknowledged that changes imposed upon the nature, form and content of probation reports are suggestive of this cultural shift, explored later in this chapter.

This is not to suggest that all aspects of the 'old' or pre-modernised service could always withstand critical scrutiny, and that the new wine of modernisation is indubitably corked. We should be reminded, lest we allow our minds to distort events by romanticising the past, previous research revealed that probation officers could propose custody inappropriately, made decisions that drew people deeper into the criminal justice system and failed to take seriously incidents of domestic violence (Bean, 1976; Bottoms and McWilliams, 1979; Cohen, 1985). Some of these points were taken up by Box (1987), who concluded that probation officers had contributed to a rising prison population by recommending tougher sentences in their reports to maintain credibility with sentencers (the phenomenon of second-guessing the magistrates). He also stated that some officers considered a number of offenders unsuitable for their professional help, which culminated in an up-tariff shift if community sentences were deemed inappropriate. Additionally, by sliding down tariffs to find clientele to maintain sufficient numbers being supervised in the community, probation officers unwittingly expanded the net of social control by advocating supervision for those who previously would have been dealt with by a financial penalty or conditional discharge. These problems, the doctrine of unintended consequences, keep repeating themselves in each new criminal justice generation (Carter, 2007).

Therefore, balance is required when explaining modernising developments during the decade prior to this research, just as much as historical accuracy is needed when excavating periods that belong to the pre-modern and the complex outcomes attached to social work rationality. In total, 54.8% of solicitors, 45.5% of clerks and 33.7% of magistrates acknowledged the shift from social work help to a law enforcement agency.

Managing risk of reoffending and harm, including public protection

These two variables capture another cultural shift, both in probation work and in criminological thinking, from a rationality of understanding and help with personal and social problems, to managing, containing, controlling and allocating offenders to various categories of risk. The language of risk is associated with reoffending and harm, and to protect the public from both is the primary task of probation. Table 5.1 presents data on more marked differential responses by solicitors, clerks and magistrates, particularly where risk is concerned – 54.8%, 81.8% and 71.3%, respectively. One clerk embellished the tick box by saying that "Yes, the focus is now on managing the risk of reoffending and harm".

Benefit Sanction

This refers to the withdrawal of a proportion of state benefits from selected offenders who did not comply with community orders in four designated areas, including 'Northtown' (but see endnote 4 in Chapter Four, which confirms that this experiment terminated in 2009). This provision was contained under sections 62–66 of the Child Support, Pensions and Social Security Act 2000 and was construed as an extra punishment against unemployed offenders imposed by New Labour (Kennedy, 2005, p 245; see also discussion in Windlesham, 2001). This measure did not apply to those offenders who were in work, which discriminated against the unemployed. This measure constituted an example of a more punitive and authoritarian state bringing the unemployed offender to heel, and probation was implicated in its delivery.

More court clerks (86.4%) were aware of this cultural shift than solicitors (35.5%) and magistrates (49.5%), mainly because the former are involved in explaining the provision to offenders in court. One clerk offered the following, perhaps surprising, observation, when she commented that the:

> "Benefit Sanction, not a lot to be said; it's there as a punishment but I'm sure it does create problems. The defendants are put under a huge amount of strain. These are the people who do not have a lot of income in any event and if they have their benefits stopped, it just seems to be an invitation to go and commit further crimes, but that's just a personal view."

In marked contrast, a magistrate said that:

> "I personally think that has been a huge step forward. I think the thought of actually losing their benefit has got to be a good sanction to have because you can clearly say 'do it again and we're going to reduce a lot of your dole'. That gets people's attention and is one of the few ways it will hit people."

More concerned with victims than offenders

Lastly, respondents were asked to consider if they thought the probation service had become more concerned with victims than offenders. This was included in the research because victim issues have acquired a raised profile over recent years (Garland, 2001; Home Office, 2005; Newburn, 2007, ch 17). However, the vast majority of these respondents were not aware that probation services are more concerned with victims than offenders – 19.4% of solicitors, 18.2% of clerks and 13.9% of magistrates. It should be noted that other organisations exist that seek to respond to the needs of victims, even though probation made a distinctive contribution in this area of work because of its own victim liaison officers. However, when discussing this theme, one of the clerks volunteered the following construction on the approach to victims by saying that "I don't think perhaps the magistrates look at the issue of the offender being a victim but there must be clear circumstances where they are".

Therefore, when perusing the data collected on all eight variables in Table 5.1, there is some evidence to suggest that these solicitors, clerks and magistrates were differentially aware of cultural change in probation between 1997 and 2007, and had different perspectives on, and understandings of, what has occurred. Let us now turn to a more limited data set from the 'Northtown' Crown Court.

It was always my intention to include a crown court perspective in this research. However, after completing the quantitative and qualitative data collection stage at the 'Northtown' Magistrates' Court, it became evident that data sets gleaned from barristers and judges would not include interviews. As mentioned earlier, the logistics at the higher court made it difficult to reach for the tape recorder to interview barristers and judges, in addition to which one could not escape from observing the prevailing political and organisational proprieties. Nor did I want to damage working relationships between the judiciary and probation. Consequently, the choice was between quantitative tick-box data or nothing at all. In settling for the former, it should be reiterated that limitations were placed upon the amount of data that could be collected.

Table 5.2: Evidence of modernisation and cultural change at 'Northtown' Crown Court

	Barristers (*n*=20)	Judges (*n*=10)
	Number (%)	Number (%)
Rigorous enforcement	8 (40)	7 (70)
From advise, assist and befriend to punishment in the community	9 (45)	8 (80)
Target-driven organisation	9 (45)	2 (20)
From social work help to a law enforcement agency	4 (20)	5 (50)
Focus on managing the risk of reoffending and harm	13 (65)	9 (90)
Public protection	16 (80)	9 (90)
Benefit Sanction	6 (30)	2 (20)
More concerned with victims than offenders	5 (25)	1 (10)

When turning to the quantitative data collected from the 20 barristers and 10 judges, the following may be cautiously observed. The analytical point underlying Table 5.1 on the 'Northtown' Magistrates' Court data sets can be tentatively extended by elucidating that there are differential responses when comparing the two sets of respondents at the 'Northtown' Crown Court in Table 5.2. The largest percentage difference is the shift from advise, assist and befriend to punishment in the community (45% of barristers and 80% of judges). By contrast, the closest they came to agreement is public protection (80% of barristers and 90% of judges). The percentages are relatively low for target-driven organisation (at 45% of barristers and 20% of judges) and Benefit Sanction (30% of barristers and again 20% of judges). The qualifying caveat is that it is unwise to engage in speculation and force unwarranted extrapolation from such limited data, particularly when it was not possible to probe what may lie behind the responses. Nevertheless, there is *some* insight into *some* of the many cultural shifts that have occurred. I now turn from cultural change to respondents' understandings of probation.

This is a more interesting and significant data set compared with Tables 5.1 and 5.2. By initially detaching the first column of data presented in rank order on solicitors, the point can be established (this applies to all three groups but in different ways) that not all 31 respondents define their understandings of probation in exactly the

Table 5.3: Understandings of probation at 'Northtown' Magistrates' Court

	Solicitors (n=31)	Clerks (n=22)	Magistrates (n=101)
	Number (%)	Number (%)	Number (%)
Understand why people offend	30 (96.8)	19 (86.4)	77 (76.2)
Awareness of offenders' personal and social circumstances	29 (93.6)	20 (90.9)	75 (74.3)
Promote criminal and social justice through court reports	28 (90.3)	20 (90.9)	85 (84.2)
Values of tolerance, care, compassion and decency	25 (80.7)	13 (59.1)	44 (43.6)
Advise, assist and befriend	24 (77.4)	14 (63.6)	36 (35.7)
Empathy	20 (64.5)	8 (36.4)	25 (24.8)
Deliver punishment in the community	18 (58.1)	18 (81.8)	81 (80.2)
Manage, contain and control	18 (58.1)	15 (68.2)	71 (70.3)
Social work ethos	17 (54.8)	6 (27.3)	23 (22.8)
Keep out of custody	14 (45.2)	7 (31.8)	39 (38.6)
Public protection	13 (41.9)	11 (50.0)	57 (56.4)
Rigorously enforce orders	7 (22.6)	17 (77.3)	66 (65.3)
Robust, tough and punitive approach	1 (3.2)	4 (18.2)	33 (32.7)
Victim support	0 (0.0)	1 (4.5)	31 (30.7)

same way. This is what I would have expected when interviewing a group of independent and strong-minded professionals. Nevertheless, a high proportion of solicitors clarified their perception of probation as: an organisation that brings an understanding of *why* people offend into the criminal justice system (96.8%); awareness of an offender's personal and social circumstances (93.6%); promotion of criminal and social justice through the provision of information contained in court reports (90.3%); an organisation with a set of identifiable values rooted in tolerance, care, compassion and decency (80.7%); in addition to advise, assist and befriend (77.4%, which, as noted earlier, is no longer a legislative requirement). Notwithstanding differential responses among the 31 solicitors in relation to the 14 variables, it is argued that these data reveal a discernible, albeit qualified, professional perspective in that some features are more important than others when thinking about and understanding the role of probation within the criminal justice system, about what they want and expect from probation.

When turning to compare percentage data across the three groups of respondents, more revealing than looking at each group in isolation, there are points of similarity between them, specifically in relation to the following variables: understanding why people offend; awareness of an offender's personal and social circumstances, which implies putting behaviour into a holistic context; promoting criminal and social justice; and keeping people out of custody (lower percentages but similarities of response at 45.2%, 31.8%, 38.6% for solicitors, clerks and magistrates, respectively). There are a number of contrasting responses that should be illustrated, as follows: certain values associated with probation (80.7% of solicitors, 59.1% of clerks and 43.6% of magistrates); advise, assist and befriend (77.4%, 63.6% and 35.7%, respectively); empathy (64.5%, 36.4% and 24.8%, respectively); whether probation should be a punishment in the community (58.1%, 81.8% and 80.2%, respectively); social work ethos (54.8%, 27.3% and 22.8%, respectively); rigorous enforcement (22.6%, 77.3% and 65.3%, respectively); and a robust, tough and punitive approach to people who offend (3.2%, 18.2% and 32.7%, respectively). These contrasting perspectives provided an insight into different operational philosophies at work within the criminal justice system and differential roles being undertaken, including criminological approaches to offenders and perhaps political allegiances.

The social work ethos variable is worth accentuating because, traditionally, probation was involved in helping offenders with their personal and social problems, rather than delivering overt forms of punishment towards those classified as failures for not playing by the rules. In other words, offenders could be constructed as the victims of an unjust and unequal capitalist socio-economic system, thus necessitating a broad explanatory context within which to analyse and explain certain forms of offending behaviour (Home Office, 1977; Walker and Beaumont, 1981). This was probation with a radical edge and campaigning voice, which constituted a challenging perspective towards those cultural shifts that have occurred over previous years. Nevertheless, the language of social work should not be used solely to convey the view that it is always associated with benign outcomes. Social work impulses have positive and negative effects and, where the latter is concerned, can suffer from the doctrine of unintended consequences, as the aforementioned research by Box (1987) indicates.

The politics of modernisation and associated cultural transformations, as Chapter One made clear, placed more emphasis on: punitive and custodial responses; a bureaucratic field of targets; reclassifying offenders as statistical units of risk (low, medium, high, very high); managing risk rather than holistically understanding the past; rigorous enforcement practices, with onerous requirements, which have inflated the prison population; and tougher attitudes towards offenders. Yet, *despite* or *precisely because of* these changes, the complex dialectics of the modernised criminal justice system among these respondents in 'Northtown' retained a place and definable space for a probation organisation associated with more benign rather than punitive impulses. Arguably, such an understanding of probation belongs more to its pre-modernised manifestation (before the 1980s). Accordingly, some of these respondents revealed that a number of pre-modernised elements had not been erased from their thinking and criminal justice responses. This finding was pertinent when considering the nature of probation developments under the NOMS structure, particularly in anticipation of those public, private and voluntary agencies that increasingly displaced probation from its monopoly position, a direct outcome of contestability.

When reflecting upon the punitive turn taken by probation within the criminal justice system, it is interesting to hear the disquiet of two magistrates: first, "the sentence that the court passes is intended as a punishment. I would not have thought that it was the aim of probation to be punitive"; and, second:

> "The punitive approach to offenders seems to me to conjure up probation staff themselves being punitive and I don't see them as doing other than delivering the punishment the court has advised, so I didn't tick it for that reason."

These data suggest that solicitors, court clerks and magistrates at the 'Northtown' Magistrates' Court were involved in a complex conversation with probation because of politically imposed modernising accretions in the criminal justice system since the 1980s. At this point, I once again turn to the findings from the crown court.

When returning to the more limited data set on how barristers and judges express their understandings of what features should define probation, the following observations can be made. A proportion of respondents understand that probation should: deliver the politically modernised features of punishment in the community (45% of barristers and 80% of judges); and manage, contain and control offenders (40% of barristers and 80% of judges). These constitute differential responses that are not without interest. The proportions are identical for public protection, at 60%. This leaves 55% of barristers and 40% of judges suggesting that probation should rigorously enforce the orders of the court (these are the orders they imposed); however, intriguingly, only

5% of barristers and 30% of judges agree that probation should be associated with a robust, tough and punitive approach. This finding challenges recent modernising drifts and cultural transformations under New Labour.

Table 5.4: Understandings of probation at 'Northtown' Crown Court

	Barristers (*n*=20)	Judges (*n*=10)
	Number (%)	Number (%)
Understand why people offend	16 (80)	7 (70)
Awareness of offenders' personal and social circumstances	16 (80)	7 (70)
Promote criminal and social justice through court reports	19 (90)	10 (100)
Values of tolerance, care, compassion and decency	9 (40)	5 (50)
Advise, assist and befriend	7 (35)	5 (50)
Empathy	6 (30)	3 (30)
Deliver punishment in the community	9 (45)	8 (80)
Manage, contain and control	8 (40)	8 (80)
Social work ethos	5 (25)	3 (30)
Keep out of custody	6 (30)	3 (30)
Public protection	12 (60)	6 (60)
Rigorously enforce orders	11 (55)	4 (40)
Robust, tough and punitive approach	1 (5)	3 (30)
Victim support	2 (10)	1 (10)

By contrast, it is interesting to observe the relatively high percentages set alongside the following variables and correspondingly high agreement between barristers and judges: probation officers should understand why people offend (80% and 70% , respectively); there should be an awareness of offenders' personal and social circumstances (again 80% and 70% , respectively); and there should be the promotion of criminal and social justice through court reports (90% of barristers but all 10 judges ticked this box). Furthermore, even though the percentages are less for the following – the values of tolerance, care, compassion and decency; advise, assist and befriend; empathy; social work ethos; and keeping offenders out of custody – a proportion of respondents associated probation with a pre-modernised vocabulary, as well as modernised reconstructions. One must be very careful with the interpretation of these data because, having been denied opportunities to interview respondents, detailed explanations and qualifications could not be sought. Nevertheless, these preliminary findings, elicited from the completion of the quantitative tick boxes, are of some interest when considering changes to the criminal justice system after 1997. Even though these respondents could not be interviewed, it is worth noting that, rather unexpectedly, six barristers added a number of unsolicited hand-written comments when handing back their responses to the tick boxes. Let us hear them articulate a veritable mixed bag of views at this juncture. First is a positive endorsement: "The probation service's value to the criminal justice system is inestimable". Second:

> "I often find that a Pre-Sentence Report [PSR] is written in negative terms because the defendant appears to deny or minimise some aspect of the offence, even where this has been agreed between prosecution and defence. Sometimes, it's obvious the PSR author has taken a dim view of the defendant or the offence. I think this occasional lack of objectivity is regrettable."

Third, on the subject of targets, another barrister stated that probation reports are "More reliant on tick-box computer programmes than experienced judgement. OASys [the Offender Assessment System] seems to dictate the outcome even though it is focused on static factors". This comment finds an echo in John Pratt (2007, pp 134–5) talking about actuarialism: "It allows bureaucratic organisations to avoid the moral consequences of their policies by relying on statistical computations rather than human judgements". Fourth, we hear that "I would like to see even more rigorous enforcement of breaches". Penultimately, the:

> Pace of change is unprecedented… Your budget-savvy managers have spotted an opportunity to deskill the service. Thus, we have hard-working officers (who may not be too well trained/experienced) cranking out FDRs [fast delivery reports] in a mechanistic fashion, which have no place for the nuances a well-qualified practitioner might have about a client and the problems he poses."

Finally, this was a powerful assessment:

> "The probation service has changed beyond recognition over the course of the last 10 years. The shift of the probation service has left the criminal justice system

unbalanced. There is too much emphasis on punishment, and a void where there should be an agency dedicated to values of befriending and assisting."

In summary, we have an endorsement, expression of frustration, two laments, support for enforcement and a concern about the nature of cultural change. After presenting quantitative data, occasionally embellished with a melange of explanatory and qualifying comments, the next substantive section focuses on interviews with court clerks and magistrates at 'Northtown' on a number of pertinent themes (see endnote 2). However, first I begin with a brief profile of my respondents.

Clerks' profile (*N* = 22)

Age

Gender

My aim was to provide a balance between male and female respondents. This was achieved to a limited degree as five male and 17 female clerks made themselves available for interview.

Table 5.5: Age of court clerks

Age	Number	%
30–39	7	31.8
40–49	11	50.0
50–59	4	18.2
Total	22	100.0

Note: The average age of these 22 clerks is 43.5 years.

Ethnicity

Even though there were a handful of clerks from a minority ethnic background working at 'Northtown', all my respondents were White British. Again, this was not planned, but emerged from a situation of those who were willing to be interviewed. One should not read anything negative into the fact that no clerks from a minority ethnic group presented themselves for interview; this was nothing more than a coincidence of the research enterprise.

Table 5.6: Number of years working as a court clerk

Years	Number	%
1–9	3	13.6
10–19	10	45.5
20–29	8	36.4
30–39	1	4.5
Total	22	100.0

Length of service

The average number of years that my respondents had been employed as a court clerk was 17.4 years. Consequently, it can be deduced that they were experienced at their work, in addition to which they were ideally placed to comment on changes to probation in the years preceding 2007.

Magistrates' profile (*N* = 20)

Age

Gender

There were 13 male and seven female respondents.

Ethnicity

All respondents identified themselves as White British, but one magistrate did not want to be pigeonholed into any ethnic category. By the summer of 2007, there were over 30,000 magistrates in England and Wales, of whom over 7% were from minority ethnic backgrounds.[4]

Table 5.7: Age of magistrates

Age	Number	%
40–49	3	15.0
50–59	6	30.0
60–69	11	55.0
Total	20	100.0

Note: The average age of these 20 magistrates is 58.7 years.

Length of service

The average number of years that my respondents had been working as a magistrate was 17.3 years, almost identical to the 22 clerks. Again, the point can be made that they were experienced magistrates and well placed to comment on probation transformations.

Table 5.8: Number of years working as a magistrate

Years	Number	%
1–9	3	15.0
10–19	11	55.0
20–29	5	25.0
30–39	1	5.0
Total	20	100.0

Purpose of probation

The literature produced by the Home Office, and since May 2007 by the newly created Ministry of Justice, promotes an image of the National Probation Service as a law enforcement agency that, since 2003–04, has been incorporated into NOMS. With its 21,000 staff located in 42 areas throughout England and Wales (in 2007), subdivided into 10 regions, its primary goals were articulated as follows:

- public protection;
- the reduction of offending;
- punishing offenders in the community;
- to ensure offenders are aware of the effects of crime on victims; and
- rehabilitation.

This list resonates with the purpose of sentencing located in the Criminal Justice Act 2003. A high proportion of staff are female, even though the vast majority of offenders are male. It had approximately 246,360 offenders under various forms of supervision, made up of 149,280 under a court order in the community and a further 97,080 being supervised pre- or post-release from custodial facilities (Ministry of Justice, 2008c). It was also preparing in the region of 250,000 reports annually for the magistrates' and crown courts.

When turning to respondents, it is not without interest to note the tone they struck when explaining how they understood the purpose of probation. After more than a decade of modernising reforms since 1997, including the punitisation of probation work (since the Criminal Justice Act 1991, reconfigured as a punishment in the community), the key word used by 10 clerks and four magistrates was 'rehabilitation'. The concept of rehabilitation has a long association with the prison system and means a return to a state of law-abidingness (Mathiesen, 2006, p 27). It is one of several sentencing aims in the Criminal Justice Act 2003, and constitutes an ideology traditionally embedded within probation, mediated through a constructive relationship between offender and officer. One clerk explained that in the long term, the purpose of probation "I guess it is for the rehabilitation of offenders in essence". This was a view complemented by illustrative comments from a further two magistrates: "I think it's to help the rehabilitation of offenders to a better life basically. It is to help them, families, and courts"; and, "Well, my view of the probation service is to support, rehabilitate where necessary and if appropriate punish".

Of course this is not the only understanding, as indicated earlier by the quantitative data and acknowledged by the magistrate just cited. Furthermore, during interviews with court clerks, as well as a number of references to rehabilitation, other voices were heard saying: being "an essential service for the courts"; "helping people if they had problems"; it is something *other than* custody; "to carry out court orders"; "assist and educate them"; as well as its modernised association with punitive responses. The tone set by magistrates is captured as follows: a dual role that involves a responsibility in the courts but also towards offenders; to prevent reoffending; the provision of support to and supervision of offenders to deal with their problems; *as* rather than *for* punishment; and public protection and monitoring. Therefore, I was presented, quantitatively and qualitatively, with a multifaceted discourse, a melange of voices, utilising concepts of varying philosophico-ideological origin to attach different meanings to the purpose of the organisation 10 years after New Labour became responsible for criminal justice. For clerks and magistrates, probation was not solely or even predominantly conceptualised by a punitive stance towards people who offend. Rather, there was a rehabilitatively positive, supportive and helping understanding. Stated differently, there is evidence of an anti-punitive discourse. Nevertheless, when summarising these responses, it must be reiterated that my respondents were engaged in a complex dialogue with the probation service in the sense of different voices clamouring for a hearing.

Purpose of probation reports

It is difficult to say exactly when police court missionaries after 1876 became involved in making enquiries on offenders before sentence (McWilliams, 1983). Nevertheless, it was probably around the Probation of First Offenders Act 1887. Subsequently, paragraph 36 of the Departmental Committee on the Probation of Offenders Act 1907 (Home Office, 1909) recorded that the first probation officers were undertaking preliminary enquiries for magistrates. Additionally, it is "obviously an advantage to the Probation Officer to know all the circumstances relating to the offence" (Home Office, 1909, para 37). In one of the earliest books ever written on the inchoate probation system in England and Wales, cited earlier, Leeson (1914, p 67) confirmed that probation officers were involved in making enquiries for the courts to determine suitable cases for probation supervision. Such enquiries were conducted by taking note of the offender's character, domestic circumstances, education and employment, associates, and habits. Arguably, this was during a period when offending behaviour was constructed by a narrative of character defects and moral weakness, rather than theorising the possibility of a behavioural response to problems generated by the political economy. By the 1930s, comprehensive advice was being issued on the preparation of written reports for the courts (Le Mesurier, 1935).

By the rehabilitative and welfare-oriented 1950s (Home Office, 1959), followed by the Streatfield Report (Home Office, 1961), part of the latter document was concerned with selecting the most effective form of treatment for offenders appearing before the sentencing courts. The probation system had by this juncture evolved beyond its theological phase (1876–1930s) to a more secular, professional and 'scientific' expression, associated with a personalised medical-treatment model of corrections. It should also be acknowledged that the Streatfield Report resulted in a burgeoning of reports for the courts (Bottoms and McWilliams, 1986; Bottoms and Stelman, 1988). There are copious references to the importance of probation reports in Haxby (1978, p 136), and by the 1980s, when some 200,000 were being prepared annually, the social enquiry report, as it was then called, was potentially an instrument for diverting offenders from custody in the post-rehabilitative era (Home Office, 1984). The Criminal Justice Act 1991 transformed the social enquiry report into the PSR in what was a more justice- than treatment-oriented criminal justice system (Whitehead and Statham, 2006). Therefore, notwithstanding the different epistemological, political and cultural frameworks within which information has been processed and reports prepared since the 1880s – theological, welfare, treatment, rehabilitative, justice and then punishment in the community – it is clear that they have constituted a central feature of probation practice for over 100 years.

Section 158 of the Criminal Justice Act 2003 continues to provide the legal basis and rationale for the preparation of reports (NOMS, 2007; House of Commons Official Report, 2007). Accordingly, a report is prepared "with a view to assisting the courts in determining the most suitable method of dealing with an offender". Furthermore, section 160 of the Act refers to *other* reports, which means that in addition to the comprehensively written PSR, other formats are possible. Several years ago, the probation officer working in the criminal courts could be asked by magistrates and judges to deliver a *stand-down report* if this was appropriate. In such circumstances, a case was stood down by the courts (between 30 minutes to 1 hour) to enable probation to conduct a brief interview before delivering verbal feedback to bring matters to an expedited sentencing conclusion (I recall undertaking this task on numerous occasions). This practice metamorphosed into the *specific sentence report*, which involved the preparation of a briefly written document that, in turn, was further refined by the FDR and currently the *oral stand-down*. Therefore, if it remains possible for the probation service to be involved in the preparation of different report formats, they required elucidation in 2007.

First, the comprehensive PSR, structured and informed by the computerised OASys and National Standards, is normally prepared within an adjournment period of 15 working days (10 days if the offender is remanded in custody). The adjournment period enables probation to conduct interviews at the office and/or home of the defendant, in addition to making relevant investigations and verifying information. This is a detailed report because it is written by taking cognisance of the following OASys headings: offending information; analysis of the offences; accommodation status and history; education, training and employability; financial management and income; relationships; lifestyle and associates; drug, alcohol and other addictions; emotional well-being; and thinking and behaviour, including the offender's attitudes. Furthermore, the author has a duty to consider risk of reoffending and harm prior to making a sentencing proposal for the magistrates' and crown courts.

Second, an FDR should ideally be completed on the day requested by the courts, certainly within five working days. In other words, interviewing and writing the document, normally undertaken by the court duty officer, should be completed within a couple of hours. This format, unlike the aforementioned full report, is structured differently by utilising a series of tick boxes to expedite the presentation of collected data. However, scope remains to include explanatory written text to expand upon tick-box data if required. This type of report, by definition briefer than the full report, also takes cognisance of the same OASys headings alluded to earlier, but without the necessity to undertake a computerised and time-consuming OASys assessment. Rather, the Offender Group Reconviction Scale (OGRS) is also applied, in addition to the OASys risk of harm screening.

Finally, it is possible for probation to be invited to prepare, or even initiate, a *verbal report* (its lineage is the former *stand-down report*) to expedite the sentencing function of the court even further. After a brief interview with the person who has offended, probation delivers verbal rather than written feedback to sentencers.

Further clarification was provided by Probation Circular 12/2007, when it stated that the standard delivery full report, fast delivery and oral format are all PSRs. The three formats are deemed to be of equal standing. It was also made clear that courts must be provided with the information they require to reach a sentencing decision, which begins to raise a number of pertinent issues. One of these, emerging from the Criminal Justice Act 2003 and supporting Circular, concerns who determines the volume of information required to facilitate a sentencing decision. For example, is the probation service the recognised lead authority or is the decision made after taking soundings from the *dramatis personae* within the magistrates' courts – court clerks as legal advisors, defence solicitors and magistrates themselves? Another pressing issue touches upon the differential distribution of power within the organisational composition of local criminal justice systems, with their conflicting ideologies, organisational dynamics and discrete agendas. Insights into these differential perspectives are expressed in Tables 5.1 to 5.4. In other words, probation officers, clerks, magistrates and solicitors have their own views on, and approaches to, offenders and offending that shape the information considered necessary and the uses to which it will be put. There will be those who are motivated by the arguments for efficiency (3Es [economy, efficiency and effectiveness] and VfM [value for money]), and others more concerned to promote criminal and social justice without recourse to cost. Accordingly, such issues and questions raise potential difficulties associated with the selection of report formats, what constitutes relevant information and evaluations of criminal and social justice, which will now be explored in more detail by resorting to these empirical findings.

A preliminary discussion with court clerks on their understanding of the purpose of reports revealed documents that assist the courts to arrive at a sentencing decision. This was clearly stated by one respondent: "To assist the courts in deciding what sentence they should reach". This echoes the rationale articulated at section 158 of the Criminal Justice Act 2003. Importantly, nine clerks juxtaposed the term "background information" with the production and rationale of reports, expanded upon by one who said that "when you get a report that has lots of information, with a strongly reasoned conclusion, that does carry a lot of weight with the magistrates". Another said that it is to give "a fuller picture of the defendant, their personal background, their offending background". Therefore, prior to arriving at a sentencing decision, relevant background information should be presented to the courts by probation.

When exploring the purpose of reports with magistrates, the responses provided were: to be as objective as possible and steer a course between defence and prosecution; to provide information on backgrounds and circumstances; and to inform decision-making. Moreover:

> "There's always a story to tell ... and I think that it is important that we hear about social backgrounds, family, and what is going on in their life, and to me, the PSRs and FDRs are of great importance before we go to sentencing."

Another stated their purpose as "To give us greater insights into the offender and to give us recommendations as to community penalties". Also, "It helps us to put the individual into context, where they've come from and why they might have done what they have done". Therefore, for nine magistrates, as well as nine court clerks, the provision of information on offenders' backgrounds and circumstances was an important probation function. In other words, information about the person (Who are you?), as well as the offence (What have you done?), is required. For both sets of respondents, there was a self-evident logic to the provision of information on offences and offenders: for clerks, it facilitated informed advice to courts; for magistrates, it facilitated the sentencing process.

Expanding upon the term "background information", Neil Hutton, albeit within a different context, makes the point that research utilising focus groups and deliberative polling has revealed that the public may not be as punitive as survey data indicate. In fact, when people are given individual cases to deal with, provided with relevant background information about the criminal justice system "and allowed to engage in dialogue with each other" (Hutton, 2008, p 205), they are less punitive and more rational and constructive about sentencing matters. The probation service at 'Northtown' used to participate in sentencing exercises with clerks and magistrates, which utilised probation reports containing background information on individual offenders they proceeded to sentence in mock exercises. Similar exercises occurred at court open days, when members of the public observed role-plays of a sentencing court in operation. However, it has become increasingly less likely that courts receive detailed background information on *all* offenders because of the prevailing emphasis on FDRs and oral reports. This is an issue that requires careful exploration because of the implications for criminal and social justice, which may be little understood because of the salient arguments for efficiency, particularly after the economic crisis of 2007–08.

Fast delivery reports and the 40% rule

When narrowing the focus to incorporate the elevated status increasingly arrogated to FDRs and oral reports, it should be acknowledged that until 2006/07, the target for FDRs was 40% of all reports being prepared in magistrates' courts. The figure of 40% remained in force to become part of a Service Level Agreement (SLA) between the 10 NOMS regions and local services, rather than a specific target, when the research was undertaken. Consequently, it was important to turn to this subject with respondents during interview. If the full report appeared destined to be restricted to more serious offenders, were there any implications or even concerns if government policy was pushing probation and the courts towards the production of shorter-format reports?

It should be clarified that there were 12 positive responses from clerks and 11 from magistrates. In other words, these respondents did not anticipate problems with a SLA of 40%. A selection of positive responses from the 12 clerks revealed:

> "I would certainly like to see a greater number of FDRs used rather than the full report. I think there are several issues with a full report – length; time; defendants not attending court; failure to attend appointments; the backlog is ultimately there."

This senior clerk also gave support for the oral report to expedite the process of bringing cases to a sentencing conclusion. Another stated:

> "The FDR is very good but it is not easy to read and I think there are a lot of tick boxes which mean very little. I think what we have found with an oral report is often much better because it sticks to the point of what the magistrates need to hear; not the tick boxes as I don't think they are very relevant and the magistrates don't find them easy to read."

Next: "The aim of the FDR I would say is speedy justice, which is something I believe in because I do think that delay isn't good. I do think the faster you deal with things the better"; "The number of cases that are going to need an in-depth enquiry that's proportionate to what we are actually going to do I think are quite slim"; and "Well, I personally agree with having FDRs in the majority of cases because I do not think in most cases that there is any need to adjourn for a full report".

When turning to responses from some of the 11 magistrates, we hear that:

> "I don't in principle have a problem with that [achieving 40% FDRs] provided that the key issues are drawn out within the time available and we are aware of all the important things that in sentencing we need to have."

It is also stated that if the FDR is not appropriate, then the safeguard of a full report exists. This is an important caveat when discussing the provision of information to the courts: "I think when I have had an

FDR it has been quite frequently just as good if not better than the PSR. I don't know whether it focuses the mind but the experience of them has been very positive". FDRs and oral reports are helpful at saving time and money, which is a benefit for the courts, and "I certainly think there are lots of occasions when a full report is requested when it is not necessary". This magistrate, because of her position on the local Bench, was acutely aware of the financial constraints pressing upon Her Majesty's Courts Service. Another magistrate commented that "I don't see that it is any different from the full report; it just means that it is delivered faster and perhaps gets to the point rather more quickly". Therefore, a number of respondents are in favour of the shorter-format reports.

By contrast, eight clerks and six magistrates raised some concerns with the FDR format in the following terms, beginning with the clerks: "I think that they are only scratching the surface with FDRs". The 40% implication is that "you might not get the full picture … you could be missing a problem in the person's history that needs addressing". Missing information, scratching the surface, their being rushed and concerns about tick boxes linked to chasing targets were mentioned:

> "Personally I don't like the FDRs, they are not easy to read. Too many ticky boxes like a magazine quiz … well I wouldn't mind an FDR like a shortened version of a full report, set out in proper paragraphs. The FDR is not user-friendly."

Additionally:

> "I think it's to get work done more quickly really. FDRs aren't terribly fascinating to read; in fact, I often skip the ticked boxes and look at the written information. I don't think the full picture is going to come out. I think it is just a way of moving the work along quickly and everybody meeting targets in terms of speed."

Corresponding comments of concern from magistrates include: "I am not a great believer in targets because I think it has got to be case-driven rather than target-driven"; and that the assessed needs of the individual offender should come first. Other comments were:

> "Everybody is very concerned to deal with cases as quickly as possible and from the victims' point of view, which is

important, there should be minimal delay. The problem I foresee with increasing the number of FDRs is that you will perhaps fail to spot the people who need more specialised disposals than they would do so if they had the opportunity to prepare a full PSR."

It may be suggested this is a pertinent point because of the increasing number of unqualified staff involved in writing FDRs. Moving on, the 40% could result in probation "rushing through things and I think a full report gives us a better understanding of the person". Moreover:

"Because of the timescale, when we got full PSRs, it was a lot easier if we wanted to come back on a case [due to the operation of the magistrates' rota]. FDRs make that more difficult and therefore I think that the defendants see more magistrates involved in their eventual penalty and I think the problem is you lose continuity of people who are eventually going to decide your punishment."

Also, "I'm a great fan of the FDR and even greater fan of oral reports … but, yes, I think you miss an awful lot". Lastly, two clerks were reluctant to express a view on this subject, and in the circumstances, I deduced that it would be unhelpful to press the respondents further; also, three magistrates' comments were difficult to categorise. Therefore, in addition to some respondents concurring with the direction of travel towards the production of shorter-format reports, by contrast, we also hear a number of expressions of concern.

Business efficiency or justice: New Public Management and morality

Penetrating even more deeply into the subject of reports for the sentencing function of the court led to a discussion on whether the criminal justice system was putting efficiency before criminal and social justice (Cook, 2006). In other words, the New Public Management agenda imposed on the public sector, which emphasised value for money, was also being applied to reports, and the emphasis on the fast-delivery format is a pertinent example (Whitehead and Statham, 2006; Whitehead, 2007, p 34). In fact, the local criminal justice environment in 2007 that contextualised the discussion with clerks and magistrates can be sketched by paying attention to the following factors that applied discernible pressures to create specific outcomes consistent with business efficiency.

Spend less money on reports

In a speech delivered at Wormwood Scrubbs prison on 7 November 2006, the Home Secretary stated that too much money was diverted to writing reports and not enough on practical help (Reid, 2006, para 14). It may be surmised that one of the reasons for this was the introduction of the computerised OASys in 2001, since when it had taken longer to prepare a full PSR – a workload weighting of 6.5 hours (formerly 8 hours) compared to 1.5 hours for an FDR. This was because in addition to interviewing and writing time, numerous items of collected data must be entered into the computer (Mair et al, 2006; Whitehead, 2007, p 28).

However, during the summer of 2009, the latest version of eOASys was released (4.3.1). It introduced the concept of *layered assessments* so that the amount of detail required is determined by the type and tier of offender. For the less serious and risky offender, assessment demands are reduced because the strains placed upon eOASys are less. On the one hand, this adds weight to my concerns that a paucity of information militates against understanding and justice. On the other hand, staff time could be freed up to engage more fully and productively with people who offend, which could, in turn, rehabilitate the category of understanding (Weberian *verstehen*).

The triple 'S' agenda

The 'Simple, Speedy, Summary' (triple 'S') justice initiative (Home Office, 2006c), which began to influence the practices of magistrates' courts towards the end of 2007, was an attempt by government to introduce a more efficient modus operandi. This initiative was consistent with the principles of New Public Management committed to the 3Es and VfM. This agenda signalled a much greater emphasis upon dealing with cases expeditiously, thus reducing the average number of hearings before a case is dealt with from five/six to an expectation of one in guilty pleas. In pursuing this objective, the logical implication is a preference for FDRs and oral reports, rather than a full report adjourned for three weeks. The triple 'S' agenda may well facilitate simple, speedy and summary justice (whatever this means), but is this the same as social justice for people who offend (Roberts and McMahon, 2007)? The Ministry of Justice endorsed the triple

'S' agenda at the Magistrates' Association Annual General Meeting on 17/18 November 2008, and we should remind ourselves that the magistrates' courts deal with approximately 95% of all criminal cases in the criminal justice system of England and Wales.

Service Level Agreement

As a consequence of the emergence of NOMS since 2004, there was a SLA between the 10 regions and local area services that 40% of all reports should be FDRs. Additionally, in a document published by the Ministry of Justice during 2008 – 'Value for money delivery agreement' – it was stated that the ratio of FDRs to standard court reports should be improved. This was taken a step further in *Probation Circular 06/2009*, which reinforced the position that the FDR should become the default sentencing instrument in magistrates' courts by raising the SLA from 40% to 70% (National Probation Service, 2009). It can be extrapolated that the preparation of reports is weighted increasingly towards briefer formats. It should also be explained that even though there is a predilection for expedited reports, in certain circumstances, an adjournment for three weeks to prepare a full report could well be the judgement of probation staff, even when the court has asked for a short-format document. This is an important safeguard. It should also be noted that the business plan of the Teesside area service, for example, specified that for 2008/09, the SLA indicative values are £318 for a full report and £79 for an FDR. On the grounds of business efficiency and fiscal rectitude, the latter is a more attractive product than the former.

Offender Management Bill and Act

It is pertinent to allude to what was a crucial debate in the House of Commons (in 2007) on the Offender Management Bill (House of Commons Official Report, 2007). It was clarified by the Home Secretary that within the NOMS structure, the preparation of reports, in addition to the supervision of offenders and breach proceedings, will remain a probation task within the public sector. However, and tellingly, this state of affairs was guaranteed to last for three years when, because of contestability, the preparation of reports could become the responsibility of another organisation, perhaps within the private sector. If this was a vision of potential future developments in 2007, carried through beyond the next general election in 2010, then the historical association of the probation service providing a range of information to the courts would end. However, the political reconfigurations imposed by the rehabilitative revolution during 2010 to 2015 (see Chapter One) confirmed that probation will continue to write reports for courts, not the 21 CRCs.

Nevertheless, questions must be posed, issues raised and concerns expressed within the operational dynamics of the criminal justice system that are relevant to the changing nature of information being provided to sentencers, ostensibly driven by cost. One of the main areas of contention is the potential conflict between the legitimate goal of ensuring efficiency when allocating taxpayers' money to criminal justice, and pursuing ideals of criminal and social justice. Of course, these two objectives are not inherently incompatible, but, in certain circumstances, they could be. Even though the aforementioned *Probation Circular* stated that the three report formats are of *equal standing* as a basis for justifying sentencing decisions, it is difficult to support this position primarily because of differential content and quality. The comprehensive standard delivery report provided much more text-based information on offenders' background circumstances, thus providing a fuller basis for sentencing than FDR (tick box-driven) and oral formats. However, governments have made it clear that the deluxe version has become an expensive luxury; justice comes with a price tag.

There will be occasions when probation formulates the judgement, and then advises the court, that it is appropriate to prepare an FDR or oral report. Certain cases, of an uncomplicated nature, are indubitably suitable for the briefer format without diluting the pursuit of justice, doing what is deemed to be morally right for the offender, victim and sentencing outcome. Nevertheless, there will be occasions when a full report is required in the interests of justice. Consequently, the complex task of sentencing offenders involves more than routinely and proportionately matching offence seriousness with the sentencing bands contained in the Criminal Justice Act 2003, complying with an SLA to achieve 70% FDRs and making decisions to achieve efficiency savings. This is because sentencing is a moral issue existing alongside and informing its technical and legal requirements, which means thinking carefully about the right thing to do for each individual having regard to *all* the circumstances. This, in turn, has implications for the selection of report formats and requisite judgements about an offender's culpability, which is beginning to change, as Table 5.9 illustrates.

These data, gleaned from the Ministry of Justice probation statistics, disclose interesting comparisons between a 12% reduction in the full standard delivery report over the course of a year, but a 15% increase in FDRs and 101% increase in oral reports. A perusal of *Probation Statistics Quarterly Briefings*, since the beginning of 2007, reveals a clear shift in

Table 5.9: Criminal reports written by the Probation Service at magistrates' courts from Quarter 4, 2006 to Quarter 4, 2007, England and Wales

	Q4 2006	Q1 2007	Q2 2007	Q3 2007	Q4 2007	% change Q4 2007
SDRs	24,737	25,618	24,249	23,584	21,787	−12
FDRs	10,833	12,183	12,492	12,957	12,506	+15
Oral	2,585	3,278	3,401	4,011	5,197	+101

the fall of the standard PSR, and corresponding rise in FDRs and orals (eg Ministry of Justice, 2009). Additionally, the *Offender Management Statistics Quarterly Bulletin* for April–June 2013 contained limited data on reports: a decline in the overall number of reports but an increased use of the FDR.

My research found that 12 clerks and six magistrates indicated that they were concerned the current system was putting efficiency before justice. Some of these clerks can be heard saying:

> "It does sometimes seem that way. I think tick-box formats can always give that impression, that the answers are too narrow."

> "Yes it appears that way. It may be that offenders who have had an FDR prepared on them are given the most appropriate order for them; it may be coincidental; but there may be the risk that with a short-format report, that information has been missed."

> "I suppose you could see it like that, yes, because it comes across as a computerised tick box, not particularly about the individual."

> "Yes definitely. And for the victims, the whole thing gets lost in the urge to get work done quickly."

Moreover, the six magistrates expressed similar concerns that efficiency trumps justice, but the replies are more nuanced. One stated that FDRs are clearly about efficiency and others embellished:

> "I don't know; it's always a worry if the FDR is done fast and we don't get all the relevant information or whether it's just we ticked the box but there might be more to add

in that box. But when I've had a FDR, we have usually been able to sentence through it."

"I mean, for the vast majority, FDRs are the way to go and I think they do have sufficient information to make me feel that I can make a decision. I just worry, and there's a little bit of tension in me, that I might be missing something and that probation might miss something that I need to know."

"Oh gosh, possibly, but I don't know that I have any evidence to be able to back that up, but I think just a gut response to the question would be 'yes, I do think so' ... I feel that there is less personal information on FDRs.... Whereas obviously a more text-based standard delivery report is more flexible and there's an awful lot more that seems to go into that, I do understand that it takes longer to produce."

Alternatively, nine clerks expressed less concern about the potential conflict between efficiency and justice and a selection of comments included initial concerns expressed that this was justice on the cheap because of the tick-box format. However, "I think I am of the opinion that the way the justice system is being run, justice being seen to be done and delivered in a very short period of time, it is helpful". This does not necessarily compromise justice as it depends on how well they are written. The public has a right to expect speedy justice, and, again, written information contained in a full report will mitigate concerns: "I think it does still aim to achieve justice, but I think a lot of it is about speed". Finally, one clerk did not express a coherent view on the matter.

When turning to the 10 magistrates who expressed fewer concerns, it was stated:

"I can see the problems that there could be, but from my perspective, I feel that defendants should be dealt with as quickly as possible and I sometimes feel that adjournments for three weeks for a full report is too long and is causing them more anxiety and problems. Whereas if it can be done efficiently and without prejudice to the defendant as an FDR, I feel that is much better for the defendant and also for the courts."

Another magistrate stated that while they initially had concerns, they no longer did because "My view is that FDRs seem to be providing the kind of service that I am happy with". Also:

> "I'm not sure that the FDR does actually make that a more difficult thing to achieve. I think we are still getting enough information and we are still ending up with a recommendation, so that we can sentence on the report."

However, concerns were expressed about the tick boxes: there are tensions, but if probation staff are around to elaborate on the FDR in court, "then I don't think justice will suffer at the hands of targets". Also:

> "Yes, but I understand that we rely on the probation service to come back and tell us it is inappropriate for an FDR, so you would hope that the probation service would still do that and request a full report."

The remaining four magistrates' responses were that one was ambiguous about the nature of our discussion; another simply restated the problems with tick boxes; and the last two did not really answer. Therefore, there is a mixed picture in that 12 clerks and six magistrates indicated concerns; by contrast, nine clerks and 10 magistrates expressed fewer concerns with some of these recent modernising developments in probation.

Punitisation of reports

This was a specific concern at 'Northtown', illustrated by repeating the following statement, which surfaced during the course of this research and that we have already encountered. It is that "Teesside Probation Service proposes custody in a high percentage of PSRs – 5.2%. This is far higher than the national average of 2.7% and is the fourth highest in the country at proposing custody" (Teesside Probation Service, 2008). Moreover, and to reiterate, the context for the qualitative interviews during the period 2006/07 with representatives from criminal justice agencies working alongside the probation service was the cultural shift towards punishment. Accordingly, I wanted to understand if respondents perceived that probation reports had become more punitive. Interestingly, but not surprisingly given the preceding statement in the Business Plan, 14 clerks and nine magistrates said that they perceived what can be described as the punitisation of reports.

Illustrative comments from clerks are as follows. As to whether probation officers are more willing to accept no alternative to custody in certain cases, answers were as follows: "Yes, definitely, and obviously it must be a general feeling as I have it commented to me as well, by magistrates, they have observed that"; and "There was a time when probation never recommended prison, but now they do and that's after legislation stated that is what they are for, to recommend a penalty rather than just recommend a probation sentence". As to whether reports are now more realistic because they can recommend custody, one clerk replied: "Yes, but I don't altogether think that is a bad thing".

Similarly, some of the nine magistrates said:

> "Yes, I think it is because of a change of emphasis of the probation service, that you are no longer seen as advise, assist and befriend; you are now seen as recommending what is the correct punishment for society, for that offender [which will result in proposals for custody]."

Also, "Yes, things have changed; the probation service is more credible compared to previously when recommendations could be unrealistic". One magistrate was unaware of more recommendations for custody but made the comment that "community sentences with requirements are more punitive and harder". Also, "Historically, there always used to be laughter that a report would never ever say custody was appropriate for a person. That does actually happen nowadays, so more punitive, more honest", and "That has definitely been a big climate change", from not recommending custody to doing so, and "I think reports are more credible because of that". Finally, proposals for custody are "a good thing" because of the injection of realism.

By contrast, the following comment is typical of the seven 'no' responses from clerks: "Haven't noticed that; it's very rare that you come across a recommendation for custody". Additionally, eight magistrates perceived that reports have not become more punitive: "No it's very, very rare that you actually recommend custody and I can understand why. I mean custody doesn't work anyway, well I don't think it does". Furthermore:

> "At one time, you would never ever see a custodial sentence recommended. I know I think only on one occasion have I actually seen it in the recent past, so although I know they

are making those recommendations now, I wouldn't say, from my experience, that there are a lot of them coming in."

This was not the case in the reports that another magistrate had been reading, deemed no bad thing because "we have to look forward to where we can be looking towards rehabilitation rather than a sentence of custody".

When reflecting on the reasons for such differential responses among respondents, it should be clarified that there are 14 courts sitting within the 'Northtown' Magistrates' Court building that function during the morning session (10am to 1pm) and during the afternoon (from 2.15pm until the business of the day is completed, which could be between 5pm and 6pm). Furthermore, clerks and magistrates form part of a court rota system, so that even though all 14 courts could be sitting concurrently each day, probation reports do not find their way into all of them. During the course of the research, there was a designated court during the afternoon session for dealing with all those cases that had been adjourned for a probation report. Accordingly, only one clerk and three magistrates, out of 20 clerks and 60 magistrates on duty, would be reading reports. In observing this organisational phenomenon, it is also possible that during each day's business at 'Northtown', probation reports could find their way into other courts, notwithstanding designated afternoon courts. Consequently, it may be surmised that there was differential exposure to reports among magistrates and clerks, which accounts for these variable findings. After allowing for court dynamics and contingencies, I draw the conclusion from this part of the research that probation practices were evidentially different to previous years. This was supported by official statistics that generated concerns and called for remedial action prior to receiving a share of the additional £40 million allocated to probation. Finally, one clerk was unsure and the remaining three magistrates did not specifically address the issue under consideration.

Verstehen and the art of probation

One area of practice explored with clerks and magistrates was: are probation reports demonstrating *less understanding* of offenders' personal and social circumstances? The somewhat slippery but important notion of understanding is arguably the distinctive contribution of probation work to the dialectics of criminal justice, primarily through the medium of court reports. Before judgements are formulated and sentencing decisions made about offending episodes, relevant factors should be collected and pondered by an organisation trained to interpret the vagaries of human conduct. In fact, the qualities looked for within probation officers were once described as "flexibility of mind and a capacity for listening to and understanding others" (Jarvis, 1974, p 268). This, of course, is a complex task, but complexity should not preclude engagement with a task associated with the pursuit of criminal and social justice (Whitehead, 2007).

Having said that, the modernised context is hardly conducive to facilitating a framework of understanding because of: the interpretive limits imposed by the tenets of neo-classical and administrative criminology (Garland, 2001); discernible shifts in the rationale of probation, as outlined in Chapter One; greater emphasis placed upon individual responsibility, associated with a punitive culture engendered by neoliberal ideology and the strictures of New Public Management; and a politics of condemnation rather than understanding, which has been a feature of criminal justice policy since 1997 (and before). The politics of coercive imposition and disavowal has fashioned a probation system disposed more to the bureaucratic management and punishment of offenders, than to an insightful sociological understanding of the human condition under transformed politico-economic conditions. This radical transformation represents the organisational logic of the neoliberal capitalist order. Garland and Sparks (2000, p 17) have stated that:

> The posture of 'understanding' the offender was always a demanding and difficult attitude, more readily attained by Liberal elites unaffected by crime or else by professional groups who make their living out of it. This posture increasingly gives way to that of condemning criminals and demanding that they be punished and controlled.

Understanding is an important organisational variable for probation work, but it is under pressure to deliver, as the following illustrates.

The bigger picture

As alluded to in previous chapters, the Keynesian post-war settlement enabled the political establishment to intervene in socio-economic matters to mediate between the competing interests of capital and labour, promoting inclusivity and solidarity through a social-democratic welfare state (Garland, 2001; Cavadino and Dignan, 2006). When this began to break down under the weight of economic turbulence during the 1970s. the rise of the neoliberal order had implications for criminal justice (Whitehead and Crawshaw, 2012). Neoliberalism has advanced to reconstruct a grand narrative of individual responsibility, fearful competition, private sector over public sector solutions, coupled with New Public Management (Leys, 2003), in addition to explaining offending as neo-classical rational choice (Harvey, 2005; Garland, 2001; Young, 1999, 2007; Wacquant, 2008, 2009).

This narrative vies with an alternative analysis located within the political economy of crime exemplified by Bonger's (1969 [1916]) criminology. The Chicago School (Smith, 1988), and Robert Merton (1968), located offending within the social structure. Taylor, Walton and Young (1973), Hall et al (1978) and Taylor (1997) argued that capitalism is criminogenic, which demands a fully social theory of deviance reaching beyond the trope of individual responsibility, culpability and punishment. This holistic sociological analysis, intellectually opposed to a reductionism that looks no further than blaming offenders, reveals how macroeconomic factors are associated with crime due to the 'extent and impact of unemployment, poverty and inequality following the collapse of the post-war Keynesian, welfare state compromise, and the social tsunami of neo-liberalism' (Reiner, 2007a, p 164). Similar points are advanced in Harvey's (2005, p 80) analysis, and a Cabinet Office (2006) document that acknowledged the relationship between adverse economic conditions and fluctuations in crime.

This body of macro-theorising is relevant for probation practice because the process of sentencing, to which it has contributed for over a century, proceeds according to parameters established by legislation and national standards, which take account of numerous variables. Some of these variables, alluded to earlier, draw attention to offence seriousness, previous convictions and aggravating and mitigating factors, which are incorporated within OASys. It is the principle of offender mitigation that should draw the courts into reflecting upon the personal histories and wider social circumstances of individuals appearing before them, historically brought to their attention by information contained within a full *social enquiry* report. This constitutes a challenge to reach beyond the offence (*What* has the offender done?), notions of individual responsibility and rational choice, to consider behavioural repertoires associated with, and sometimes a rational response to, adverse socio-economic factors. On a daily basis, the probation service, other court personnel and now the 21 CRCs come into contact with people from adverse social backgrounds, educational and employment disadvantages, differential life chances, relative deprivation, and associated alcohol and drugs problems. Such matters are well documented in the literature and constitute the staple ingredients of probation practice (Walker and Beaumont, 1981; Stewart and Stewart, 1993; Stewart et al, 1994; Wilkinson and Pickett, 2009).

If the principle is reaffirmed that decision-making ought to take account of the social circumstances of offenders, and that the pursuit of criminal and social justice should be informed by such dynamic consideration, then the weight placed upon FDRs and oral reports may not always be conducive to just and right outcomes. The lurking danger is in superficially skirting over salient background information that should be brought to the courts' attention by probation. It is not possible to reduce complex human behaviours to tick-box formats completed within a couple of hours because of fiscal constraints. Sometimes, the stories of people's lives require careful analysis and diligent recounting. Therefore, to return to our question, *are reports demonstrating less understanding of the lives of offenders*? It is of interest to observe that according to nine clerks, probation reports are demonstrating *less understanding* of offenders. There is a concern that tick boxes entail less background information and "less feeling for how the person has ended up where they are": "On the old-style full PSRs, I would say 'no', I haven't noticed that, but maybe a little on the FDRs, yes"; and "I think the full PSR still looks at the offender as well as the offence, but again I think that's possibly a problem with the FDRs, they don't look at the personal circumstances of the offender so much". Other voices commented that there have been good reports, but the FDR cannot get into the issues as well as a full report. There are issues with the FDR format in that they provide little time for the offender to open up to probation staff. One clerk said that "There used to be a very strong emphasis towards the individual, explanations for offending and underlying problems with the offender's circumstances. It has changed to a degree; they are looking more at the offence".

Only two magistrates said that reports are demonstrating less understanding:

> "The full PSR, done properly, does cover the ground that the Social Enquiry Report used to, but yes, by and large, there is less of that and more emphasis on offence analysis."

> "Not in an SDR [standard delivery report], but I think in an FDR.... Going back to the FDR, there is the danger that there could be issues with the individual concerned that don't come to light so the longer you take, the longer time you have to prepare the report."

By contrast, 10 clerks and 14 magistrates indicated that reports are certainly not compromising on the principle of understanding. Illustrative comments from clerks were:

> "I think that depends on the author of the report. Some reports we have had have been excellent where they have really looked at the offender's personal circumstances and how they can be helped. Other reports you sometimes feel that they have picked bits, set phrases, that they think fit that person."

Additionally, "I don't think they have changed that much in that respect" – reports still look at background issues and are not demonstrating less understanding. When hearing from magistrates it was said that, first:

> "I don't think so; I think that is one baby that we haven't thrown out with the bath water. I think we still have a considerable amount of understanding of social deprivation, of social problems, that lead to offending and I don't think that we have necessarily thrown that out when we lean more to punishment or enforceability. I think we still have that but it is more measured and tempered with public protection issues."

Second, "Overall I would say the vast majority of reports that we get are full of detail. They seem to have become extended to what they were". Third:

> "I have to be perfectly honest, the reports that I have had lately have been excellent and there's been a fine balance between how their lifestyle has got them to where they are and what the offence is. So it's a fine balance and I think it is important that we do know some of the deeper structure of people's lives."

Fourth, "I still think you have a very similar level of understanding of the offender's personal and social circumstances. I think reports have got better". Finally, another said:

> "I think it is more balanced than it used to be. I think the digging, the antecedent history, more importantly the social background perhaps, used to be the major part of some

reports and now we are getting a more balanced report about what they have done, why they did it and even what should be done about it."

Nevertheless, one magistrate stated somewhat exceptionally: "certainly the opposite. I find it more for the offender than punishment now. Personally, I don't think that some reports tally with the offence or their behaviour". In the last analysis, three clerks did not elaborate, and one of the four magistrates who found it difficult to express a clear view stated that it is "difficult to make a judgement" on this matter.

It is possible to argue that the analytical category of *human understanding* pursued within the context of writing court reports is associated with the exercise of discretion, differential treatment and responses. It is possible for the exercise of discretion to produce malign outcomes, as illustrated by questionable sentencing practices (Freiberg and Gelb, 2008). By contrast, it can be construed as a positive factor when exercised in adverse social circumstances. Hudson argued for discretion that facilitates leniency in sentencing practices because of poverty. Similarly, Tonry alludes to social adversity mitigation, which would provide sentencers with the licence to have regard to the 'particular difficulties faced by impoverished, unemployed, and otherwise disadvantaged offenders' (quoted in Zedner, 2004, p 192; see also Cook, 2006; Roberts and McMahon, 2007). Indubitably, this is a contentious issue, both professionally and politically, in circumstances where there has been a profound cultural shift of emphasis towards the law-abiding majority rather than focusing on the needs of offenders. Exercising discretion can be seen as making excuses and condoning offending, but it is also informed by the principle of understanding, which can establish a basis for advancing arguments for greater leniency. There are serious problems reconciling these competing interests, but probation work has a moral duty to operate within a framework of understanding, and to exercise discretion if it wants to make a serious contribution to criminal and social justice. However, to repeat, the modernised context in the form of NOMS and the privatisation of the probation system will make this task harder to achieve. At this point, I want to turn again to NOMS by addressing the subject of contestability, which was important in 2007 and even more so between 2010 and 2015.

The National Offender Management Service and contestability – court clerks

Table 5.10: Clerks' understanding of NOMS

	Number	%
No understanding	11	50.0
Some understanding	9	40.9
Clearer understanding	2	9.1
Total	22	100.0

When probing the awareness and understanding that court clerks had of NOMS, remarkably, 11 (50%) declared no understanding of the new organisational structure that brought prisons and probation closer together after 2003, or had considered potential implications. A further nine disclosed some understanding and two were clearer in their grasp of NOMS. When hearing from the 11 clerks who had *no understanding* of NOMS, typical yet surprising comments were: "Never heard of it"; "No idea. I don't know what NOMS is"; "I don't think I know a great deal about it; and it's not something that we are involved in". Next, for those nine who expressed some understanding, we hear: "The new name for probation"; "I don't know, probably the governing body of the probation service"; "I assumed that was a fancy umbrella name for the whole of the probation service. I've heard of it, yes, but it's never really registered to be honest"; and "It's the probation service. That's my understanding of it; it's just a new name for it". Finally, two clerks with a clearer understanding stated as follows:

> "My understanding is that it's a service in its own right and comprises the probation service and the prison service. I'm not sure if anyone else is involved but it's to manage offenders both in the community and in prison and following release and it's therefore both those agencies combined in effect."

> "It's a service that incorporates probation, the prison service, others, and basically it is a service that joins up and manages someone from the time they are sentenced to the time that they finish their sentence. A joined-up service if you like, including one or two different agencies."

Furthermore, I thought it would be of interest to find out if any of the 22 court clerks had heard of contestability. The findings are equally instructive, as Table 5.11 suggests.

Given that NOMS, with its commitment to contestability, would have radical implications for the delivery of offender services going forward from 2007, it was surprising that only one clerk was familiar with the term: "Yes, it's another word for competition" (correct answer).

Table 5.11: Clerks and contestability

	Number	%
Yes	1	4.5
No	21	95.5
Total	22	100.0

The National Offender Management Service and contestability – magistrates

When turning to the 20 magistrates, it was discovered that 12 of them expressed no understanding of this significant organisational development, but that four had some understanding, as one stated, it is "another name for probation". By contrast, the remaining four were clearer that the term incorporates probation and prison. One commented:

Table 5.12: Magistrates' understanding of NOMS

	Number	%
No understanding	12	60.0
Some understanding	4	20.0
Clearer understanding	4	20.0
Total	20	100.0

"My understanding is that it has been created within the Home Office, three or four years ago now, to bring together probation and prison services and principally with a need for I think the phrase is end-to-end offender management. It has also created a regional structure in order to do so."

Again, when turning to whether magistrates had heard of contestability, the findings in Table 5.13 are surprising.

From Table 5.13, we can observe that four magistrates said that they had heard of contestability (compared to only one court clerk), one of whom acknowledged that it means work that could be provided by another body or services. The one I located

Table 5.13: Magistrates and contestability

	Number	%
Yes	4	20.0
No	15	75.0
Qualified	1	5.0
Total	20	100.0

in the qualified category said that "I've heard of it, but I'm not quite sure what it entails". The remaining 15 said that they had not heard of contestability. One of these 15 proceeded to comment that "If it's actually a buzzword, it's not quite clicking". Another commented incorrectiy, and bizarrely, that "Well, yes, where someone is not happy with a report, or an action within court, they have the right to contest. Is this right?". Again, it is surprising, but also disconcerting, that there is such a lack of awareness of NOMS and the implications of contestability for probation and the operation of the courts. As I proceed towards the end of this research-based chapter, I want to include some final material that emerged from talking to the respondents about how they saw the future of the probation service. First, clerks should be allowed to speak for themselves.

Last word on the future of probation from clerks

It was acknowledged during the course of the interviews conducted 10 years after New Labour came to power, and three years before the rehabilitation revolution of 2010–15, that even though the future was contingent upon political decisions outside their control, there were concerns that focused on the rationale of targets and the considerable pressure on probation. Due to these pressures, one clerk stated that probation should be split "so that you've got, on one side, the more traditional approach and then one that is more punitive and monitoring of the more serious offenders". This clerk was unaware that her suggestion echoed, to some degree, the thesis of Robert Harris (1980), alluded to in a previous chapter. Other voices of concern were:

> "I will have to be slightly negative and say that I can see services being led down the path which is controlled by financial constraints and by the need to meet targets, which I don't think the probation service and the criminal justice system as a whole is all about. It's the same with the clerks, we are very much pushed not to grant adjournments, not to do this, not to allow that, whereas in reality, in the interests of justice, you should be allowing it and you should be doing x, y and z. We are criticised at meetings when we don't meet our targets and it also has funding implications if we don't meet our targets and I suspect the probation services are probably under the same pressures. Really, I think that the probation team that work at the courts are extremely helpful, really pleasant, excellent at their job despite the fact

that they are put under a lot of pressure and the majority of the reports that are written are really good and I don't have any problems with the probation service at all, I think they are very helpful."

This was a revealing comment from a court clerk who had been working at 'Northtown' for over 20 years. Next, we hear that:

"I think if you continue to go down the road of increased government interference, the justice system both in terms of the courts, particularly lower courts such as magistrates and a body like the probation service, will lose its independence and will gradually lose the values that have made the justice system in this country so good. It's very strange and I would imagine that the same is happening to you as is happening to other public service bodies. I can definitely see it happening with us."

It was also stated:

"Well, sadly, it's going to depend on politics and I feel it's quite difficult to predict. As soon as there is a change of government, there is a change of policy, a change of ideas. Without a change of government, there's a change of Prime Minister, so I wouldn't like to predict. We seem to go in cycles of clamping down on punishment I suspect, lengthening prison sentences and perhaps recommending prison more often and then, of course, it swings the other way and it looks at a whole new way of managing offenders in the community. I really wouldn't like to predict which way it will go."

Concerns included that there is going to be more of the same: prisons overcrowded, pressure to keep more people out of custody and so probation will be more overworked. Furthermore:

"I suppose with the set-out of reports and things, I see it as being unfortunately more computerised and more people in a big building somewhere rather than coming to court and actually physically being there to speak to people and help people. I mean, I hope it won't happen but I see that it is more tick boxes than actually getting behind why somebody's committing offences."

Then again:

"Well, I think pretty much the way it has been at present (and over the last five years) but it is becoming, and I'm sorry if I keep repeating it ... I don't want to say punishment as in sending people to prison but punishment in the community."

Also mentioned were: that there could be new community penalties; probation changing and moving back to a more social work-based service; and a lament for the dilution of contact between probation and court and the severing of these links. Also, the introduction of NOMS and privatisation are seen as a retrograde step:

"I think you have all this highly trained pool of people and certainly the ones I come across seem very effective, and they should just be allowed to get on with the job and they shouldn't be sidetracked into punishment. If they want people to punish, use a different organisation and use probation for what they were originally set up for, leaving other people to do the punishment. So that is my opinion."

This constitutes yet another reference to the separation of care and control in the work of Robert Harris. Therefore, a melange of concerns were articulated in relation to time constraints and resources, chasing targets, pressures from government, constant change, bureaucratic routines, more punishment and the loss of professionalism. However, no one could have predicted what would happen between 2010 and 2015.

Last word from magistrates

Concerns were raised by magistrates when turning to the future beyond 2007 about: privatisation and contestability; more prisons being built; and concerns about resources and staff run off their feet, with one implication being that members of staff would not "get a proper chance to build relationships with people who would certainly benefit". This was an insightful comment. Additionally, disquiet was expressed about 'softer' sentences: "I have no confidence that the Ministry of Justice is going to do what society wants". However, then again:

"My concern is that it becomes too target-driven, as I've referred to earlier, that can be at the expense of a professional approach that might need more time. So I worry about professional standards being maintained as resources become tighter."

Finally, there was a desire to retain flexibility in circumstances of national standards and targets and the danger of too much central control. Therefore, there are similarities between the concerns of magistrates and court clerks as they looked ahead.

Conclusion

As suggested in previous chapters, bodies of social theory, personalist impulses and moral sensibilities facilitate a critical exploration and explanation of what modernised and transformed probation has become since 1997. Additionally, this chapter provokes a challenging response on what it ought to be through assimilating the views of solicitors, court clerks, magistrates, barristers and judges. This research, which I conducted nearly a decade into the criminal justice politics of New Labour, represents a slice of criminal justice history at an important juncture. It disturbed the surface of events to excavate, theoretically and empirically, political impositions and organisational transformations from the perspective of those institutions existing alongside probation. If Chapter Four put to work theories and sensibilities assembled earlier in the book, Chapter Five adds another layer of empirical complexity. The final chapter, to which we now turn, re-evaluates the conclusions contained in the first edition by assimilating the complementary themes of modernisation and transformation.

Notes

[1]   It should be acknowledged that there is a paucity of published research on defence solicitors and magistrates' court clerks. By contrast, there is more research data on magistrates, barristers and judges. See, for example, Brown (1991) and Gelsthorpe and Raynor (1995); see also relevant Home Office Research Studies that have been published over a number of years, Noaks and Wincup (2004) and King and Wincup (2007).

[2]   The first stage of this research project involved interviewing solicitors at 'Northtown'. For further details, see Whitehead (2007, ch 5), where these findings are presented in full.

[3]   Ethical issues are significant when undertaking empirical research and are touched upon in the introduction to the current chapter. For further information on this subject, see, for example, Dohan (2003, p 241), when undertaking ethnographic research in the US.

[4] For additional information on the ethnic composition of the magistracy, one can be directed to the following publication: *Magistrate* (2007), 63(5). Furthermore, it should be acknowledged that there were just over 30,000 magistrates in post when the research was conducted in 2006/07, and some progress made towards diversity. In 2002, the percentage of magistrates from black and minority ethnic backgrounds was just over 6%, but by 2006, this had risen to approximately 7.3%. Some recent figures from the Ministry of Justice confirm that in 2014, there were 22,160 magistrates in England and Wales, 7,110 fewer than 2009.

SIX

Modernising monstrosities and transformational traumas: social theory, criminal justice and morality

Introduction

The first four chapters chronologically elongated and reconstructed the modernising transformations in probation and criminal justice that occurred between 1997 and 2010, and then 2010 and 2015. These chapters include a refined and extended grid of theoretical reference points that are put to work for the purpose of analysis and critique. Also, within the historical time frame of New Labour, opportunities were presented to research probation within one local criminal justice system in the north-east of England. The research chapter is retained to rectify what is a paucity of empirical research on solicitors, clerks, magistrates, barristers and judges. The first section of the final chapter reprises the period under review before assimilating the research findings. I also incorporate some concluding reflections prior to refining the task of theorising the criminal justice system.

Probation and criminal justice, 1997–2015

There have been occasions since 1945 when the term 'modernisation' has been applied within the UK (Marr, 2008). Nevertheless, it acquired an exalted status under New Labour and is synonymous with a political phenomenon that emerged during the 1990s, stimulated by Clinton Democratic politics in the US. Previously, it was acknowledged how the term was applied to developments extending throughout the whole public sector, which includes the criminal justice system. Let us reprise some of these modernising and transformational features.

Modernisation signalled a discernible shift in criminal justice policy to 'old' Labour, which had provided an explanatory framework that accommodated compensatory social welfare and help towards rehabilitation. A new compass bearing was taken towards a muscular approach, which enabled New Labour modernisers to compete with the Conservatives on law and order. However, there was a contradiction in New Labour's soul because even though criminal justice had been reconfigured in a more punitive direction, the Social Exclusion Unit and the Cabinet Office Strategy Unit acknowledged the link between adverse socio-economic conditions created by periodic downturns in capitalist markets and property offences (Newburn, 2007, p 55). This explains why New Labour addressed child poverty and introduced the New Deal to assist young people into work. It also established the Sure Start programme to benefit disadvantaged families.

Modernisation was manifested in fast-tracking young people through the youth justice system, reforming the Crown Prosecution Service and the police, and introducing anti-social behaviour orders (ASBOs), which criminalised lower-level forms of disorder. Modernisation resonated with the expansion of surveillance technology and a torrential flow of new criminal legislation (Auld, 2001; Carter, 2007). A change in penal philosophy signalled by the Criminal Justice Act 2003 ensured that sentencing would become incrementally tougher for persistent offending. This undermined the just desserts approach of the Criminal Justice Act 1991. There was a war being waged against crime, the fight taken to the enemy within an atmosphere of zero tolerance and the axis tilted towards victims and witnesses, which rebalanced the system. One of the clearest indications of a radical transformation in penal policy is the expansion of the prison system. Between 1993 and 2012, the prison population in England and Wales increased by 41,800 to 86,000 (Ministry of Justice, 2013e). At the end of December 2015, it stood at 85,641 – 81,735 male and 3,906 female prisoners – and is projected to rise to 90,000 by 2020 (Ministry of Justice, 2014). As the 2010 general election approached, there was little to choose between Labour and Conservative approaches to criminal justice.

Modernisation signalled profound cultural transformations in probation, illustrated by the creation of a national service in 2001. Moreover, the centralisation of command and control established by the National Probation Service (NPS) was quickly followed by the National Offender Management Service (NOMS) during 2003/04. The latter created the politically imposed conditions for a mixed economy of offender provision (*contestability*), which penetrated deeply after 2010 on the platform of competition, marketisation and privatisation. The NPS and NOMS rerouted probation into the circuits of bureaucratic centralism and punitive controlism (Burnett et al, 2007). Although rehabilitative language remains part of NOMS, modernisation repositioned the organisation towards the punitive-controlling end of the care–control continuum.[1]

The conjuncture of political impositions and media representations elevated crime within the national consciousness as a phenomenon for which individuals are primarily accountable, rather than behavioural disturbances under neoliberal conditions. Accordingly, the war on crime is fought primarily against people from certain groups marked by the stigmata of vulnerability, poverty and disadvantage to create the relegated urban outcast, rather than fighting the differential impacts of neoliberal capitalist structures and attendant inequalities (Cavadino and Dignan, 2006; Reiner, 2007a; Wacquant, 2008, 2009; Wilkinson and Pickett, 2009). Macro-structures are not conducive to creating a climate of trust, loyalty and respect between people in local communities. The Respect campaign was foregrounded in the strategic front line as the solution to curing behavioural problems associated with crime (Pratt, 2007, p 121). Probation was rigorously modernised after 1997, politically manipulated, then marketised and privatised after 2010 to exist in the new dispensation established by political fiat. Nevertheless, there were voices of disquiet from within the criminal justice system prior to the rehabilitation revolution.

Respondents' doubts and challenges

The significance of the research findings gleaned from solicitors, court clerks and magistrates, and to a lesser extent barristers and judges, is that *at certain points* modernising developments under New Labour received some support. By contrast, there were concerns at the way the system had evolved after 1997. In fact, there were doubts about, and challenges to, modernisation erupting from a pre-modern direction.

The *quantitative insights* reveal some points of similarity between solicitors, clerks and magistrates on their operational knowledge of probation, which should demonstrate an understanding of offending, an awareness of personal and social circumstances, promoting criminal and social justice, and keeping people out of custody. Nevertheless, there are differential responses to other variables elucidated in Table 5.3 in Chapter Five. It is clear that the politics of modernisation created a climate of robust responses, bureaucratic targets, offenders categorised as units of risk and rigorous enforcement procedures, sculpting a musculature bulked up on punitive steroids. By contrast, there is evidence for retaining the services of an organisation associated with benign rather than punitive instincts in response to complex human problems. Accordingly, there is more to criminal justice than punishment, and respondents were involved in a complex, not always consistent, conversation with probation. Table 5.4 is a more limited data set, yet it provides further support for a number of *pre-modern* features among barristers and judges.

Interviews with clerks and magistrates constitute a rich source of *qualitative responses*. It emerged that the purpose of probation retains a rehabilitative element, complemented by providing a service to people requiring help, assistance and remedial education, as well as engaging with the dominant language of punishment. To some degree, the information gleaned from respondents reinforced what are *mixed* messages emanating from the tick-box data tables. Importantly, probation has a dual role because of its responsibilities towards the courts and offenders.

When turning to reports, a critical function throughout probation history that it still retains after the rehabilitative revolution, there were concerns contingent upon the simple, speedy, summary (triple 'S') and New Public Management agendas. Until this research was conducted in 2006/07, there was a Service Level Agreement for probation to produce 40% of reports in the fast delivery report (FDR) format. By 2009, this had risen to 70% (National Probation Service, 2009). In a climate of recession (late 2008/09), there were mounting pressures to anoint the FDR as the default document in the magistrates' court. The rationale of the probation report is to assist the court to determine the most suitable sentence, which relies upon furnishing *all relevant information* on the background of offenders. For nine clerks and nine magistrates, "background information" defined the rationale of reports. However, the focus upon fast delivery compromised this objective, which has serious implications for achieving criminal and social justice. This remains pertinent for magistrates' courts, which deal with 95% of criminal cases. The FDR, or oral stand-down, indubitably reduces costs and expedites answering '*What have you done?*' questions, yet it contributes little to exploring the more sociologically probing '*Why have you done it?*'. Interestingly, 12 clerks and 11 magistrates did not anticipate problems with FDRs. By contrast, eight clerks and six magistrates raised insightful concerns by acknowledging that they only scratch the surface, appear rushed and exemplify chasing central government targets. It is possible to tick all the boxes and achieve the targets, yet fail to engage effectively with offenders. Similarly, all the boxes can be ticked within the National Health Service (NHS) and fail patients.[2]

The report problemmatic should be confronted head on as the FDR, or oral stand-down, represents a false document, a system canard, specifically because of its incomplete methodology and self-evident inadequacy, being incomplete and inadequate because it abstracts and truncates offending and offenders in the material interest of the 3Es (economy, efficiency and effectiveness). It promotes poor probation practice by stating the obvious yet concealing the vital. There were tensions between the pursuit of efficiency within the New Public Management agenda and achieving just outcomes. It was also clear that there was a noticeable shift in direction towards FDRs and away from full pre-sentence reports (PSRs): 12 clerks and six magistrates expressed concern that recent developments in the criminal justice system amounted to elevating business efficiency above the notion of justice. By contrast, nine clerks and 10 magistrates articulated less concern about this growing tension.

There was some evidence for the punitisation of reports at 'Northtown', supported by evidence supplied by central government (in the Teesside Area Business Plan for 2008/09 [Teesside Probation Service, 2008]): 14 clerks and nine magistrates perceived that this was the case in proposals for custody and punishment in the community. Then again, other respondents were less convinced. Furthermore, the notion of *understanding* (Weberian *verstehen*) is under pressure. Arguably, the macro-context of neoliberalism is highly pertinent for the criminal justice system because it provides an explanatory context for offending episodes. To some degree, the Offender Assessment System (OASys) facilitates an exploration of offenders' lives, from personal and family factors to wider social circumstances. However, we saw how the prevailing culture of FDRs, in addition to the triple 'S' and New Public Management agendas, undermined an insightful exploration of individual stories: nine clerks and two magistrates said that probation was demonstrating *less* understanding of offenders. Alternatively, 10 clerks and 14 magistrates indicated that probation was not diluting the contribution made to understanding people who offend. Intriguingly, version 4.3.1 of OASys, released in the summer of 2009, implied that probation staff would spend less time processing computerised data through the mechanism of layered assessments.

It is disquieting that although NOMS had been in existence since 2003/04, few respondents had any meaningful grasp of what it was, or its likely implications. This finding constituted a cause for concern in 'Northtown', particularly after assimilating the rehabilitation revolution between 2010 and 2015, which normalised competition between the public, private and voluntary sectors, internal markets, and privatisation (see Deering and Feilzer, 2015). Contestability during 2006/07 became fearful competition during 2010–15, which reflects and reproduces the organisational logic of neoliberal political economy and New Public

Management. NOMS was critical to the future of criminal justice but only one clerk and four magistrates had heard of contestability.

When reflecting upon *what probation had become* under New Labour, stimulated by the empirical findings, some respondents restored a semblance of balance to the operational dynamics of criminal justice by retaining, if not reinstating, pre-modern features. Rutherford's (1994) *Criminal Justice and the Pursuit of Decency* included interviews with 28 practitioners between 1988 and 1991. The comments by a Chief Probation Officer are worth repeating:

> I have no qualms that we are part of the criminal justice system. But our prime task is to be a social work service 'core', and that buys in a set of principles which we do not abandon because other bits of the criminal justice process find them uncomfortable. (Rutherford, 1994, p 153)

Rutherford concluded that hope lies with practitioners if the criminal justice system is to be oriented around a set of principles that can be classified as decent and humane. However, since 1997, particularly after 2001, and now 2010–15, this has become increasingly difficult because of inbalances injected into the system by the political class.

The great *un*balancing act under New Labour

The comment from a barrister with over 25 years' experience at 'Northtown' should be repeated:

> "The probation service has changed beyond recognition over the course of the last 10 years. The shift of the probation service has left the criminal justice system unbalanced. There is too much emphasis on punishment and a void where there should be an agency dedicated to values of befriending and assisting."

In an undated message to staff during 2008, Jack Straw, Secretary of State, and Permanent Secretary Suma Chakrabarti (Ministry of Justice Priorities and Performance and Efficiency Programme) clarified that the primary purpose of the Ministry of Justice is to secure justice, protect the public and punish lawbreakers. There must be justice for the law-abiding and victims of crime and the message suggested a further bout of modernisation could be required, without any hint of future transformational activity.

After serious reflection on what occurred after 1997, and taking account of some of the findings in Chapter Five, rebalancing *un*balanced the criminal justice system. Barbara Hudson (1987) reminded us that the pursuit of justice should not be equated with punishment. Additionally, justice is not necessarily found patiently waiting at the end of modernising reflexes, constant change, expanding organisational bureaucracies or transforming probation into a power to punish. Justice may not even be located in the direction of expanding the criminal justice estate, tinkering with penal policy, building new prisons, heightening its emotional tone or reducing the cultural divide between probation and prisons. Instead, dialogue surrounding criminal and social justice must take account of the circumstances of offenders, including the macro-context of neoliberalism and its differential impacts on individuals, families and communities.[3]

The lives of people who offend, and who appear before magistrates and judges, should be understood within a holistic explanatory context. By doing so, it is logical to argue that there should be an organisation charged with the responsibility to explore and explain factors of relevance to sentencers. Modernising impositions have weakened this critical faculty, acutely illustrated by the changing nature of reports by fiscal constraints. Accordingly, rebalancing has *un*balanced the system in the direction of punishment rather than enhancing the category of insightful understanding, which is necessary for making careful judgements about people who offend. Probation should be: drawing attention to human casualties not compromising its historic mission; critically challenging the rationale of punitive excesses; a signpost towards alternatives to custody and punishment rather than a weathervane that catches the prevailing political wind; and maintaining the professional capacity to engage with offenders to recount their life stories. Modernising processes, gilded by hideous transformations, have undermined these organisational functions.

Rebalancing *un*balanced the relationship between probation and prisons. It was surprising that most court clerks and magistrates, but also solicitors, did not have a sufficient grasp of NOMS, particularly contestability. Additionally, NOMS was restructured during 2008/09 to transform the two organisations by electing prison the dominant partner. This can be recounted as follows. First, there were 17 members of the Ministry of Justice ministerial team and Corporate Management Board in London. However, there was no probation representation at the highest strategic and decision-making level by 2010. Second, a parliamentary answer to Neil Gerrard MP on 21 January 2009 revealed that there were 113 former probation employees working within NOMS headquarters, compared to 3,445 prison service staff. In other words, on the brink of the transforming rehabilitation agenda, probation accounted for only 3.2% of the total staffing complement in what was described as the 'new agency' (information contained in the National Association of Probation Officers briefing paper on 9 March 2009). Third, roles and responsibilities were rationalised at a regional level by coalescing prison area managers and regional offender managers into the post of Director of Offender Manager (DOM). Most of the 10 DOMs were appointed by February–March 2009 but only one had a background in probation – Roger Hill, who left his post as Director of Probation, which was not replaced, to become the first DOM of the South-East region.

From the highest strategic level (NOMS headquarters), then into the 10 regions, not forgetting that only approximately 50% of front-line employees were professionally trained, probation was under-represented in a modernised organisation dominated by the prison by 2010. This made it difficult, if not impossible, for probation to argue its case and defend its principles, values, history, culture and distinctive contribution to the criminal justice system. The point where probation and prison overlap is when prisoners are being prepared for release into the community. Accordingly, the primary tasks of these organisations are self-evidently different as the prison system is concerned with humane containment, while probation is concerned with the supervision of offenders in the community. Both sets of staff require different skills when working with prisoners in conditions of secure confinement and offenders on community orders in conditions of freedom. Of course, there are points of interaction, but the primary tasks are fundamentally different and it is absurd to think otherwise. Therefore, bringing both organisations closer to each other within one organisational structure constituted an affront to logic, and a disturbing display of ignorance by the Ministry of Justice that it repeatedly compounds. For example, during the autumn of 2015, the probation training scheme pursuant to the rehabilitation revolution – 'Community Justice Learning' – was reviewed by Martin Narey, a non-executive director in the Ministry of Justice. I am probably oversensitive and decidedly too picky, but I am not aware that he was either trained or worked as a probation officer, supervised offenders, or prepared reports. In other words, if you have not done the job that you have been asked to review, where is the legitimacy? Why not come clean: 'I am not equipped for the task'.

What should be clear by now is that modernisation between 1997 and 2010 constructed the politico-ideological platform to impose the rehabilitation revolution between 2010 and 2015. The revolution eroded the sphere of probation influence by the creation of 21 Community Rehabilitation Companies (CRCs), which constitutes the new order of things. Before returning to the thematic structure of this book, I want to reflect on whether the period from 1997 to 2015 was inevitable. Just because things are as they are does not mean that they have to be like this.

'What if' and 'if only'

Ian Kershaw's (2007) *Fateful Choices: Ten Decisions That Changed the World 1940–1941* can be extrapolated to question the recent history of criminal justice and penal policy. The 10 decisions were: Britain fighting alone in the spring of 1940 rather than negotiate peace with Germany; Hitler's decision to attack the Soviet Union in 1940, which occurred in 1941; Japan seizing her opportunities; Mussolini deciding to grab his share of the spoils; Roosevelt deciding to lend a hand; Stalin's refusal to take seriously the German threat to his country; Roosevelt declaring war; Japan's decision to attack Pearl Harbour; Hitler declaring war on the US; and, lastly, Hitler's decision to eradicate the Jews in Europe. Kershaw asserts that these decisions were made by a handful of people in Britain, Germany, Japan, Italy and the US, but his central task is to explore those diverse and certainly complex influences that culminated in these world-altering decisions. Kershaw poses the question: were the decisions taken inevitable, or were other courses of action feasible? Significantly, were there opportunities before the final and fateful decisions were taken to pursue alternative courses of action? He answers:

> In retrospect, what took place seems to have been inexorable. In looking at the history of wars, perhaps even more than at history generally, there is an almost inbuilt teleological impulse, which leads us to presume that the way things turned out is the only way they could have turned out. (Kershaw, 2007, p 6)

Kershaw argues that this was not the case. Decisions imply choices and alternative judgements and decisions could have been made amid the welter of variables, pressures and national and international contingencies that interacted with each other. James Joyce, in *Ulysses*, addressed the nightmare of history that imposes itself with a heavy hand. Joyce, long before Kershaw, and one might add the great speculators of history, including Vico, Hegel, Comte and Marx (Mazlish, 1968), was troubled by the thought that it could have been other than it is. What if Pyrrhus had not fallen or Julius Caesar knifed to death? 'But can those have been possible seeing that they never were? Or was that only possible which came to pass? Weave, weaver of the wind' (Joyce, 1992, p 30).

Other decisions could have been made according to Kershaw's historical analysis. Moreover, the creation of the NPS in 2001 was neither desirable nor inevitable. It should be recalled that arguments for a national probation service were mooted as early as 1962 but rejected (Home Office, 1962). The Carter proposals in 2003 to create NOMS could have been dispensed with (do not forget, a step too far during 1997/98 but a step in time after 2003). There were, and are, alternatives to competition, marketisation, privatisation, computer technology, numerical targets, centralisation and bureaucratisation, including the management of 'problem populations' via punitive strategies, just as much as there are alternatives to the neoliberal order of things (Saad-Filho and Johnston, 2005). It is rank stupidity to think otherwise. A series of decisions were made by the political modernisers, implemented by apparatchiks *and probation managers*, but they were not inevitable. We can agree with Kershaw that things might have turned out differently – decisions imply choices – but imposition and collusion seized the day.

Garland (2001) argued that today's crime control strategies are a response to late-modern crime issues associated with increased levels of insecurity, the decline of rehabilitative efficacy and social welfare. The state has taken up the fight against those most affected by late-modern socio-economic conditions engendered by neoliberalism, primarily the urban poor, welfare claimants, minority groups and offenders as the excluded 'other' (Garland, 2001, p 195). Within this context, probation has been *forced to adjust* to reflect the latest political, electoral and penal realities that have been emerging since the 1970s. Choices have been made that incorporate punitive retaliation and acting out to maintain the rule of law, social order and control. These choices have not been inevitable, but more likely because of late-modern conditions and the problems they spawn. However, 'what if' and 'if only' other choices had been exercised in the direction of more integrative social policies to reduce structural inequality (Wilkinson and Pickett, 2009), rather than hardening the state's penal arteries? What if and if only probation with greater determination resisted modernising overtures by defending its core values, organisational ideals and professional integrity? Why has probation allowed itself to be turned over within such a relatively short period of time into a spectre of its former self? Why have respected social workers of the courts allowed themselves to be manipulated into punishment workers, when other judgements could have been formulated, decisions made and actions taken? Has the organisation been ethico-culturally transformed beyond all recognition? *This was the question I posed in 2009 before the revolutionary transformations of 2010–2015* (see Whitehead, 2010, p 160).

There is evidence in Chapter Five to suggest that the 'Northtown' probation service had an ally among some court clerks, magistrates, solicitors, barristers and judges circa 2006/07 but did not realise it. These local relationships could have been cultivated to reshape events – a new twist to multiagency working. Instead, my research was perceived as a threat by some of my senior colleagues, rather than a source of support in what were difficult operational circumstances.

Theorising probation and criminal justice

I have exposed the under-theorised domains of probation and criminal justice to theoretical excavation in order to illuminate politically induced empirical complexity. As noted earlier, social theory constitutes an essential tool in scholarly activity to explore and analyse features of social phenomena, including institutional practices. The theorisation of criminal justice cannot support a single interpretive approach, any more than crime can be theorised by resort to one criminological theory. Accordingly, theories constitute the 'conceptual means of interpreting and explicating information. They come into competition only when they offer alternative and incompatible explanations of the same data' (Garland, 1990, p 13). The theoretical spine of this monograph, in conjunction with its empirical content, constructs the intellectual resources to analyse and critique discrete periods of modernisation and transformation within the criminal justice system, with particular attention directed towards probation. Those modernising forays of New Labour from 1997 to 2010, followed by the rehabilitation revolution imposed by the Coalition government between 2010 and 2015, are bathed in clearer light by the application of social theory, the religio-personalist tradition and the penetrating lens of moral economy. In pursuing this approach, we are confronted with the distance travelled from the probation and civilisational ideal (see Chapter Three). A sequence of political convulsions has exacerbated organisational dissonance beyond anything envisaged by Harris (1980), and distorted its distinctive historical contribution to the dialectics of criminal justice (see Whitehead, 2015b).

Probation represented a discernible configuration of governmental-supported approaches and values. Of course, the supporting Keynesian social-democratic dispensation was not perfect, there was no golden age, but it was intellectually and morally different to what currently exists after repeated bouts of modernisation and transformational incursions. Governmental intervention since the 1990s has pitched economics before ethics, markets before morality, to establish the organisational logics of neoliberalism. The former reproductive mechanisms of symbolic efficiency – the probation ideal (Whitehead, 2015b, pp 34–5), the rehabilitative ethic, personalism, inclusive citizenship and an aversion to punishment and prison – have fractured under the weight of the market state. According to this monograph, modernisation and transformation, the raw constituents of a forceful political act violently imposed *from above*, have constructed a multifaceted organisational phenomenon, elucidated by condensing the aforementioned extended grid of intellectual resources:

- The articulation of heightened emotional responses through expressive punishment, acting out and displays of sovereign power as a symbolic spectacle of reassurance in the fight against crime (Durkheim).
- From the individual offender as the primary unit of analysis to controlling aggregates of risk. Greater emphasis on bureaucratic management, the 3Es,[4] value for money (VfM), procedures, processes and impersonal systems, as well as National Standards, business audits, targets, computerisation, NOMS and contestability (Weber).
- Probation implicated in government's punitive strategy directed against the poor. Forced integration into, rather than instead of, the repressive capitalist state apparatus that it reflects and reproduces (Marx). Probation's reconstruction by fearful competition, privatisation and marketisation.
- The offender manager casts a disciplinary and normalising gaze over offenders, the eye and ear of the regulatory state. Deviant populations have their minds and bodies cognitively redirected to promote compliant citizenship. Accredited programmes, such as Think First, induce *normal* thinking through social and problem-solving skills conducive to docile behavioural drills (Foucault).
- The Lacanian/Žižekian conceptual framework can be applied to organisational analysis and critique (as well as human subjectivity), illustrated in the single case study of probation. Under the Keynesian dispensation, probation and criminal justice were components of the post-war welfare state and supported a rehabilitative ethic. Under the neoliberal order, probation has been jettisoned out of the *Symbolic*

order and accompanying accoutrements of symbolic efficiency, into the capitalist *Real* by the forces of privatisation, marketisation and competition. Payment by results is the material signifier of the new politico-economic, ideological and material dispensation.

- Religion, personalist impulses and a moral economy of humane sensibilities combine to work with offenders within the context of social work *relationships*, as well as to provide support and help for personal and social problems, rather than punishment. A distinctive set of attitudes and values promote respect for persons and treat people as ends not means. Helping strategies to promote rehabilitation remain a feature of NOMS, although less in evidence than formerly (see Chapter Three).

Remaining with the last facet in the preceding list, there are scattered deposits of hope in probation and the 21 CRCs, a vestige of muted voices, rather than organisational resistance and opposition to modernising transformations (see Mawby and Worrall, 2013; Deering and Feilzer, 2015; Cowburn et al, 2015; Whitehead, 2015b, ch 5). However, these deposits are not taking on the forces of modernisation, but desperately cohabiting, trying to cling on and survive in the interstices of a state-driven hegemony. Probation must excavate its history (Whitehead and Statham, 2006) to reconnect with its distinctive ideological resources in order to move forward in conjunction with the CRCs. The impedimenta forced onto probation and, in turn, the criminal justice system, flushed to the surface by the theoretical construction of this book, must be systematically dismantled to return to reasoned debate on ethics and criminal and social justice. This is why the rediscovery and reassertion of a probation historico-ideology is so urgent and vital.

Ideology constitutes a set of beliefs, axiological commitments and value orientations by which to transform and transcend our current neoliberal predicament, not simply cohabit in the new order of things – ideology in the sense not of distorting reality, but of fundamental beliefs and values by which to restructure the macro-political economy, the organisations of civil society and human subjectivity (see Winlow et al, 2015). My earlier work on *Reconceptualising the Moral Economy of Criminal Justice* (Whitehead, 2015b) advances the intellectual resources to construct an ideology to resist and transform, not collaborate with, our current predicament – in other words, to build our way out of raw nature, and the penetrative encroachment of the *Real*, towards ethics that constitute the renewal of vision in a good and just society. Ideology transcends the present after a sustained period of disavowal at the injudicious hands of modernisers and transformers. This is, as a matter of logic, a basic requirement in a people-facing organisation and moral leadership is required to vigorously defend probation, not collaborate with the principalities and powers of the age. Moral leadership is urgently required to stimulate a moral core that dispels the moral void left by the mutilators of an honourable profession.

What is swirling around beneath our feet, violently erupting from below the surface of the criminal justice system, is a vortex of exchange relations, material signifiers, fearful competition and the new orthodoxy of privatisation. The generative core of the neoliberal market state has reconfigured organisational rationalities and probation is a notable scalp. If we despair at the construction of the new order of things, it is urgent and imperative to *transform* the criminal justice domain, not reform it piecemeal by tinkering at its operational edges to enhance effectiveness or efficiency. Specifically, it is in the realm of politics proper where we need to raise basic questions of ethics and moral obligation that, in turn, have implications for the renewal of organisational life. With this in mind, a case can be made for: more advise, assist and befriend and less punishment and prison; more attention to ethics and less to the material priorities of the market state; and more intrinsic right and good than utility at the political and organisational level. It is in the realm of politics where we must urgently decide what kind of society we want to construct, its defining anthropological characteristics and the organisations we want to sustain it. This will involve the demanding task of forging a rapprochement between politics, ethics and justice, systematically eroded by successive governments, specifically the Ministry of Justice.

Epilogue

Probation, at its idealistic best, its most exalted and fondly remembered – perhaps this was always its promissory note to the criminal justice system – was located at the epicentre of a human drama of offending behaviours. It was anxious and curious about the fracturing of the *Symbolic* order, debilitating acts of theft and burglary, and the preparedness of some citizens to inflict serious damage on others. Probation offered to understand and explain the repertoire of behaviours through exercising its existential, aetiological and hermeneutical skills, and flexing moral responsibility towards offenders, victims, courts and the local community. However, this responsibility has been eroded by a sequence of politico-economic convulsions. Probation has been roughed up, knocked about and coerced into line to reflect and reproduce the ideological and material contours of the neoliberal order of things. Modernising monstrosities and transformational traumas constitute the blunt instruments of reconstructive organisational surgery. Incontrovertibly, the political elite botched the operation by the repeated excision of what was of inestimable value to the criminal justice system. Its blunt-edged scalpel hacked away at healthy organisational tissue, assaulted its vital organs and, in turn, destabilised the arterial flow of justice. The extended theoretical construction of this monograph adds academic weight to this contention.

A series of hinges to promote critical excavation are 1979, 1992–93, 1997, 2001 (NPS), 2003 (NOMS) and the misnomer of the rehabilitation revolution from 2010 to 2015. The year 2015 signals the final, or latest, phase in what is a long project of ideological and material reconstruction that began in the 1970s. Since then, the generative core of capitalism, previously insulated by the regulatory jacket of Keynesian social democracy, represented in the criminal justice system by probation, has expanded and penetrated. This is the transition from Keynesian to neoliberal governance, from nation-state to market state. The anti-ethical *Real* has fractured the contours of symbolic efficiency. We must lament this historical event and express concern at its present and future consequences.

The probation system, or what remains of it, in conjunction with the 21 CRCs, has a duty and moral obligation to transcend the politics of imposition and embed the civilisational ideal in the criminal justice system. However, it cannot do this unless and until it also exercises the duty and moral obligation to challenge a political economy that has released amoral forces into the system, starkly manifested in the erosion of the probation service. Unless this debate is enjoined – unless we proceed from piecemeal reforms that tinker at the edges to radical transformation – then more of the same will ensue between 2015 and 2020.

Notes

[1] Some years ago, I located what were referred to as different models of probation on a care–control continuum (Whitehead, 1990). First, a number of *academic models* from the contributions of Robert Harris (1977, 1980) at the care end of the continuum, to Griffiths (1982a, 1982b) at the control-punitive end. Additionally, I introduced a *bureaucratic model* associated with the *Statement of National Objectives and Priorities* (Home Office, 1984), and made reference to a National Association of Probation Officers *professional model*. Finally, there was a *local area service model* of probation practice.

[2] The introduction of an objective-driven and later target culture into the public sector during the 1980s and 1990s, continued after 1997, elicited numerous comments in the national press, which can be illustrated as follows. First, we were told that a consultant gynaecologist quit the NHS 'over the tyranny of targets and tick-boxes' (*Daily Mail*, 8 June 2006). Second, Simon Jenkins, in the *Sunday Times* (24 September 2006), headlined his article with the words 'Set a silly target and you'll get a really crazy public service'. Jenkins explored targets in education and the NHS, arguing that a public service and professional ethos had been replaced with a target-driven culture imposed by central government, with adverse effects. Next, Peter Riddell, in an article on treasury targets in *The Times* (19 July 2007), exclaimed that 'No one will miss targets when they're gone'. The next two examples begin to raise deep concerns about the effects of targets when we read, in *The Times* (24 August 2007) again: 'Children taken from parents and adopted to meet ministry targets'. Also, *The Guardian* (3 April 2008) states: 'Police criminalising young to hit targets, says charity'. Sixth, the G2 section of *The Guardian* (19 March 2009) stated that 'A hospital is able to tick all the boxes, yet still utterly fail patients'. Finally, for a critique of targets in probation, see Whitehead (2007, pp 39–46).

[3] Castellano and Gould (2007) refer to three types of justice: procedural, distributive and restorative. Where the first two are concerned, it is argued that procedural justice refers to the processes and procedures adopted by organisations by which disputes are resolved. Therefore, within a criminal justice context, it may be suggested that the dilution of discretion and autonomy, particularly within the probation service, in addition to putting the procedural emphasis upon the FDR rather than standard delivery report, may not enhance the cause of criminal and social justice. Furthermore, distributive justice alludes to the economic system and the equitable distribution of material resources throughout society (which relates to the arguments advanced in Wilkinson and Pickett [2009] already considered and referenced in this book).

[4] During 2008 and 2009, the Ministry of Justice made it clear in numerous documents that budgets would be cut during the next three years. Where the probation service was concerned a Briefing Note compiled by Harry Fletcher (National Association of Probation Officers, 2009) made the following observations in response to Ministry of Justice projections. The probation budget for 2008/09 was £914 million; for 2009/10, it should be £894 million; subsequently there will be a further reduction of £50 million in 2010/11; and a further £50 million reduction in 2011/12. Therefore, by 2012, the probation budget was £794 million, which constituted a total reduction of £120 million. Significantly, the Briefing Note provided a breakdown of the implications within 30 area services and it was summarised that 'The consequence of the cuts are dire and coupled with the recession are likely to have a major impact on crime. The average cumulative cut is about 20%, and therefore most areas will have to cut frontline jobs' (National Association of Probation Officers, 2009, p 6). Harry Fletcher, on behalf of the National Association of Probation Officers, concluded that the probation service faces 'meltdown if the current cuts go ahead and crime soars in the recession' (National Association of Probation Officers, 2009, p 11). These could be the conditions in which the third sector will flourish in the criminal justice system. This was before the transforming rehabilitation events of 2010–15 and the privatisation of part of probation through the creation of the 21 CRCs.

References

Albrow, M. (1970) *Bureaucracy*, London: Macmillan.

Allen, K. (2004) *Max Weber: A Critical Introduction*, London: Pluto.

Aristotle (2000) *Nicomachean Ethics* (trans and ed R. Crisp), Cambridge: Cambridge University Press.

Auld, Lord Justice (2001) *Review of the Criminal Courts of England and Wales*, London: The Stationery Office.

Badiou, A. (2003) *Saint Paul: The Foundations of Universalism*, Stanford, CA: Stanford University Press.

Bailey, R. (1980) 'Social workers: pawns, police or agitators?', in M. Brake and R. Bailey (eds) *Radical Social Work and Practice*, London: Edward Arnold.

Bailey, R. and Brake, M. (eds) (1975) *Radical Social Work*, London: Edward Arnold.

Barber, M. (2007) *Instruction to Deliver: Tony Blair, Public Services and the Challenge of Achieving Targets*, London: Politico's.

Bean, P. (1976) *Rehabilitation and Deviance*, London: Routledge and Kegan Paul.

Bean, P. (1981) *Punishment*, Oxford: Martin Robertson.

Beirne, P. (1993) *Inventing Criminology: Essays on the Rise of Homo Criminalis*, Albany, NY: State.

Belsey, C. (2002) *Poststructuralism: A Very Short Introduction*, Oxford: Oxford University Press.

Bendix, R. (1960) *Max Weber: An Intellectual Portrait*, London: Heinemann.

Beynon, H., Hudson, R. and Sadler, D. (1994) *A Place Called Teesside: A Locality in a Global Economy*, Edinburgh: Edinburgh University Press.

Biestek, F.P. (1961) *The Casework Relationship*, London: George Allen and Unwin Ltd.

Bochel, D. (1976) *Probation and After-Care: Its Development in England and Wales*, Edinburgh: Scottish Academic Press.

Bonger, W. (1969 [1916]) *Criminality and Economic Conditions*, Bloomington, IN: Indiana University Press.

Bonhoeffer, D. (1955) *Ethics* (ed E. Bethge), London and New York, NY: Macmillan.

Bottoms, A.E. (1983) 'Neglected features of contemporary penal systems', in D. Garland and P. Young (eds) *The Power To Punish: Contemporary Penality and Social Analysis*, London: Heinemann Educational Books.

Bottoms, A.E. and McWilliams, W. (1979) 'A non-treatment paradigm for probation practice', *British Journal of Social Work*, 9(2): 159–202.

Bottoms, A.E. and McWilliams, W. (1986) 'Social enquiry reports twenty-five years after the Streatfield Report', in P. Bean and D. Whynes (eds) *Barbara Wootton Social Science and Public Policy: Essays in Her Honour*, London and New York, NY: Tavistock Publications.

Bottoms, A.E. and Stelman, A. (1988) *Social Inquiry Reports: A Framework for Practice Development*, Community Care Practice Handbooks, Aldershot: Wildwood House.

Bourgois, P. (2003) *In Search of Respect: Selling Crack in El Barrio* (2nd edn), Cambridge and New York, NY: Cambridge University Press.

Box, S. (1987) *Recession, Crime and Punishment*, Basingstoke: Macmillan Education Ltd.

Brake, M. and Hale, C. (1992) *Public Order and Private Lives: The Politics of Law and Order*, New York, NY, and London: Routledge.

Brody, S.R. (1976) *The Effectiveness of Sentencing*, London: HMSO.

Brown, S. (1991) *Magistrates at Work: Sentencing and Social Structure*, Buckingham: Open University Press.

Brown, S. (2005) *Understanding Youth and Crime: Listening to Youth?* (2nd edn), Buckingham: Open University Press.

Bryant, G.A. (1985) *Positivism in Social Theory and Research*, Basingstoke: Macmillan.

Bryant, M., Coker, J., Estlea, B., Himmel, S. and Knapp, T. (1978) 'Sentenced to social work?', *Probation Journal*, 25(4): 110–14.

Buchdahl, G. (1969) *Metaphysics and the Philosophy of Science: The Classical Origins Descartes to Kant*, Oxford: Basil Blackwell.

Burke, R.H. (2008) *Young People, Crime and Justice*, Devon, Cullompton: Willan.

Burnett, R., Baker, K. and Roberts, C. (2007) 'Assessment, supervision and intervention: fundamental practice in probation', in L. Gelsthorpe and R. Morgan (eds) *Handbook of Probation*, Devon, Cullompton: Willan.

Burrow, J. (2009) *A History of Histories: Epics, Chronicles, Romances and Inquiries from Herodotus and Thucydides to the Twentieth Century*, London and New York, NY: Penguin.

Cabinet Office (1999) *Modernising Government*, presented to Parliament by the Prime Minister and the Minister for the Cabinet Office, London: The Stationery Office.

Cabinet Office (2006) *Prime Minister's Strategy Unit Policy Review, Crime, Justice and Cohesion*, London: Cabinet Office.

Cabinet Office (2008) *Engaging Communities in Fighting Crime* (Casey Report), London: Home Office and Ministry of Justice.

Cabinet Office (2010) *Modernising Commissioning: Increasing the Role of Charities, Social Enterprises, Mutuals and Cooperatives in Public Service Delivery*, London: Cabinet Office.

Cabinet Office and HM Treasury (2007) *The Future Role of the Third Sector in Social and Economic Regeneration: Final Report*, London: The Stationery Office.

Cabinet Office and Prime Minister's Strategy Unit (2006) *Policy Review: Crime, Justice and Cohesion*, London: Stationery Office.

Callinicos, A. (2007) *Social Theory: A Historical Introduction*, Cambridge: Polity.

Campbell, A. (2007) *The Blair Years: Extracts from the Alistair Campbell Diaries*, London: Hutchinson.

Canton, R. (2007) 'Probation and the tragedy of punishment', *Howard Journal*, 46(3): 236–54.

Canton, R. (2011) *Probation: Working with Offenders*, London: Routledge.

Carter, P. (2003) *Managing Offenders, Reducing Crime: A New Approach*, London: Home Office and Strategy Unit.

Carter, P. (2007) *Securing the Future: Proposals for the Efficient and Sustainable Use of Custody in England and Wales*, London: Ministry of Justice.

Castellano, T.C. and Gould, J.B. (2007) 'Neglect of justice in criminal justice theory: causes, consequences, and alternatives', in D.E. Duffee and E.R. Maguire (eds) *Criminal Justice Theory: Explaining the Nature and Behaviour of Criminal Justice*, New York, NY, and London: Routledge.

Cavadino, M. and Dignan, J. (2002) *The Penal System: An Introduction* (3rd edn), London, Thousand Oaks, CA, and New Delhi: Sage.

Cavadino, M. and Dignan, J. (2006) *Penal Systems: A Comparative Approach*, London, Thousand Oaks, CA, and New Delhi: Sage.

Chadwick, O. (1990) *The Secularisation of the European Mind in the 19th Century* (Canto edn), Cambridge and New York, NY: Cambridge University Press.

Chambers, M. (2013) *Expanding Payment by Results: Strategic Choices and Recommendations*, London: Policy Exchange.

Charman, S. and Savage, S. (1999) 'The new politics of law and order: Labour, crime and justice', in M. Powell (ed) *New Labour, New Welfare State? The 'Third Way' in British Social Policy*, Bristol: The Policy Press.

Chernomas, R. and Hudson, I. (2007) *Social Murder and Other Shortcomings of Conservative Economics*, Winnipeg: Arbeiter Ring Publishing.

Chiricos, T.G. and Delone, M.A. (1992) 'Labour surplus and punishment: a review and assessment of theory and evidence', *Social Problems*, 39(4): 421–46.

Chui, W.H. and Nellis, M. (eds) (2003) *Moving Probation Forward: Evidence, Arguments and Practice*, London and New York, NY: Pearson-Longman.

Clarke, J., Gewirtz, S. and McLaughlin, E. (2000) *New Managerialism, New Welfare?*, London, Thousand Oaks, CA, and New Delhi: Sage.

Clarke, P. (2004) *Hope and Glory: Britain 1900–2000* (2nd edn), London and New York, NY: Penguin Books.

Clay, W.L. (1969) *Prison Chaplain*, Glen Ridge, USA: Patterson Smith.

Cohen, S. (1985) *Visions of Social Control*, Cambridge: Polity Press.

Conservative Party (2008) *Prisons with a Purpose: Our Sentencing and Rehabilitation Revolution to Break the Cycle of Crime, Security Agenda Policy Green Paper Number 4*, London: Conservative Party.

Cook, D. (2006) *Criminal and Social Justice*, London, Thousand Oaks, CA, and New Delhi: Sage.

Copleston, F. (2003 [1953]) *A History of Philosophy, Volume 3, Late Mediaeval and Renaissance Philosophy* (paperback edn), London and New York, NY: Continuum.

Copleston, F. (2003 [1959]) *A History of Philosophy, Volume 5, British Philosophy: Hobbes to Hume* (paperback edn), London and New York, NY: Continuum.

Copleston, F. (2003 [1960]) *A History of Philosophy, Volume 6, the Enlightenment: Voltaire to Kant* (paperback edn), London and New York, NY: Continuum.

Copleston, F. (2003 [1963]) *A History of Philosophy, Volume 7, 18th and 19th Century German Philosophy* (paperback edn), London and New York, NY: Continuum.

Copleston, F. (2003 [1966]) *A History of Philosophy, Volume 8, Utilitarianism to Early Analytic Philosophy* (paperback edn), London and New York, NY: Continuum.

Coser, L.A. (1977) *Masters of Sociological Thought: Ideas in Historical and Social Context* (2nd edn), New York, NY, and London: Harcourt Brace Jovanovich Publishers.

Cousins, M. and Hussain, A. (1984) *Michel Foucault*, Hampshire and London: Macmillan.

Cowburn, M., Duggan, M., Robinson, A. and Senior, P. (eds) (2015) *Values in Criminology and Community Justice*, Bristol: The Policy Press.

Cowling, M. (2008) *Marxism and Criminological Theory: A Critique and Tool Kit*, Hampshire: Palgrave.

Crawshaw, P., Bunton, R. and Gillen, K. (2002) 'Modernisation and Health Action Zones: the search for coherence', in L. Bauld and K. Judge (eds) *Learning from Health Action Zones*, Chichester: Aeneas.

Davis, C. (2010) 'Paul and subtraction', in J. Milbank, S. Žižek and C. Davis (eds) *Continental Philosophy and the Future of Christian Theology*, Grand Rapids: Brazos Press.

De Angelis, M. (2007) *The Beginning of History: Value Struggles and Global Capitalism*, London: Pluto.

Deering, J. and Feilzer, M.Y. (2015) *Privatising Probation: Is Transforming Rehabilitation the End of the Probation Ideal?* Bristol: The Policy Press.

De Giorgi, A. (2006) *Rethinking the Political Economy of Punishment: Perspectives on Post-Fordism and Penal Politics*, Aldershot: Ashgate.

Dohan, D. (2003) *The Price of Poverty: Money, Work, and Culture in the Mexican Barrio*, Berkley, Los Angeles, CA, and London: University of California Press.

Downes, D. and Morgan, R. (1997) 'Dumping the "hostages to fortune"? The politics of law and order in post-war Britain', in M. Maguire, R. Morgan and R. Reiner (eds) *The Oxford Handbook of Criminology* (2nd edn), Oxford and New York, NY: Oxford University Press.

Downes, D. and Rock, P. (1988) *Understanding Deviance: A Guide to the Sociology of Crime and Rule Breaking* (2nd edn), Oxford: Clarendon Press.

Driver, S. and Martell, L. (1998) *New Labour: Politics after Thatcherism*, Cambridge: Polity.

Duff, A. and Garland, D. (eds) (1994) *A Reader On Punishment*, Oxford and New York, NY: Oxford University Press.

Duffee, D.E. and Maguire, E.R. (eds) (2007) *Criminal Justice Theory: Explaining the Nature and Behaviour of Criminal Justice*, New York, NY, and London: Routledge.

Duménil, G. and Lévy, D. (2004) *Capital Resurgent: Roots of the Neoliberal Revolution*, Cambridge and London: Harvard University Press.

Durkheim, E. (1915 [1912]) *The Elementary Forms of the Religious Life*, London: Allen and Unwin.

Durkheim, E. (1938 [1895]) *The Rules of Sociological Method*, New York, NY: The Free Press.

Durkheim, E. (1952 [1897]) *Suicide: A Study in Sociology*, London and Henley: Routledge and Kegan Paul.

Durkheim, E. (1984 [1893]) *The Division of Labour in Society, with an Introduction by Lewis Coser* (trans W.D. Halls), Basingstoke: Macmillan.

Durkheim, E. (2002) *Moral Education* (trans and with a preface by E.K. Wilson and H. Schnurer), Mineola, NY: Dover Publications.

Eagleton, T. (2009) *Trouble with Strangers: A Study of Ethics*, Chichester: Wiley-Blackwell.

Easton, S. and Piper, C. (2005) *Sentencing and Punishment: The Quest for Justice*, Oxford and New York, NY: Oxford University Press.

Elliott, A. (2005) 'Psychoanalytic social theory', in A. Harrington (ed) *Modern Social Theory: An Introduction*, Oxford and New York, NY: Oxford University Press.

Emirbayer, M. (ed) (2003) *Emile Durkheim: Sociologist of Modernity*, Oxford: Blackwell.

Eribon, D. (1989) *Michel Foucault*, London and Boston, MA: Faber and Faber.

Fairclough, N. (2000) *New Labour, New Language?*, London and New York, NY: Routledge.

Faulkner, D. and Burnett, R. (2012) *Where next for criminal justice?* Bristol: Policy Press.

Fielding, N. (1984) *Probation Practice: Client Support under Social Control*, Aldershot, Hampshire: Gower.

Foucault, M. (1970) *The Order of Things: An Archaeology of the Human Sciences*, London: Tavistock Publications.

Foucault, M. (1977) *Discipline and Punish: The Birth of the Prison*, England and New York, NY: Penguin.

Frayn, M. (2006) *The Human Touch: Our Part in the Creation of the Universe*, London: Faber and Faber.

Freiberg, A. and Gelb, K. (2008) *Penal Populism, Sentencing Councils and Sentencing Policy*, Devon, Cullompton: Willan.

Fullwood, C. (1994) 'Policy and management implications', in J. Stewart, D. Smith and G. Stewart, with C. Fullwood (eds) *Understanding Offending Behaviour*, Harlow, Essex: Longman.

Garland, D. (1985) *Punishment and Welfare: A History of Penal Strategies*, Aldershot: Gower.

Garland, D. (1990) *Punishment and Modern Society: A Study in Social Theory*, Oxford and New York, NY: Oxford University Press.

Garland, D. (2001) *The Culture of Control: Crime and Social Order in Contemporary Society*, Oxford and New York, NY: Oxford University Press.

Garland, D. and Sparks, R. (2000) 'Criminology, social theory, and the challenge of our times', in D. Garland and R. Sparks (eds) *Criminology and Social Theory*, Oxford and New York, NY: Oxford University Press.

Garland, D. and Young, P. (eds) (1983) *The Power To Punish: Contemporary Penality and Social Analysis*, London and New Jersey, NJ: Heinemann Educational Books.

Gay, P. (1967) *The Enlightenment: An Interpretation. The Rise of Modern Paganism*, New York, NY: Alfred A Knopf.

Gay, P. (1969) *The Enlightenment, An Interpretation; the Science of Freedom*, New York, NY, and London: W. W. Norton and Company.

Gelsthorpe, L. and Morgan, R. (eds) (2007) *Handbook of Probation*, Devon, Cullompton: Willan.

Gelsthorpe, L. and Raynor, P. (1995) 'Quality and effectiveness in probation officer reports to sentencers', *British Journal of Criminology*, 35: 188–200.

George, V. and Wilding, P. (1991) *Ideology and Social Welfare*, London and New York, NY: Routledge.

Gerth, H.H. and Mills, C.W. (eds) (1948) *From Max Weber*, London: Routledge and Kegan Paul.

Giddens, A. (1971) *Capitalism and Modern Social Theory: An Analysis of the Writings of Marx, Durkheim and Max Weber*, London and New York, NY: Cambridge University Press.

Giddens, A. (1972) *Emile Durkheim: Selected Writings*, London and New York, NY: Cambridge University Press.

Giddens, A. (1978) 'Positivism and its critics', in T. Bottomore and R. Nisbet (eds) *A History of Sociological Analysis*, London: Heinemann.

Giddens, A. (1982) *Profiles and Critiques in Social Theory*, Basingstoke: Macmillan.

Giddens, A. (1989) *Sociology*, Cambridge: Polity Press.

Gilbert, B.B. (1966) *The Evolution of National Insurance in Great Britain: The Origins of the Welfare State*, London: Michael Joseph.

Glover, E.R. (1956) *Probation and Re-Education* (rev 2nd edn), London: Routledge and Kegan Paul.

Goodman, A. (2003) 'Probation into the millennium: the punishing service?', in R. Matthews and J. Young (eds) *The New Politics of Crime and Punishment*, Devon, Cullompton: Willan.

Grayling, A.C. (2005) *Descartes: The Life of Rene Descartes and Its Place in His Times*, London: Free Press.

Griffiths, W.A. (1982a) 'A new probation service', *Probation Journal*, 29(3): 98–9.

Griffiths, W.A. (1982b) 'Supervision in the community', *Justice of the Peace*, 21 August.

Gutting, G. (ed) (1994) *The Cambridge Guide to Foucault*, Cambridge and New York, NY: Cambridge University Press.

Gutting, G. (2005) *Foucault: A Very Short Introduction*, Oxford and New York, NY: Oxford University Press.

Haines, K. and Morgan, R. (2007) 'Services before trial and sentence: achievement, decline and potential', in L. Gelsthorpe and R. Morgan (eds) *Handbook of Probation*, Devon, Cullompton: Willan.

Hall, A.R. (1954) *The Scientific Revolution 1500–1800: The Formation of the Modern Scientific Attitude*, London and New York, NY: Longman.

Hall, S. (2012) *Theorizing Crime and Deviance: A New Perspective*, London: Sage.

Hall, S., Critcher, C., Jefferson, T., Clarke, J. and Roberts, B. (1978) *Policing the Crisis: Mugging, the State and Law and Order*, Basingstoke: Macmillan.

Harari, Y.N. (2014) *Sapiens: A Brief History of Humankind*, London: Harvill Secker.

Harrington, A. (2005) *Modern Social Theory: An introduction*, Oxford: Oxford University Press.

Harris, R. (1977) 'The probation officer as social worker', *British Journal of Social Work*, 7(4): 433–42.

Harris, R. (1980) 'A changing service: the case for separating "care" and "control" in probation practice', *British Journal of Social Work*, 10(2): 163–84.

Harvey, D. (2005) *A Brief History of Neoliberalism*, Oxford and New York, NY: Oxford University Press.

Haxby, D. (1978) *Probation: A Changing Service*, London: Constable.

Hay, D. (1975) 'Property, authority and the criminal law', in P. Linebaugh, J.G. Rule, E.P. Thompson and C. Winslow (eds) *Albion's Fatal Tree: Crime and Society in Eighteenth Century England*, Harmondsworth: Pantheon Books.

Hinde, R.S.E. (1951) *The British Penal System 1773–1950*, London: Gerald Duckworth and Co. Ltd.

HM Government (2011) *Open Public Services*, CM 8145, London: The Stationery Office.

Hobsbawm, E. (1994) *Age of Extremes: The Short Twentieth Century 1914–1991*, London: Michael Joseph.

Home Office (1895) *Report of the Departmental Committee on Prisons* (Gladstone Committee) C7702, London: HMSO.

Home Office (1909) *Report of the Departmental Committee on the Probation of Offenders Act 1907*, Cmnd 5001, London: HMSO.

Home Office (1922) *Report of the Departmental Committee on the Training, Appointment and Payment of Probation Officers*, Cmnd 1601, London: HMSO.

Home Office (1936) *Report of the Departmental Committee on the Social Services in Courts of Summary Jurisdiction*, Cmnd 5122, London: HMSO.

Home Office (1959) *Penal Practice in a Changing Society: Aspects of Future Development (England and Wales)*, Cmnd 645, London: HMSO.

Home Office (1961) *Report of the Inter-Departmental Committee on the Business of the Criminal Courts (Streatfield Report)*, Cmd 1289, London: HMSO.

Home Office (1962) *Report of the Departmental Committee on the Probation Service (Morison Committee)*, Cmnd 1650, London: HMSO.

Home Office (1977) *A Review of Criminal Justice Policy 1976*, London: HMSO.

Home Office (1984) *Probation Service in England and Wales. Statement of National Objectives and Priorities,* London: The Stationery Office.

Home Office (1998) *Prisons–Probation: Joining Forces to Protect the Public*, London: HMSO.

Home Office (2001a) *Criminal Justice: The Way Ahead*, Cm 5074, London: The Stationery Office.

Home Office (2001b) *Making Punishments Work: The Report of a Review of the Sentencing Framework for England and Wales (Halliday Review)*, London: The Stationery Office.

Home Office (2004a) *Confident Communities in a Secure Britain: The Home Office Strategic Plan 2004–2008*, Cm 6287, London: The Stationery Office.

Home Office (2004b) *Cutting Crime, Delivering Justice: A Strategic Plan for Criminal Justice 2004–2008*, Cm 6288, London: The Stationery Office.

Home Office (2005) *Rebuilding Lives: Supporting Victims of Crime*, Cm 6705, London: HMSO.

Home Office (2006a) *A Five Year Strategy for Protecting the Public and Reducing Re-Offending*, Cm 6717, London: The Stationery Office.

Home Office (2006b) *Rebalancing the Criminal Justice System in Favour of the Law Abiding Majority: Cutting Crime, Reducing Re-Offending and Protecting the Public*, London: The Stationery Office.

Home Office (2006c) *Delivering Simple, Speedy, Summary Justice*, London: Criminal Justice System.

Home Office (2006d) *Improving Prison and Probation Services: Public Value Partnerships*, London: The Stationery Office.

Home Office (2007) *Re-offending by Adults: Results from the 2004 Cohort*, London: Home Office.

Homer, S. (2005) *Jacques Lacan*, London and New York, NY: Routledge.

Hope, T. and Walters, R. (2006) *Critical Thinking About the Uses of Research*, London: Centre for Crime and Justice Studies.

Hough, M., Allen, R. and Padel, U. (2006) *Reshaping Probation and Prisons: The New Offender Management Framework*, Bristol: The Policy Press.

House of Commons Justice Committee (2014) *Crime Reduction Policies: A Coordinated Approach? Interim Report on the Government's Transforming Rehabilitation Programme*, 12th Report of Session 2013–13, 14 January, London: House of Commons.

House of Commons Official Report (2007) *Parliamentary Debates* (*Hansard*), Wednesday 28 February, vol 457, no 51.

Howard, J. (1973 [1777]) *The State of Our Prisons*, Montclair, NJ: Warrington.

Hudson, B.A. (1987) *Justice through Punishment: A Critique of the 'Justice' Model of Corrections*, Basingstoke: Macmillan.

Hudson, B.A. (2003) *Understanding Justice: An Introduction to Ideas, Perspectives and Controversies in Modern Penal Theory* (2nd edn), Buckingham and Philadelphia, PA: Open University Press.

Hughes, R. (1987) *The Fatal Shore: A History of the Transportation of Convicts to Australia 1787–1868*, London: Pan Books.

Hugman, B. (1977) *Act Natural*, London: Bedford Square Press.

Hutton, N. (2008) 'The Sentencing Commission for Scotland/ institutional mechanisms for incorporating the public', in A. Freiberg and K. Gelb (eds) *Penal Populism, Sentencing Councils and Sentencing Policy*, Devon, Cullompton: Willan.

Ignatieff, M. (1978) *A Just Measure of Pain: The Penitentiary in the Industrial Revolution, 1750–1850*, Basingstoke: Macmillan.

Jameson, F. (1991) *Postmodernism, or, the Cultural Logic of Late Capitalism*, London: Verso.

Jarvis, F.V. (1972) *Advise, Assist and Befriend: A History of the Probation and After-Care Service*, London: National Association of Probation Officers.

Jarvis, F.V. (1974) *Probation Officers' Manual*, London: Butterworths.

Jones, T. and Newburn, T. (2004) 'The convergence of US and UK crime control policy: exploring substance and process', in T. Newburn and R. Sparks (eds) *Criminal Justice and Political Cultures: National and International Dimensions of Crime Control*, Devon, Cullompton: Willan.

Joyce, J. (1992) *Ulysses*, London and New York, NY: Penguin.

Katz, M.B. (1989) *The Undeserving Poor: From the War on Poverty to the War on Welfare*, New York, NY: Pantheon Books.

Kehlmann, D. (2007) *Measuring the World*, London: Quercus.

Kennedy, H. (2005) *Just Law: The Changing Face of Justice – and Why it Matters to Us All*, London: Vintage.

Kershaw, I. (2007) *Fateful Choices: Ten Decisions That Changed the World 1940–1941*, New York, NY: The Penguin Press.

Kiberd, D. (2009) *Ulysses and Us: The Art of Everyday Living*, London: Faber and Faber.

King, J.F.S (1964) *The Probation Service* (2nd edn), London: Butterworths.

King, R.D. and Wincup, E. (2007) *Doing Research on Crime and Justice* (2nd edn), Oxford and New York, NY: Oxford University Press.

Knight-Markiegi, A. and Quinn, A. (2013) *Comparing Payment by Results across Public Services and in Housing Related Support*, London: Sitra.

Kuehn, M. (2001) *Kant: A Biography*, Cambridge: Cambridge University Press.

Lacan, J. (2001) Écrits, Abingdon: Routledge.

Laffargue, B. and Godefroy, T. (1989) 'Economic cycles and punishment: unemployment and imprisonment', *Contemporary Crises*, 13: 371–404.

Leeson, C. (1914) *The Probation System*, London: P. and S. King and Son.

Le Mesurier, L. (1935) *A Handbook of Probation and Social Work of the Courts*, London: NAPO.

Leys, C. (2003) *Market-Driven Politics: Neoliberal Democracy and the Public Interest*, London and New York, NY: Verso.

Löwith, K. (1993) *Max Weber and Karl Marx*, London: Routledge.

Lukes, S. (1973) *Emile Durkheim His Life and Work: A Historical and Critical Study*, Harmondsworth, Middlesex: Penguin.

Macey, D. (1993) *The Lives of Michel Foucault*, London: Hutchinson.

Mack, M.P. (1962) *Jeremy Bentham: An Odyssey of Ideas 1748–1792*, Melbourne, London and Toronto: Heinemann.

MacRae, D.G. (1987) *Weber*, London: Fontana Press.

Mair, G., Burke, L. and Taylor, S. (2006) 'The worst tax form you've ever seen? Probation officers' views about OASys', *Probation Journal*, 53(1): 7–24.

Marquand, D. (2014) *Mammon's Kingdom: An Essay on Britain, Now*, London and New York, NY: Allen Lane.

Marr, A. (2008) *A History of Modern Britain*, Basingstoke: Macmillan.

Marx, K. (1964 [1932]) *The Economic and Philosophic Manuscripts of 1844*, New York, NY: International Publishers.

Marx, K. (1976 [1867]) *Capital: A Critique of Political Economy Volume 1*, Harmondsworth, Middlesex: Penguin.

Marx, K. and Engels, F. (1947 [1845]) *The German Ideology Part 1*, New York, NY: International Publishers.

Marx, K. and Engels, F. (1967 [1848]) *The Communist Manifesto, with an Introduction by A.J.P. Taylor*, Harmondsworth, Middlesex: Penguin.

Mathiesen, T. (2006) *Prison on Trial* (3rd edn), Winchester: Waterside Press.

Matthews, R. (1999) *Doing Time*, Basingstoke: Macmillan.

Mawby, R.C. and Worrall, A. (2013) *Doing Probation Work: Identity in a Criminal Justice Occupation*, London: Routledge.

Mazlish, B. (1968) *The Riddle of History: The Great Speculators from Vico to Freud*, Massachusetts: Minerva Press.

McIvor, G. and McNeill (2007) 'Probation in Scotland: past, present and future', in L. Gelsthorpe and R. Morgan (eds) *Handbook of Probation*, Devon, Cullompton: Willan.

McLellan, D. (1976) *Karl Marx: His Life and Thought*, St Albans Hertfordshire: Paladin.

McLellan, D. (1986) *Marx* (2nd edn), Hammersmith, London: Fontana Press.

McNay, L. (1994) *Foucault: A Critical Introduction*, Cambridge: Polity.

McNeil, F. and Weaver, B. (2010) 'Changing lives? Desistance research and offender management', The Scottish Centre for Crime and Justice Research, Report Number 03/2010, University of Glasgow and Strathclyde.

McWilliams, W. (1983) 'The mission to the English police courts 1876–1936', *Howard Journal of Criminal Justice*, 22(1–3): 129–47.

McWilliams, W. (1985) 'The mission transformed: professionalisation of probation between the wars', *Howard Journal of Criminal Justice*, 24(4): 257–74.

McWilliams, W. (1986) 'The English probation system and the diagnostic ideal', *Howard Journal of Criminal Justice*, 25(4): 241–60.

McWilliams, W. (1987) 'Probation, pragmatism and policy', *Howard Journal of Criminal Justice*, 26(2): 97–121.

McWilliams, W. (1992) 'The rise and development of management thought in the English probation system', in R. Statham and P. Whitehead (eds) *Managing the Probation Service: Issues for the 1990s*, Harlow, Essex: Longman.

Mead, R. (2014) *The Road to Middlemarch: My Life with George Eliot*, London: Granta.

Merquior, J.G. (1985) *Foucault*, Hammersmith, London: Fontana.

Merquior, J.G. (1986) *From Prague to Paris: A Critique of Structuralist and Post-Structuralist Thought*, London: Verso.

Merton, R. (1968) *Social Theory and Social Structure*, New York, NY: The Free Press.

Millard, D. (1979) 'Broader approaches to probation practice', in J.F.S. King (ed) *Pressures and Change in the Probation Service* (Cropwood Conference Series No 11), Cambridge: Institute of Criminology, University of Cambridge.

Ministry of Justice (2008a) *Punishment and Reform: Our Approach to Managing Offenders*, London: Ministry of Justice.

Ministry of Justice (2008b) *Working with the Third Sector to Reduce Re-Offending, Ministry of Justice and NOMS, Securing Effective Partnerships*, London: Ministry of Justice.

Ministry of Justice (2008c) *Probation Statistics Quarterly Brief, January to March 2008*, London: Ministry of Justice.

Ministry of Justice (2009) *Probation Statistics Quarterly Brief, January to March 2009*, London: Ministry of Justice.

Ministry of Justice (2010) *Breaking the Cycle: Effective Punishment, Rehabilitation and Sentencing of Offenders*, London: Ministry of Justice.

Ministry of Justice (2011) *Competition Strategy for Offender Services*, London: Ministry of Justice.

Ministry of Justice (2012a) *Punishment and Reform: Effective Community Sentences*, Consultation Paper CP8/2012, London: Ministry of Justice.

Ministry of Justice (2012b) *Punishment and Reform: Effective Probation Services*, Consultation Paper CP7/2012, London: Ministry of Justice.

Ministry of Justice (2012c) *Swift and Sure Justice: The Government's Plans for Reform of the Criminal Justice System*, CM 8388, London: Ministry of Justice.

Ministry of Justice (2013a) *Transforming Rehabilitation: A Revolution in the Way We Manage Offenders*, Consultation Paper CP1/2013, London: Ministry of Justice.

Ministry of Justice (2013b) *Transforming Rehabilitation: A Strategy for Reform*, CM 8619, Response to Consultation CP (R) 16/2013, London: Ministry of Justice.

Ministry of Justice (2013c) *Target Operating Manual: Rehabilitation Programme*, London: Ministry of Justice.

Ministry of Justice (2013d) *'Best in the Business' Bidding to Rehabilitate Offenders*, London: Ministry of Justice.

Ministry of Justice (2013e) *Story of the Prison Population 1993–2012 England and Wales*, London: Ministry of Justice.

Ministry of Justice (2013f) *Statistical Notice: Interim Re-Conviction Figures for the Peterborough and Doncaster Payment by Results Pilots*, London: Ministry of Justice.

Ministry of Justice (2013g) *Transforming Rehabilitation: A summary of evidence on Reducing Reoffending*, London: Ministry of Justice.

Ministry of Justice (2014) *Prison Population Projections 2014–2020 England and Wales*, London: Ministry of Justice.

Ministry of Justice and NOMS (National Offender Management Service) (2009) *Strategic Business Plans 2009–10 to 2010–11*, London: Ministry of Justice.

Morgan, R. (1997) 'Imprisonment: current concerns and a brief history since 1945', in M. Maguire, R. Morgan and R. Reiner (eds) *The Oxford Handbook of Criminology* (2nd edn), Oxford and New York, NY: Oxford University Press.

Morrison, K. (1995) *Marx, Durkheim, Weber: Formations of Modern Social Thought*, London, Thousand Oaks, CA, and New Delhi: Sage.

Mounier, E. (1952) *Personalism*, London: Routledge and Kegan Paul.

Muncie, J. (2009) *Youth and Crime* (3rd edn), London, Thousand Oaks, CA, and New Delhi: Sage Publications.

Myers, T. (2003) *Slavoj Žižek*, Abingdon: Routledge.

NAPO (National Association of Probation Officers) (2007) *Changing Lives: An Oral History of Probation*, London: NAPO.

NAPO (2009) *Probation under Stress: A Briefing Paper*, (BRF06-09) compiled by H. Fletcher, London: NAPO.

National Offender Management Service (2006) *The NOMS Offender Management Model*, London: NOMS.

National Offender Management Service (2007) *Probation Circular 12/2007: Pre-Sentence Reports*, London: NOMS.

National Probation Service (2009) *Probation Circular 06/2009, Determining Pre-Sentence Report Type*, London: National Probation Service.

Nellis, M. (1999) 'Towards "the field of corrections": modernising the probation service in the late 1990s', *Social Policy and Administration*, 33(3): 302–23.

Nellis, M. (2007) 'Humanising justice: the English probation service up to 1972', in L. Gelsthorpe and R. Morgan (eds) *Handbook of Probation*, Devon, Cullompton: Willan.

Newburn, T. (2007) *Criminology*, Devon, Cullompton: Willan.

Noaks, L. and Wincup, E. (2004) *Criminological Research: Understanding Qualitative Methods*, London, Thousand Oaks, CA, and New Delhi: Sage.

Office for National Statistics (2015) 'Crime in England and Wales year ending March 2015', 16 July. Available at: http://ons.govt.uk/ons/taxonomy/index.html?nscl=Crime+and+Justice (accessed September 2015).

Oldfield, M. (2008) 'Probation resources, staffing and workloads 2001–2008', Centre for Crime and Justice Studies.

O'Neil, O. (2002) *A Question of Trust*, Cambridge and New York, NY: Cambridge University Press.

Orwell, G. (1933) *Down and Out in Paris and London*, London: Penguin.

Outhwaite, W. (1975) *Understanding Social Life: The Method Called Verstehen*, London: George Allen and Unwin.

Outram, D. (2013) *The Enlightenment* (3rd edn), Cambridge: Cambridge University Press.

Parenti, C. (1999) *Lockdown America: Police and Prisons in the Age of Crisis*, London and New York, NY: Verso.

Pashukanis, E.B. (1978) *Law and Marxism: A General Theory*, London.

Piaget, J. (1971) *Structuralism*, London: Routledge and Kegan Paul.

Piketty, T. (2014) *Capital in the Twenty-First Century*, Cambridge, MA, and London: The Belknap Press of Harvard University.

Platt, A. (1977) *The Child Savers: The Invention of Delinquency* (2nd edn), Chicago, IL, and London: The University of Chicago Press.

Porter, R. (2000) *Enlightenment: Britain and the Creation of the Modern World*, London and New York, NY: Penguin.

Pratt, J. (2007) *Penal Populism*, Key Ideas in Criminology Series, London and New York, NY: Routledge.

Pratt, J., Brown, D., Brown, M., Hallsworth, S. and Morrison, W. (eds) (2005) *The New Punitiveness: Trends, Theories and Perspectives*, Devon, Cullompton: Willan.

Radzinowicz, L. (1958) *Preface to the Results of Probation. Report of the Cambridge Department of Criminal Science*, Basingstoke: Macmillan.

Radzinowicz, L. (1999) *Adventures in Criminology*, London and New York, NY: Routledge.

Radzinowicz, L. and Hood, R. (1990) *The Emergence of Penal Policy in Victorian and Edwardian England*, Oxford and New York, NY: Oxford University Press.

Rahman, Z.H. (2014) *In the Light of What We Know*, Basingstoke: Macmillan.

Raynor, P. (1985) *Social Work, Justice and Control*, Oxford: Basil Blackwell.

Raynor, P. (2002) 'Community penalties: probation, punishment, and "what works"', in M. Maguire, R. Morgan and R. Reiner (eds) *The Oxford Handbook of Criminology* (3rd edn), Oxford and New York, NY: Oxford University Press.

Raynor, P. and Vanstone, M. (2002) *Understanding Community Penalties: Probation, Policy and Social Change*, Buckingham and Philadelphia, PA: Open University Press.

Raynor, P. and Vanstone, M. (2007) 'Towards a correctional service', in L. Gelsthorpe and R. Morgan (eds) *Handbook of Probation*, Devon, Cullompton: Willan.

Reid, J. (2006) 'Check Against Delivery', speech by the Home Secretary on offender management, HMP Wormwood Scrubs, 7 November.

Reiman, J. (1998) *The Rich Get Richer and the Poor Get Prison: Ideology, Class, and Criminal Justice* (5th edn), Boston, MA, and London: Allyn and Bacon.

Reiner, R. (2006) 'Beyond risk: a lament for social democratic criminology', in T. Newburn and P. Rock (eds) *The Politics of Crime Control: Essays in Honour of David Downes*, Clarendon Studies in Criminology, Oxford and New York, NY: Oxford University Press.

Reiner, R. (2007a) *Law and Order: An Honest Citizen's Guide to Crime and Control*, Cambridge: Polity.

Reiner, R. (2007b) 'Political economy, crime, and criminal justice', in M. Maguire, R. Morgan and R. Reiner (eds) *The Oxford Handbook of Criminology* (4th edn), Cambridge: Oxford University Press.

Ritzer, G. and Goodman, D.J. (1997) *Classical Sociological Theory* (4th edn), London, Boston, MA, and New York, NY: McGraw Hill.

Roberts, R. and McMahon, W. (eds) (2007) *Social Justice and Criminal Justice*, London: Centre for Crime and Justice Studies.

Rodger, J.J. (2008) *Criminalising Social Policy: Anti-Social Behaviour and Welfare in a De-Civilised Society*, Devon, Cullompton: Willan.

Rose, G. (1961) *The Struggle for Penal Reform: The Howard League and its Predecessors*, London and Chicago, IL: Stevens and Sons Limited and Quadrangle Books, Inc.

Rose, J. (1994) *Elizabeth Fry*, London: The History Press Ltd.

Roshier, B. (1989) *Controlling Crime*, Buckingham and Philadelphia, PA: Open University Press.

Roudinesco, E. (2014) *Lacan: In Spite of Everything*, London and New York, NY: Verso.

Rusche, G. and Kirchheimer, O. (1968 [1939]) *Punishment and Social Structure*, New York, NY: Russell and Russell.

Russell, B. (1996 [1946]) *History of Western Philosophy*, London and New York, NY: Routledge.

Rutherford, A. (1994) *Criminal Justice and the Pursuit of Decency*, Winchester: Waterside Press.

Saad-Filho, A. and Johnston, D. (eds) (2005) *Neoliberalism: A Critical Reader*, London and Ann Arbor, MI: Pluto Press.

Safranski, R. (2003) *Nietzsche: A Philosophical Biography*, London: Granta Books.

Sampson, R.V. (1956) *Progress in the Age of Reason: The Seventeenth Century to the Present Day*, London and Toronto: Heinemann.

Sandel, M. (2012) *What Money Can't Buy: The Moral Limits of Markets*, London and New York, NY: Allen Lane.

Sayer, D. (1991) *Capitalism and Modernity: An Excursus on Marx and Weber*, London and New York, NY: Routledge.

Scheurich, J.J. and McKenzie, K.B. (2005) 'Foucault's methodologies: archaeology and genealogy', in N.K. Denzin and Y.S Lincoln (eds) *The Sage Handbook of Qualitative Research* (3rd edn), London, Thousand Oaks, CA, and New Delhi: Sage.

Schwan, A. and Shapiro, S. (2011) *Foucault's Discipline and Punish*, London: Pluto.

Schweitzer, A. (1929) *Civilisation and Ethics: The Philosophy of Civilisation, Part II* (2nd edn), London: A. and C. Black.

Sen, A. (2009) *The Idea of Justice*, London and New York, NY: Allen Lane.

Sim, J. (2009) *Punishment and Prisons: Power and the Carceral State*, London, Thousand Oaks, CA, and New Delhi: Sage.

Simon, J. (2007) *Governing Through Crime: How the War on Crime Transformed American Democracy and Created a Culture of Fear*, Oxford and New York, NY: Oxford University Press.

Simon, W.M. (1963) *European Positivism in the Nineteenth Century: An Essay in Intellectual History*, Ithaca, NY: Cornell University Press.

Sinnerbrink, R.S. (2008) 'The Hegelian "night of the world": Žižek on subjectivity, negativity, and universality', *International Journal of Žižek Studies*, 2(2): 1–21.

Smith, A. (2009 [1759]) *The Theory of Moral Sentiments* (Intro A. Sen), London and New York, NY: Penguin.

Smith, D. (1988) *The Chicago School: A Liberal Critique of Capitalism*, Basingstoke: Macmillan.

Smith, D. (2006) 'Making sense of psychoanalysis in criminological theory and probation practice', *Probation Journal*, 53(4): 361–76.

Solomon, E. and Garside, R. (2008) 'Ten years of Labour's youth justice reforms: an independent audit', Centre for Crime and Justice Studies.

Solomon, E., Eades, C., Garside, R. and Rutherford, M. (2007) 'Ten years of criminal justice under Labour: an independent audit', Centre for Crime and Justice Studies.

Solomon, R.C. (1988) *Continental Philosophy since 1750: The Rise and Fall of the Self*, Oxford: Oxford University Press.

Spitzer, S. (1975) 'Punishment and social organisation: a study of Durkheim's theory of penal evolution', *Law and Society Review*, 9(4): 613–38.

Statham, R. (ed) (2014) *The Golden Age of Probation: Market v Mission*, Sherfield-on-Loddon: Waterside Press.

Stelman, A. (1980) 'Social work relationships: an exploration', *Probation Journal*, 27: 85–94.

Stevenson, L. and Haberman, D.L. (1998) *Ten Theories of Human Nature*, Oxford and New York, NY: Oxford University Press.

Stewart, G. and Stewart, J. (1993) *Social Circumstances of Young Offenders under Supervision*, London: Association of Chief Probation Officers.

Stewart, J., Smith, D. and Stewart, G., with Fullwood, C. (1994) *Understanding Offending Behaviour*, Harlow, Essex: Longman.

Straw, J. (2009) 'Probation and community punishment', speech to trainee probation officers at the Probation Study School, University of Portsmouth, 4 February.

Sztompka, P. (1986) *Robert K. Merton: An Intellectual Profile*, Basingstoke: Macmillan.

Tarnas, R. (1991) *The Passion of the Western Mind: Understanding the Ideas That Have Shaped Our World View*, London: Pimlico.

Taylor, I. (1997) 'The political economy of crime', in M. Maguire, R. Morgan and R. Reiner (eds) *The Oxford Handbook of Criminology* (2nd edn), Oxford and New York, NY: Oxford University Press.

Taylor, I., Walton, P. and Young, J. (1973) *The New Criminology: For a Social Theory of Deviance*, London, Boston, MA, and Henley: Routledge and Kegan Paul.

Taylor, R., Wasik, M. and Leng, R. (2004) *Blackstone's Guide to the Criminal Justice Act 2003*, Oxford and New York, NY: Oxford University Press.

Teesside Probation Service (2008) 'Teesside area plan for additional funding: business plan 2008–2009 (draft 2)'.

Thompson, E.P. (1971) 'The moral economy of the English crowd in the eighteenth century', *Past and Present*, 50: 76–136.

Thompson, K. (1976) *Auguste Comte: The Foundation of Sociology*, London: Nelson.

Thompson, K. (1982) *Emile Durkheim: Key Sociologists*, New York, NY: Tavistock Publications.

Thorpe, D.H., Smith, D., Green, C.J. and Paley, J.H. (1980) *Out of Care: The Community Support of Juvenile Offenders*, London: George Allen and Unwin.

Tierney, J. (2006) *Criminology: Theory and Context* (2nd edn), Harlow, Essex: Pearson Education.

Townsend, P. (1979) *Poverty in the United Kingdom: A Survey of Household Resources and Standards of Living*, London: Penguin.

Traugott, M. (1978) *Emile Durkheim: On Institutional Analysis*, Chicago, IL, and London: University of Chicago Press.

Turner, B.S. (ed) (1996) *The Blackwell Companion to Social Theory*, Oxford and Cambridge, MA: Blackwell.

Valier, C. (2002) *Theories of Crime and Punishment*, Harlow, Essex: Longman.

Wacquant, L. (2004) *Body and Soul: Notebooks of an Apprentice Boxer*, Oxford and New York, NY: Oxford University Press.

Wacquant, L. (2008) *Urban Outcasts: A Comparative Sociology of Advanced Marginality*, Cambridge: Polity.

Wacquant, L. (2009) *Punishing the Poor: The Neoliberal Government of Social Insecurity*, Durham and London: Duke University Press.

Walker, M. and Beaumont, B. (1981) *Probation Work: Critical Theory and Socialist Practice*, Oxford: Blackwell.

Weber, M. (1958 [1904–05]) *The Protestant Ethic and the Spirit of Capitalism*, New York, NY: Scribner's Press.

Weber, M. (1968 [1922]) *Economy and Society: An Outline of Interpretive Sociology* (ed G. Roth and C. Wittich), New York, NY: Bedminster Press.

Whimster, S. (eds) (2004) *The Essential Weber: A Reader*, London and New York, NY: Routledge.

Whitehead, P. (1990) *Community Supervision for Offenders: A New Model of Probation*, Aldershot and Brookfield: Avebury.

Whitehead, P. (2007) *Modernising Probation and Criminal Justice: Getting the Measure of Cultural Change*, Crayford, Kent: Shaw and Sons.

Whitehead, P. (2010) *Exploring modern probation: Social theory and organisational complexity*, Bristol: Policy Press.

Whitehead, P. (2011) 'Evaluation report of research at six community chaplaincy projects in England and Wales', Community Chaplaincy Association and Teesside University.

Whitehead, P. (2015a) 'Payment by results: the materialist reconstruction of criminal justice', *International Journal of Sociology and Social Policy*, 35(5/6): 290–305.

Whitehead, P. (2015b) *Reconceptualising the Moral Economy of Criminal Justice: A New Perspective*, Houndmills: Palgrave.

Whitehead, P. and Crawshaw, P. (2012) *Organising Neoliberalism: Markets, Privatisation and Justice*, London and New York, NY: Anthem Press.

Whitehead, P. and MacMillan, J. (1985) 'Checks or blank cheque? Justifying custody of juveniles', *Probation Journal*, 32(3): 87–9.

Whitehead, P. and Statham, R. (2006) *The History of Probation: Politics, Power and Cultural Change 1876–2005*, Crayford, Kent: Shaw and Sons.

Whitehead, P. and Thompson, J. (2004) *Knowledge and the Probation Service: Raising Standards for Trainees*, Assessors and Practitioners, Chichester: Wiley.

Wilkinson, R. and Pickett, K. (2009) *The Spirit Level: Why More Equal Societies Almost Always Do Better*, London: Allen Lane.

Windlesham, Lord (1993) *Responses to Crime, Volume 2: Penal Policy in the Making*, Oxford and New York, NY: Clarendon Press.

Windlesham, Lord (2001) *Responses to Crime, Volume 4: Dispensing Justice*, Oxford and New York, NY: Clarendon Press.

Windlesham, Lord (2003) 'Ministers and modernisation: criminal justice policy, 1997–2001', in L. Zedner and A. Ashworth (eds) *The Criminological Foundations of Penal Policy: Essays in Honour of Roger Hood*, Clarendon Studies in Criminology, Oxford and New York, NY: Oxford University Press.

Winlow, S. and Hall, S. (2013) *Rethinking Social Exclusion: The End of the Social?*, London: Sage.

Winlow, S., Hall, S., Treadwell, J. and Briggs, D. (2015) *Riots and Political Protest: Notes from the Post-Political Present*, London and New York, NY: Routledge.

Young, A.F. and Ashton, E.T. (1956) *British Social Work in the Nineteenth Century*, London: Routledge and Kegan Paul.

Young, J. (1999) *The Exclusive Society: Social Exclusion, Crime and Difference in Late Modernity*, London, Thousand Oaks, CA, and New Delhi: Sage.

Young, J. (2007) *The Vertigo of Late Modernity*, London, Thousand Oaks, CA, and New Delhi: Sage.

Young, P. (1976) 'A sociological analysis of the early history of probation', *British Journal of Law and Society*, 3: 44–58.

Zedner, L. (2003) 'Useful knowledge? Debating the role of criminology in post-war Britain?', in L. Zedner and A. Ashworth (eds) *The Criminological Foundations of Penal Policy: Essays in Honour of Roger Hood*, Clarendon Studies in Criminology, Oxford and New York, NY: Oxford University Press.

Zedner, L. (2004) *Criminal Justice*, Clarendon Law Series, Oxford and New York, NY: Oxford University Press.

Zedner, L. (2006) 'Opportunity makes the thief-taker: the influence of economic analysis on crime control', in T. Newburn and P. Rock (eds) *The Politics of Crime Control: Essays in Honour of David Downes*, Clarendon Studies in Criminology, Oxford and New York, NY: Oxford University Press.

Žižek, S. (1992) *Looking Awry: An Introduction to Jacques Lacan through Popular Culture*, Cambridge, MA, and London: The MIT Press.

Žižek, S. (2006) *How to Read Lacan*, London: Granta Books.

Žižek, S. (2008) *The Fragile Absolute, or, Why is the Christian Legacy Worth Fighting For?*, London and New York, NY: Verso.

Žižek, S. (2009) *The Ticklish Subject: The Absent Centre of Political Ontology*, London: Verso.

Žižek, S. (2010) 'A meditation on Michelangelo's *Christ on the Cross*', in J. Milbank, S. Žižek and C. Davis (eds) *Paul's New Moment: Continental Philosophy and the Future of Christian Theology*, Michigan, MI: Brazos Press.

Žižek, S. (2014) *Trouble in Paradise: Communism after the End of History*, London: Allen Lane.

Index

Note: Page numbers in *italics* indicate tables and figures and page numbers followed by an "n" refer to end-of-chapter notes.